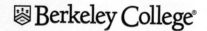

Change.edu

she says. "It's about growing as an individual and learning more about yourself and defining your values."

To most of us today, Erika's experience embodies the upward mobility enabled by the American higher education system; we see it as a proud reflection of the social opportunity our society offers. But her experience might have been puzzling to some of the men who founded Berkeley in the Civil War era. They would have wondered, what do football games and bone marrow drives have to do with education?

Berkeley's history highlights the long-running debate over the purpose of a college education. Should it be a free-form opportunity for only the highest-achieving students to develop their intellects—a place where students can foster curiosity, skepticism, and critical thinking through a meandering process in which outside-the-classroom diversions can be just as important as the coursework? Or should college be a practical and directed experience accessible to a wide swath of students—a place where tuition dollars deliver a measurable return through specific skills that will help a graduate advance in his career? And should taxpayers, who pay a huge portion of the bill for America's roughly $430 billion higher education industry[1] (including most of the cost of Erika's experience), have a say in the matter?

During Berkeley's earliest days, the school attempted to be both intellectual and practical—and then, as now, no one was entirely satisfied. The institution has its origins in two different schools. The first, called the College of California, was founded in the 1850s and was modeled after Harvard and Yale; its all-male student body took Latin, Greek, history, English, math, and natural history.[2] The College of California was led by Henry Durant, an energetic minister and scholar from Massachusetts who had the foresight to acquire farmland for his nascent campus in the foothills north of Oakland. But Durant's institution was land rich and cash poor: in its early years, it struggled to pay its bills.[3] So, in 1868, it merged with the nearby Agricultural, Mining and Mechanical Arts College, a state-funded school that was one of the first "land-grant" colleges, created under a new federal law aimed at providing practical education to the nation's farmers. By 1869 this new University of California had just ten faculty and forty students—some who wanted to study Socrates, and some who wanted to learn smarter ways to squeeze crops from their acreage.

Tension between the two groups ran high. "Who needs philosophy, music, or the humanities?" activist farmers in the Granger Movement complained, urging California legislators to keep this new college at Berkeley focused on practical, agriculture-oriented studies. On campus, however, the more scholarly students condescended to their farmer classmates, insulting them as "Granger-looking men" who didn't deserve to be attending college in the first place.

Today, Berkeley is a world-class institution that has made tremendous contributions to society. Its researchers first identified the flu virus and vitamin E. Its graduates have helped invent the personal computer (Steve Wozniak, co-founder of Apple), reinvented the way America eats (chef Alice Waters), and helped pilot the starship *Enterprise* (George Takei, the actor who played Mr. Sulu on *Star Trek*). Berkeley's faculty includes twenty Nobel laureates. *U.S. News & World Report* calls it the best public university in America—and the twenty-first best national university, public or private. Berkeley is also a pacesetter when it comes to social mobility: some one-third of its undergraduate students, including Erika, are eligible for federal Pell Grants, and 25 percent of admitted freshman are, also like Erika, first-generation college students with neither parent having a four-year college degree.[4]

That said, there's also no denying that much of the modern Berkeley experience stretches the boundaries of practicality. In a typical semester, students can take courses such as Chinese Music: Learn to Play the Erhu; Beginner's Scrabble: Strategy, Knowledge, and Fun; or Whiskey: Its History, Culture, and Appreciation.[5] And much of what goes on in the buildings that fill Berkeley's 1,232-acre campus is far removed from what happened in the unadorned classrooms and labs of Berkeley's early history. After class, Berkeley undergrads go home to dormitories like the ten residence halls at the Clark Kerr Campus. These feature Spanish mission architecture, a private swimming pool, tennis courts, a skating park, barbecue pits, and Ping-Pong[6]—a list of amenities that sounds a bit like those offered at a Napa Valley resort.[7]

Not long ago, undergrads at a typical college might have ridden an exercise bike at the gym. Today at Berkeley, students can choose from four "student recreational complexes," four swimming facilities, two weight rooms, and two tracks.[8] They can book massages or personal trainers through an online appointment system.[9] Starting with the 2011/2012 academic year, more than four hundred student athletes from some thirteen different teams will have access to the Student-Athlete High Performance Center, a $100 million-plus facility[10] that will be devoted to weightlifting, physical therapy, and the tutoring necessary to keep athletes eligible to play their sports.[11] In many ways, modern-day Berkeley doesn't resemble a school so much as a conglomerate. During the 2009/2010 academic year it had more than twenty-four thousand employees, a $1.8 billion budget, seven museums, and a full-service veterinary hospital.[12] And while Berkeley remains more affordable than an Ivy League school, you can hardly call it cheap. During the 2010/2011 academic year, it's estimated that a state resident living in an on-campus resident hall spends an average of $31,044 on tuition, fees, and other expenses, while an out-of-state undergrad's tab can hit an average of $53,923.[13]

A few hours' drive south of Berkeley, a student named Elisha Rey finished her education by taking a very different path. Rey became pregnant near the end of high school, so she didn't go to college immediately after graduating, as many of her classmates did. Instead, a year later—after she became acclimated to taking care of Brittany, her daughter—she enrolled in Cerro Coso Community College, where she earned an associate's degree in social science. She planned to continue on for a bachelor's degree, but "life kept getting in the way," she says. By 2005 she was a thirty-year-old single mother with a twelve-year-old daughter and was earning less than $18,000 a year as the office manager at a real estate company. She needed to find a way to improve her earning power. So she enrolled in an online program at a for-profit college to pursue a bachelor's degree in criminal justice.

Rey admits she had some doubts about the "online" degree, but she checked around, and employers seemed willing to accept it. Just as important, the schedule allowed her to study while still working full time and caring for her daughter—most nights, she studied from 10:00 P.M. to midnight. Indeed, she was able to complete her courses without ever setting foot on a campus; all of her classes and all of her classmates came to her, at home or at work, via her computer.

Despite the convenience, the courses were hard. "It was a lot of studying, a lot of writing; it took a lot of time," she says. But she felt that the professors went to great lengths to support her. "A lot of them took extra time to explain things, to give me that extra one-on-one that was nice to have," she says. Once again, life interrupted her studies: halfway through the program, she perception of a Berkeley education, Erika will soon plug into a different America than the one she knew growing up. "My parents didn't get the opportunity I'm getting," she says. "I know for a fact I'll be earning a better living than they do, and that I'll be able to provide my family with a house"—a big step up from the apartments in which her parents, Francisco and Maria, raised their children. Already Erika has spent her college summers interning at firms such as Northrop Grumman and KPMG, and after graduation she'll almost certainly be working in a prestigious white-collar job—and will rest comfortably in the knowledge that her own children will likely follow in her path to an elite school and even more success.

At school, Erika is a serious student: a political economics major with a minor in public policy who carries a 3.2-grade-point average. She is also involved in a variety of leadership programs. In her spare time, she mentors inner-city Latino students and organizes bone marrow donor drives to benefit indigenous Peruvian children afflicted by a rare disease.

She likes to have fun, too. She's a midfielder on an intramural soccer team that, despite losing every game last season, manages to have good time on the field. She's a season ticket holder at Cal football games, and on Saturday afternoons, she dresses in blue and yellow and tailgates with friends. She has her own room in a comfortable three-bedroom, off-campus co-op apartment, which has its own social committee to plan parties. During the summer of 2010, she spent raucous afternoons cheering for World Cup soccer matches while roommates worked the barbecue.

As she looks ahead to graduation, she expects that the friends she's made at Berkeley will remain her best friends for life. "I think that college for me is not only about going into a major that's going to help you obtain a job after you graduate,"

Introduction

Meet Erika Ballesteros, American dream.

Erika is the twenty-one-year-old daughter of Mexican immigrants. Her father is unemployed. Her mother works on a production line making Hot Pockets frozen sandwiches at a food factory in the San Fernando Valley. In 2012, when Erika graduates from the University of California at Berkeley, she will have transformed from striving immigrant to American elite, all in a single generation.

Her parents, who crossed over from Mexico in the late 1980s in search of a better life, encouraged Erika to work hard at Canoga Park High School in California. But when it came to her college search, she was largely on her own. "My parents only went to school until sixth grade, so they had no clue what I had to do" to get into college, says Erika. So she researched colleges, applied to a variety of University of California campuses, and was accepted to Berkeley, where she's won scholarships and been awarded Pell Grants that have paid the full cost of her attending. If history is any guide, because of the quality and

Contents

To Marcelle,
whose love, happiness and creativity
sustain me and make me a better person.

And to Danielle and Jake,
who make me proudest with their
kindness and humanity.

© 2011 by Andrew S. Rosen
Published by Kaplan Publishing, a division of Kaplan, Inc.
395 Hudson Street
New York, NY 10014

Designed and typeset by: Cassandra J. Pappas

Printed in the United States of America.

10 9 8 7 6 5 4 3 2 1

Library of Congress Cataloging-in-Publication Data

Rosen, Andrew S.
  Change.edu : rebooting for the new talent economy / Andrew Rosen S.
    p. cm.
  ISBN 978-1-60714-441-0 (hardback)
  1. For-profit universities and colleges—United States. 2. Public universities and colleges—United States—Finance. 3. Education, Higher—Aims and objectives—United States. I. Title.
  LB2328.52.U6R67 2011
  378'.010973--dc23   2011027722

ISBN: 978-1-60714-441-0

Kaplan Publishing books are available at special quantity discounts to use for sales promotions, employee premiums, or educational purposes. For more information or to purchase books, please call the Simon & Schuster special sales department at 866-506-1949.

Change.edu

Rebooting for the New Talent Economy

ANDREW S. ROSEN

KAPLAN PUBLISHING
New York

was laid off, changed apartments, and lost computer access, which stalled her progress. But soon she was back in class, and by July of 2009 she had earned her bachelor of science degree.

With the four-year degree in hand, she was immediately promoted to a financial analyst position at the Department of Defense, where she had taken a job as a technician during her time at the college. When she enrolled, she was earning $8.50 an hour. Today she earns $19.60 an hour. And soon after graduating, she re-enrolled to pursue a master's degree in criminal justice, which she hopes to use to launch a career in a parole or probation department.

WHEN MANY AMERICANS talk about "college," we tend to imagine a place that looks like Berkeley, not a for-profit college. That image is partly driven by the recollections of those of us who went to traditional colleges: our memories of tree-lined quads, dorm parties, new independence, first loves, and social awakenings. Traditional colleges offer a bundle of experiences, and a process in which socialization and maturation sometimes seem as important as the education.

Yet there are real costs when we assume this fantasy image is the only way to access "college." Over the last century, our country's world-class universities such as Harvard, Yale, and Berkeley have played an essential role in vaulting the United States into worldwide economic, military, and sociopolitical primacy, and they are indispensable to maintaining that position. But our obsessive focus on and considerable investment in these exclusive institutions, and the many others that emulate them, sometimes lead us to pay too little attention to the more inclusive schools that serve far more students, in far less glamorous surroundings. As taxpayers, we're helping to fund an increasingly lavish, resort-style college experience at institutions that cater to the few, when there are more cost-effective alternatives. Meanwhile, the selectivity and high costs of traditional colleges serve to exclude too many.

We're living in a time of profound economic challenges, and unlike in the Gold Rush era during which Berkeley was founded, the country's greatest resource today isn't in the ground; it's in the minds of our citizens, who urgently need education to develop their talents. For some, an elite education is a wonderful way to develop those talents. Indeed, if we could afford it, it would be a tremendous boon to countless others. But for many, many more, there are legitimate alternatives that will give them tools to move up: to help the kid sweeping the drugstore learn to work the register or manage the shop; to help the register clerk become a technician or a pharmacist; to help the pharmacist become the store owner or even own a chain of stores. Our country doesn't have a person to waste—a reality President Obama has recognized repeatedly by calling for a vast expansion in the number of Americans attending college.

Our myopic view of college is a major obstacle to that goal, and it's one that ignores both the history of higher education and the challenges of many of its long-established players. In the chapters ahead I'll develop this argument, but for now I'll summarize it in five points:

- First, while higher education may seem like the most staid of industries—one where the strongest players have dominated for many decades, even centuries—in fact, it's a field with a rich history of "disruptive innovation," in which new entrants seized market segments that incumbents were ignoring and thereby changed the nature of the market. Frequently, this innovation has served to create new opportunities for people who have been shut out by the prestigious institutions. Higher education in America has experienced three major waves of disruptive innovation: the establishment of land-grant colleges in the second half of the 1800s, the dramatic expansion of community colleges in the post–World War II era, and the recent wave of for-profit, or "private-sector," universities. The colleges that resulted from these bursts of innovation were each greeted with condescension, criticism, and charges of illegitimacy. Over time, however, land-grant universities and community colleges have become a critical and accepted part of America's educational landscape; some, such as Berkeley, have even gained elite status. In time, the newer private-sector universities will achieve the same level of acceptance.

• Second, despite the noble intentions that led to their founding, many of the institutions that were born during earlier bursts of innovation have succumbed to a powerful force I call "Harvard Envy." Schools that were created to be practical and accessible have too often morphed into places that are elaborate, pretentious, and costly. Harvard Envy has led to a well-established and nearly unshakeable set of rules under which university constituents—administrators, faculty, students, communities, funders, and others—measure themselves primarily by the prestige and attractiveness of the institution, often to the exclusion of other, seemingly more obvious measures like student learning outcomes, responsiveness to student or economic needs, training for student career opportunities, or even institutional financial viability. I've come to think of the former set of incentives and motivating forces as the Ivory Tower Playbook. Together they dictate the way most traditional colleges operate.

• Third, our higher education funding system should be focused on providing diverse, quality educational alternatives for a wide range of prospective students, not on subsidizing the *noneducational* competition of institutions in their search for an edge in attracting students or faculty. The American taxpayer foots the bill, directly and indirectly, for more than $200 billion in higher education costs because higher education is a critical driver of our economy and our civil society. Yet our universities have surprisingly little idea of what the students in their classrooms are *learning*, and for the most part they do not compete with one another on their relative ability to enable student learning. Instead, they're asking the taxpayer to fund their competition for students with amenities like athletic complexes, residence halls, and dining facilities (once known as gyms, dorms, and cafeterias) rather than classrooms. These expensive comforts are weapons that help them win students from one another and compete in the college rankings arms race, but don't do a thing to educate students. When the taxpayer is expected to participate in Illinois State University's building of a $50 million fitness center whose main role will be to aid ISU in attracting students who otherwise might have gone to the University of Illinois, while also subsidizing the University of Illinois's own massive, recently renovated recreation complex to lure those same prospective students back, something is wrong— particularly when tens of thousands of less advantaged students can't find a place in class at the local community college due to lack of funding.[14] The years ahead offer the potential for enormous improvement in the quality of education, driven in part by the rise of technology and analytics that can make learning more effective, efficient, personalized, global, and inexpensive. Our economic future requires us to refocus our taxpayer higher-ed spending on achieving these improvements in learning—and expanding access to the fruits of higher education—rather than building ever-more-comfortable and ever-more-expensive resort experiences for the few.

• Fourth, the pedagogy used by the new generation of private-sector colleges is sound and proven—and in some cases they may do a better job of educating students than traditional institutions. Traditional colleges are more likely to know how many students attended last night's basketball game than how many attended this morning's economics lecture. They know how much their alumni donated but often not what jobs they acquired after graduation. Too often, traditional colleges measure inputs, not outputs. Many of them could learn much from private-sector colleges, which are doing the most innovative work to use technology, pedagogy, and measurement systems to make sure students are really learning, and to build virtuous cycles that will continue to improve the quality of learning outcomes for many years to come.

• Fifth, despite recent criticism from the media and regulators over private-sector colleges' recruiting tactics and use of taxpayer funding, the private-sector schools are generally acting effectively and appropriately—and when you look at the numbers, as I do in chapter 5, it's clear that this sector on the whole is using taxpayer dollars more efficiently, and graduating students more successfully, than many traditional schools. While this book is not aimed at defending the for-profit education sector from this latest round of regulatory scrutiny—indeed, I wrote much of this book before the U.S. Senate began holding hearings on private-sector colleges during 2010/2011 (which I'll also describe in more detail in chapter 5)—I will address the larger criticisms that face the for-profit industry, most of which have been around for years.

Universities, of course, are many things to many people, and the emotions they inspire in graduates and supporters sometimes cloud clear thinking about what such institutions' goals should be. The traditional purposes of the university are often described as including the "dissemination of knowledge" (teaching) and the "production of knowledge" (research). To be clear, this book is *not* about the research role of American universities, which has brought unimaginable innovation to fields such as medicine, technology, food and agriculture, materials, policy—indeed, virtually every part of our economy and society. Rather, it addresses whether institutions of higher education are incentivized to deliver excellent learning outcomes for a broad range of students; whether America is getting its money's worth for its investment; and most important, whether we're getting what we need from our higher education system in an era of increasingly intense global economic competition.

When I think about America's misperceptions about what college really is, I sometimes recall the old Rodney Dangerfield movie *Back to School*. In it, Dangerfield plays Thornton Melon, a wealthy entrepreneur in his sixties. When Melon's son begins struggling as a college freshman, Melon decides to enroll in college himself—both to help his son and to get the formal education he never had.

In many ways, *Back to School* is a typical fish-out-of-water comedy, where the laughs come from watching a ribald older parent experience dorm parties, the school diving team, and final exams.[15] But there's an irony to this plotline: in fact, today the average college student bears little resemblance to the nineteen-year-olds cast alongside Dangerfield in *Back to School*, and a growing number bear more than a passing resemblance to Thornton Melon himself.

The latest fall enrollment figures, from 2008/2009, show some nineteen million Americans enrolled in graduate or undergraduate degree-granting institutions, and only about seven million of them fit the classic profile of an eighteen- to twenty-four-year-old enrolled full time in a four-year school. Thirty-nine percent of these postsecondary students attend college part time, 36 percent go to two-year schools, and about 37 percent are twenty-five years or older. Very few of those part-time students spend their weekends rowing for the crew team; they're generally busy at work or raising their families.

These were the type of people that a Vermont senator named Justin Smith Morrill had in mind when he first proposed the land-grant colleges back in the 1850s. "[These people] snatch their education, such as it is, from the crevices between labor and sleep," Morrill said. "They grope in twilight. Our country depends upon them as its right arm to do the handiwork of the nation."[16]

There's something inspiring about older, working adults persevering to further their education. In fact, we all benefit from their toil because our country desperately needs more skilled workers. But the sad fact is that too often these nontraditional students come to understand the phrase Dangerfield made famous: No Respect. And that has to change.

TO THE EXTENT that my thesis sounds critical of the elite, traditional college experience, there's an irony, because I'm a product of that experience myself. Professionally and personally, I love spending time at colleges. I've visited hundreds of campuses on five continents and rarely leave a new city without stopping by the local university. I find it inspiring to see young people grow from being exposed to new ideas and new perspectives, getting engaged in community projects, and learning to think critically about the world around them—all of which happens regularly on good college campuses. I loved my four years as an undergraduate at Duke University: my professors, lifelong friends, sunny days on the quad, basketball games. I'm certain my experiences there were important in shaping who I was to become, academically and otherwise. I met my wife at Duke, and as we raised our own children we always assumed that when they went to college, they would study full time, live in a dorm, and attend a classic, traditional university, as indeed our oldest daughter now does.

But a few years after I got out of Duke and Yale Law School, my career took an unlikely turn that gave me a new perspective on what the typical college experience is—or should be. In the early 1990s, I went to work for Kaplan, the education company then best known for its test prep courses. Kaplan's history has been all about opening doors. The company was founded in the 1930s in a Brooklyn basement by an energetic young tutor named Stanley H. Kaplan, and for decades his main clientele was composed of striving ethnic New Yorkers who hoped that higher scores on standardized tests might help them compete against prep-schoolers with Ivy League legacies. Stanley Kaplan challenged society with the notion of meritocracy by helping students who would ordinarily have been shut out of prestigious colleges win admission by virtue of high test scores.[17] Starting in the 1990s, my friend and longtime colleague Jonathan Grayer expanded Kaplan from a modest-size test prep firm to a diversified global educational powerhouse.[18]

In the last decade, Kaplan, of which I am now chairman and CEO, has evolved to have an even more expansive mission than Stanley's original vision. Today, the largest part of Kaplan is higher education, through more than seventy-five college campuses and online programs around the globe. Our largest single unit is Kaplan University, an accredited institution offering associate's, bachelor's, and master's degrees and serving primarily working adults. When I've presided at Kaplan

University graduation ceremonies, I look out on an auditorium in which the moms and dads are usually the graduates, not just the people who paid the tuition. Kaplan is a for-profit institution, but my colleagues and I see our work as mission-driven: by making highly effective higher education accessible to people who've been shut out by traditional institutions, we truly believe we're building futures. While some extraordinary students such as Erika Ballesteros, the first-generation Berkeley student, are able to thread the needle and gain access to the most prestigious institutions America has to offer, many others—often minorities, working adults, and single parents such as Elisha Rey—desperately need a hand up to help them on the path to their American dream. Along with many others—including community colleges, many state schools, and other private-sector institutions—we offer that hand.

Still, the public and private institutions that focus on addressing the needs of the underserved are not always welcomed with enthusiasm by traditional academia—or by those whose main experiences with higher education have been in traditional universities. Private-sector institutions are particularly suspect. To the traditionalists, our open admissions policies, online teaching methods, the perceived motives of for-profit status, or just the fact that we don't have Gothic buildings or two-million-volume physical libraries are cause for suspicion and sometimes condescension. Due to our newness, graduates of for-profit institutions sometimes face questions about the legitimacy of their degrees. This repeats a long historical pattern in which innovators in higher education have always been initially viewed with skepticism, but over time I've come to view this distrust as fundamentally elitist and wrong. College shouldn't be about sunny afternoons on the campus quad, but about the actual learning that students take away from the process. It's also time people took a hard look at what their tax dollars are actually subsidizing at traditional colleges—and at the high-quality, cost-effective alternatives that private-sector schools are offering.

That's not to say our industry is perfect. None is. Private-sector colleges are producing hundreds of thousands of satisfied graduates whose careers are flourishing, but they're serving a student population that consistently struggles to complete their programs, an issue they share with community colleges. (I'll talk in chapter 5 about the challenges of helping "high-risk" students graduate.) Some of these students are worse off after they matriculate because they've taken on loans to finance a degree that they never complete, a problem that's less severe at community colleges, which receive heavy direct taxpayer subsidies that permit students to take on less debt. Further, there have been documented cases of for-profit institutions too aggressively recruiting students by misrepresenting their chances of success or the economic benefits they're likely to receive from completing a program. These are serious issues. Legislators and regulators are right to give scrutiny to private-sector colleges, as they should to all higher education institutions. Ultimately, students, taxpayers, and the schools themselves will benefit from it.

That's true because, in the long term, all educational institutions succeed or fail based on their reputations. If the outcomes for students at certain schools are not good enough, or the debt loads are too high relative to students' earnings increases, those schools won't last for long in the highly competitive education landscape. If well-considered, well-constructed regulations can help improve the odds of strong, cost-efficient student outcomes, everyone benefits: the students, the taxpayers, and the institutions that get the benefit of good word of mouth.

At Kaplan, we have a little perspective on inherent governmental skepticism of for-profit education, because the company has lived through this cycle before. In the late 1970s, the federal government launched an investigation of Kaplan's test prep business, which had advertised that students who prepared with Kaplan subsequently scored higher on their standardized tests. The test makers said that this was impossible—the exams were designed to be study-proof, they explained. During the several-year, highly-publicized investigation, Stanley Kaplan, who knew his programs worked, was depicted as a charlatan. In 1979, the government concluded its investigation with a report showing that, sure enough, students who attended Kaplan really did score higher on standardized tests—a conclusion that is now viewed as entirely obvious. While the investigation was unpleasant, it ultimately vindicated the work Stanley Kaplan was doing and served as an affirmation of his business. I'm hopeful that this latest round of scrutiny will likewise affirm what we know to be the enormously positive outcomes our students experience—and help us find ways to ensure that even more students experience that success.

This book, however, is not ultimately about the scrutiny of the for-profit sector that emerged as I was writing it. Instead, it seeks to focus on the evolution of challenger institutions across the history of American higher education, including, most recently, private-sector colleges. It also seeks to provide insight into how these new institutions have impacted, and will impact, the American economy, society, and higher education system. As will be clear in the chapters ahead, I view the private-sector colleges as the newest inheritors of the mission that sparked the creation of the land-grant and community colleges. Today they play a vital, complementary role in the evolving landscape of higher education. Our country's need for talented individuals who can propel our economy forward should transcend any political agenda. There are real consequences for our nation if we fail to offer a diverse set of higher education alternatives that fit the equally diverse needs of our population. The traditional view of college as a single phase in life, something you do from age eighteen to twenty-four, is becoming outdated. Increasingly, college is a place you return to at periodic intervals, to retool and reload for the next phase of life's journey.

WHEN I THINK about the ways in which our modern economy requires workers to have more education in order to break into the middle class, I sometimes think about a story my boss, Washington Post Company chairman Don Graham, tells. In 1969, after graduating from Harvard and volunteering for two years of service in Vietnam, Graham became a patrolman for the Washington, D.C., Metropolitan Police Department, a job he held for eighteen months. "I spent enough time with my colleagues to learn why they became police officers," Graham says. "The answer was clear: it was the best job you could get in large numbers in Washington with only a high school diploma." Today, however, in most places, you can't get a job as a police officer without at least two years of college—and you probably won't get promoted to a higher rank without earning a bachelor's degree or, in some cases, even a master's degree. "Police officials will tell you the requirements have changed because the job has changed," Graham says. "Police today use sophisticated technology, and their job is heavily influenced by data analysis."[19]

The same trend is affecting many different fields. Today only about half of all preschool and kindergarten teachers hold a bachelor's degree, but in states such as Massachusetts, a four-year degree is a requirement for kindergarten teachers in public schools.[20] Several states have legislation pending that would require nurses with only an associate's degree to go back to school to earn a bachelor's degree within ten years of graduating from their associate's program.[21] These requirements are a continuation of a long-running trend. Between 1973 and 2008, the percentage of jobs in the U.S. economy that required postsecondary education more than doubled, rising from 28 percent to 59 percent.[22]

As that bar climbs even higher, America's colleges are failing to produce enough graduates to supply the nurses, teachers, police officers, and other professionals we need. In 2010, Georgetown labor economist Anthony Carnevale and his colleagues crunched the numbers to figure out the size of this shortfall. By 2018, their findings show, we'll need twenty-two million new college graduates—and due to a growing demand for workers with higher levels of education, we'll fall short by at least three million postsecondary degrees. By 2018, 63 percent of all jobs will require postsecondary education. "High school graduates and dropouts will find themselves largely left behind in the coming decade as employer demand for workers with postsecondary degrees continues to surge," Carnevale and his colleagues write.[23]

It may seem counterintuitive to engage in hand-wringing over a shortage of educated workers right now. Given the historically high unemployment rates of the last several years, some economists have argued that America's biggest domestic problem for the foreseeable future—economically, socially, and perhaps politically—will be too few jobs, not too few educated workers. But all economists agree that when employers eventually resume hiring, the workers they will be bringing on will need more education than they did in the past.

When it comes to producing these educated workers, America has become a notable laggard. In 1995, the United States was a world leader among the seventeen countries in the Organisation for Economic Co-operation and Development with comparable data when it came to the percentage of our twenty-five- to thirty-four-year-old population with postsecondary credentials. By 2007, we'd dropped to twelfth place—and one of the few postsecondary stats in which the United States ranked first was the rate at which its students drop out of college.[24]

In fact, it's downright embarrassing—something President Obama acknowledged in an address to Congress soon after taking office in 2009. Referring directly to the college drop-out rate, he said, "This is a prescription for economic decline, because we know that countries that out-teach us today will out-compete us tomorrow." In the same speech, Obama laid out an audacious goal: "By 2020, America will once again have the highest proportion of college graduates in the world."[25] Like many grand political plans, however, it's not clear how this promise can be met.

America has faced pressures like this before, particularly after World War II, when our nation decided to send millions of returning GIs to college. During that period, the U.S. government addressed the problem in a simple way: by throwing money at it. That won't work in these times, given the dismal fiscal condition of the federal and state governments. States are slashing budgets to keep pace with falling tax dollars; instead of seeking to add seats to classrooms in state universities, legislators in many states are being forced to make sharp cuts in student enrollment to try to bring budgets closer to balance.

At a time when we desperately need more students like Erika Ballesteros and Elisha Rey to gain access to a high-quality college education, more spending won't be available to smooth the way. Instead, America needs to make the dollars it spends on higher education work more efficiently. To do that, we must better understand and debate the ways in which we're currently spending these resources. Ultimately, we'll have to make choices between providing immersive, amenity-rich, and socially focused residential college experiences for a select few, or focusing more on issues of educational quality and access and offering less elaborate but more focused high-quality education for a vastly larger group of Americans, even if the latter approach comes without the frills and perks that are too often embedded in the modern understanding of the "college experience."

BACK IN THE pre-Internet days, when I was deciding where to go to college, we mailed away for thick brochures that became our key source of information about the various schools. Today students do most of this data-gathering on the Internet. But there's still a critical ritual that most students experience in person: the college tour. You've probably participated in these walkabouts yourself, following an attractive, personable undergrad as he (or, usually, she) walks backward around the campus talking up the institution's best attributes.

In the chapters ahead, I intend to give a different kind of college tour. We'll look at how many traditional colleges have evolved to a point where they sometimes seem to be focused on everything except the vital interaction between student and professor. We'll look at how institutions created to provide broader access have strayed from their central purpose. And we'll look at how the new world of for-profit colleges—the world I inhabit—can mature into institutions that play a vital role in arming American workers with the skills they need for their economic future.

Let's start walking.

Harvard Envy

Why Too Many Colleges Overshoot

Harvard.

It's the strongest and most celebrated brand name in higher education. Surely, then, it must have been named after an extraordinary man.

Well, not necessarily. In fact, only the barest details of John Harvard's life are known. He was born in a London suburb in 1607, the son of a butcher. He had a half-dozen brothers and sisters, but in 1625 the plague killed his entire family except for his mother and one brother.[1] From 1627 to 1635, John studied at Cambridge, earning bachelor's and master's degrees.[2] Within weeks of his college graduation, his mother died, too.

His family's deaths played a vital role in this young man's life. After the plague killed his father, John Harvard inherited £300. His mother quickly remarried a wealthy man, who died five months later, leaving her with sizable wealth. So upon her death in 1635, John inherited even more money—including a profitable saloon called the Queen's Head Inn.[3] In 1637, eager to flee the Old World that had brought so much sorrow, twenty-nine-year-old John Harvard and his new wife, Anne, sailed to New England. As cargo, they brought along John's three-hundred-some-odd-volume library, which included Homer, Plutarch, and Bacon's essays.[4] Within months of landing, they bought land in Charlestown, Massachusetts. They began building a house, and John started preaching at a local church. But after just thirteen months in America, he died of consumption. He was thirty years old.

Harvard's life would have been sad and entirely anonymous but for one decision: he left one half of his estate, and his entire library, to a new college that was taking root across the Charles River in Cambridge. During his life, John Harvard had little to do with the formation of the college: its founders were laying plans for its creation months before he left England, and it's unclear if he had even visited the nascent institution, though according to one sketchy account, he may have once had dinner there.[5] And it's unclear exactly what happened to the £779 he bequeathed the school. According to one historian, half of it was likely squandered or embezzled by the headmaster.[6] John Harvard's books provided only a passing benefit, too: a 1764 fire wiped out most of the Harvard library, and just a single volume from his original bequest survives today.[7]

Nonetheless, the school's founders decided to celebrate John Harvard's modest largesse by naming their college after him. It was a surprising gesture—particularly since, unlike the founders of institutions such as Stanford or Cornell, Harvard's namesake was uninvolved in its creation. In fact, when Harvard alumni decided to put up a memorial on the spot where John Harvard is buried, no one could figure out exactly where that was, since the death of the obscure minister had not been particularly noteworthy at the time. A student had to serve as a model for the statue of "John Harvard" (unveiled in 1884) that now sits in Harvard Yard, as no images of John Harvard exist.

No one who knew John Harvard could possibly have predicted his lasting fame. And just as surely, no one involved in the early days of the tiny Massachusetts college to which his name is attached could have conceived the outsize importance that Harvard University would have on American higher education. It is a truly remarkable institution. There's hardly any parent who wouldn't be thrilled at the prospect of having a child attend and graduate from Harvard, nor hardly a professor or college administrator who wouldn't love to be able to say that he or she was employed there. And while this idealization may be natural and deserved, the near-universal veneration of Harvard can be a harmful force—one that drives far too many colleges to emulate Harvard in ways that aren't beneficial to the majority of students, or to the country.

The desire to imitate Harvard is nothing new. For much of American history, the small handful of colleges that existed were modeled on the pioneering New England institution, which was itself patterned on the great English universities. In fact, the defining visual elements of the traditional American college—the grass-covered "quad" and the Gothic buildings—are features mimicked directly from Cambridge and Oxford.[8]

In the early days, very few students were able to enjoy these bucolic settings: for centuries, American colleges attracted the tiniest sliver of the population. According to historian John Thelin, only nine colleges—Brown, Columbia, Dartmouth, Harvard, Penn, Princeton, Rutgers, William and Mary, and Yale—that survive today existed in the United States in 1781,[9] nearly a century and a half after Harvard's founding. (The number that existed in 1800 is just twenty-five.[10]) As best anyone can tell, roughly 1 percent of the colonial population attended college during this era (essentially all of them white Protestant men from privileged northeastern families), and many of them didn't stay long. "One peculiar characteristic of colonial colleges in their first decades is that there was little emphasis on completing degrees," Thelin writes. "Many students matriculated and then left college after a year or two, apparently with none of the stigma we now associate with 'dropouts.'"[11]

In these early years, there was only the loosest connection between going to college and the career one would pursue as an adult. Many people think these early colleges specialized in educating clergymen, and that's true to some extent, but that perception is overblown: none of these schools had divinity programs or could ordain ministers, though half of a typical Harvard class would enter the ministry.[12] Nor were these early colleges educating doctors or lawyers. Well into the 1800s, these professions were learned via apprenticeship, and there was no requirement that aspirant physicians or barristers attend college.[13] For many families, sending a child to college was as much about social position as it was about education. "A main purpose of the colleges was to identify and ratify a social elite," Thelin writes. "The college was a conservative institution that was essential to transmitting a relatively fixed social order."[14] In fact, for many years, the names of the men—and until the mid-1800s, they were almost always men[15]—being granted degrees at Harvard's commencement ceremony weren't read off alphabetically; they were recited in the order of the graduates' social rank.[16]

By the 1800s, however, the number of colleges began to grow quickly. And as the higher education market expanded and matured, a pecking order emerged, as it does in most markets over time. Colleges such as Harvard and Yale remained at the pinnacle of the evolving higher education landscape. And as newer, less pedigreed colleges entered the scene, many of them focused considerable energy and resources on trying to move up this food chain, to be more like their elite, upmarket competitors.

THIS EVER-UPWARD PHENOMENON has become familiar to people who watch the evolution of business, thanks largely to the work of Clayton Christensen. Christensen is a former Rhodes Scholar from Utah who spent the 1980s as a manager at an industrial ceramics company. In 1989, nearing age forty and with five children, he took the highly unusual move of chucking his managerial career to pursue a doctorate in business administration. "It was very risky," he recalls, but jumping into academia in midlife had its advantages. "I had a lot of questions that were relevant to the world that managers live in."[17]

While working on his degree at Harvard Business School, Christensen began studying the history of industries such as disc drives and earth excavators. In doing so, he continually found examples of established players being challenged by upstarts whose new products, in contrast to the accepted competitive strategies, were *worse* than existing goods on the market. By 1997, he was explaining his theory—which he called "disruptive innovation"—in a book called *The Innovator's Dilemma*, which would go on to sell five hundred thousand copies.[18]

In the book, Christensen explains how most companies focus too much energy on "sustaining innovations," that is, adding new and improved features to existing products. Eventually these companies "overshoot" their customers' needs, delivering overly complicated products that have too many unnecessary bells and whistles and cost too much.

In contrast, Christensen identified a new breed of competitors that thrived by focusing their development efforts on "disruptive innovations" that *underperformed* existing products, and were "typically cheaper, simpler, smaller, and, frequently, more convenient to use."[19] Christensen points to dozens of examples of disruptive innovations that were presenting huge challenges to dominant companies—and that had the potential to topple entire industries. Among the 1990s-era examples he cites: digital photography (which would render film cameras nearly obsolete), mobile telephony (creating huge problems for providers of landline phone service), and drone aircraft (which would reduce the military's demand for manned bombers).[20] During the early years of the twenty-first century, that list has only grown, as free Internet sites have undermined newspapers, Google Docs has challenged Microsoft's Office suite, Skype introduced millions to the joy of free telephone calls, and inexpensive Flip video cameras began replacing pricey camcorders before being overtaken themselves by smartphones, which also upended alarm clocks, video games, wristwatches, cameras, and countless other single-purpose devices.

The producers and users of incumbent devices scoffed at all of these newcomers. Serious photographers ridiculed early digital cameras, whose photos were not nearly as clear as those produced with film, and later felt the same about smartphones, whose pictures were not as good as quality digital cameras. Most consumers sneered at MCI, then the early mobile phones, and later Skype, for their poor sound quality and lack of consistency compared with standard phones. These defects limited customer acceptance to fringe markets at first, and incumbent companies viewed the nascent products as low end and uncompetitive with their own high-quality devices or services. As the new competitors improved their products, however, more and more customers were willing to accept tradeoffs in exchange for the lower prices, increased convenience, or other advantages of the newer products. In time, the new products were able to match the incumbents on most fronts and exceed them on others, fundamentally shifting the market dynamics.

Although most colleges don't behave exactly like businesses, Christensen's framework is essential for understanding the forces that drive higher education. Just as companies tend to focus too much energy on improving products to create "sustaining innovations," there is a powerful impulse in higher education for institutions to move upmarket—in short, to become a bit more like Harvard. It's a force I refer to as "Harvard Envy." I define Harvard Envy as the emotional tug that exerts itself on college leaders—presidents, trustees, administrators, and faculty—and forces them to manage their institution toward gaining more prestige, oftentimes without specific linkage to actual student learning. Whenever you hear a college president talking about the average SAT scores of his institution's incoming class—a measure of exclusivity that's often directly correlated with how many students the college is able to deny for admission—you're seeing a manifestation of Harvard Envy. If you were to sit in on the trustees' meeting at a traditional college and use a stopwatch to measure how much of the discussion was focused on donations, endowment growth, and the master construction plan for more buildings from impressive architects to fill the campus, you'd be seeing evidence of Harvard Envy. If you were able to measure the number of hours a typical professor at one of these colleges devoted to writing up esoteric research papers for obscure journals or politicking over which junior faculty would or would not get tenure, instead of actually interacting with students, you'd be seeing one of the effects of Harvard Envy.

It's a phenomenon George Dehne sees all too often. Dehne runs a consulting firm that helps colleges define and refine their strategic position, by helping them understand their strengths and weaknesses versus those of competing institutions. "I see [Harvard Envy] all over the place," Dehne says. "The real driving force behind it is the governance system." Thanks in large part to the lifetime employment offered by the tenure system, the faculty are an enormously powerful constituency at most colleges, and the fact that college presidents almost always begin their pre-administrative lives as faculty members only increases their loyalty to this key stakeholder. As scholars, faculty can be especially driven by prestige: if a college can attract brighter students and move up in the rankings, its faculty have more cachet and are likely to be surrounded by yet more impressive colleagues and students. In the same way that businesspeople have a natural drive to grow their companies—allowing them to manage bigger budgets and a bigger staff, and earn bigger salaries along the way—college presidents have a natural instinct to grow their colleges. They want more buildings, a bigger and better faculty, higher-caliber students, and a bigger endowment to feed their "institutional ego," to use Dehne's phrase.

Harvard Envy tends to exert itself on virtually every constituency at a typical university. When a university increases endowments, constructs new buildings, and upgrades the quality of the faculty and student body, everybody associated with the school wins. Administrators get raises or roles at bigger universities; faculty get more prestige and access to bigger grants; alumni and students see the value of their degrees increase; and donors are held in even higher esteem, because they matter to a more important institution. On the other hand, a university that stands still while others are improving loses on all the same fronts. When you add these forces together, they create an Ivory Tower Playbook, a set of rules that govern the day-to-day behavior of college leaders as directly as the football team's playbook guides the action of the quarterback. And in the Ivory Tower Playbook, the only permissible strategy is to climb the prestige ladder. This can be a significant contributor to the creation of academic excellence on a campus, but it can also lead to serious misallocation of resources.

The biggest problem with the Ivory Tower Playbook is that it showers ever more resources on the select group of students who are already college bound. Under the existing rules of higher education, a college is defined as "better" by turning away more potential students—no different than a nightclub that's "hot" because its system of bouncers and velvet ropes leaves a critical mass of people on the outside, noses pressed to the glass. The trouble is, as universities spend more and more money making themselves ever more unattainable, they're spending money that could be better used to make education more accessible, rather than out of reach, to those who can't afford the price of admission. Top universities could enable more students to access their excellence by expanding their student bodies, or by building partnerships with less prestigious universities or community colleges. As a society, we need to use our resources to expand opportunity—to make more room inside the club—instead of watching those resources flow to the one-upmanship efforts of institutions trying to exclude more and more people, just to achieve a tiny extra sliver of prestige.

The silver lining to Harvard Envy is that it creates opportunity—not for students, mind you, but for innovators in the field of higher education. Every time a college tries to do something to enhance its prestige, it's creating an opening for a disruptive entrant to make a play for the students it is overshooting. While higher education isn't as dynamic as the market for computer gadgets or telephone services, in fact it has a rich history of disruptive innovation. And the first and biggest disruptor came in the most unlikely guise of a Vermont congressman born in 1810.

JUSTIN SMITH MORRILL was the son of a blacksmith. Morrill graduated elementary school and spent just six months in high school; he couldn't afford to attend college. But he spent much of the rest of his life reading books and trying to make up for the formal education he lacked.[21]

Starting as a teenager, Morrill began working in a general store, eventually becoming a partner in the enterprise. As a businessman he was savvy and successful—so much so that at the age of thirty-eight, he sold his interest in the establishment and was able to retire.[22] At that point, his interest turned to politics. By 1854, at the age of forty-four, he was elected to Congress, where he'd eventually serve for forty-three years—becoming, at the time, the longest-serving congressman in American history.[23]

Soon after arriving in Washington, Morrill began agitating for the government to make changes to America's system of higher education. Morrill was a believer in the Jeffersonian philosophy that America would be a nation of educated, active farmers—but the farming class remained shut out from higher education.[24] At the same time, he became concerned about a more practical worry: the agricultural output of U.S. farms was declining, and American farmers seemed behind the curve when it came to adopting the latest science-based farming practices being implemented in Europe. In particular, European farmers were becoming far more sophisticated in their use of crop rotation, shifting between crops in a careful cadence designed to leave the soil with enough nitrogen to dramatically improve per-acre output.[25] Morrill began to advocate for the creation of a new kind of college, one specifically aimed at educating farmers.

While Morrill is considered a giant figure in the history of American education, historians point out that his critique of the existing system of higher education was part of a broader rethinking—and that he wasn't the first to conceive of the idea of schools for farmers. As Morrill biographer Coy Cross notes, "workingmen's colleges" already existed in Europe, and for decades before Morrill began making proposals in Congress there had been enthusiastic discussion about creating agricultural colleges. At least two such agricultural colleges already existed, in Michigan and New York, before Morrill ever brought up the idea in the nation's capital.[26] Furthermore, the notion of "industrial" colleges that would focus on "mechanical arts" (which would come to include engineering) had been receiving vocal support since the 1850s, by an Illinois education advocate named Jonathan Baldwin Turner. In an 1851 speech to a farmers' convention, Turner noted that out of one hundred American workers, society needed just five employed in "professional" jobs but ninety-five to work in "industrial"-class jobs. "Where are the universities, the apparatus, the professors and the literature, specifically adapted to any one of the industrial classes?" Turner asked.[27]

In 1856, Morrill began talking up a scheme that would create colleges for farmers that would be modeled after West Point. Tuition would be free—all bills would be covered by taxpayers—and, ever the politician, Morrill proposed that each member of Congress be allowed to designate a student for admission. In arguing for the plan, Morrill saw an investment in America's farmers as essential to the country's development—and comparable to government support for railroads, harbor improvements, and coastal surveys.[28] Over time, however, the proposal morphed into something else: a measure that would give states wide swaths of federal land, which they could sell to raise money to fund these new "land-grant" colleges, at least one per state.

Morrill's plan proved controversial. "Some lawmakers believed that the issuance of land script would open the door to the land speculators who would take advantage of the procedure to reap huge profits," write historians Ray Herren and John Hillison. (Even if it dramatically expanded educational opportunity, they didn't feel good about educational legislation leading to *profit*.) "However, the greatest opposition came from Southern legislators. In the 1850s, the raging debate in government was over the power of the federal government versus the power of the states. Because the Constitution made no provision for any type of nationally funded education, Southerners considered the bill to be not only unconstitutional, but another means by which proponents of a strong central government could seize more power."[29] Indeed, one Alabama senator called it "one of the most monstrous, iniquitous, and dangerous measures which have ever been submitted to Congress."[30]

In 1859, the bill passed Congress but was vetoed by President James Buchanan, who believed that the bill was unconstitutional, that the proposed colleges would be unsuccessful, and that agriculture and mechanics weren't legitimate fields of study for colleges.[31] But Morrill was undeterred, and in 1862—with the benefit of a new Congress, a new president, and the secession from the Union of many of the southern states whose congressmen had objected to the bill's expansion of federal power—another iteration of the bill was signed into law by Abraham Lincoln.[32]

Passage of the bill, however, hardly stilled the controversy. Leaders at traditional colleges bristled at the idea of the government wasting so much money to educate farmers, a group that elitists didn't see as warranting the investment. "Some of us, when we learned [the Land-Grant College Act] was quietly passing the House and Senate, courageously set ourselves against the allocation of so large a sum of money to so narrow and sectional a purpose," Princeton president James McCosh told the convention of the National Education Association in 1873. "We argued that, so far as these schools were simply agricultural ones, they were not accomplishing so great a good as to entitle them to so large an endowment."[33]

Critics derided the idea of aspirant farmers sitting in front of blackboards instead of working with their hands. The sensitivity to this issue was so great that when some states set up their land-grant colleges, they emphasized that students would be engaged in several hours a day of routine manual farm work. The purpose, historian Edward Danforth Eddy, Jr., writes, was to ensure they "would not be 'educated away from the farm' by this new method of 'book farming.'"[34]

Filling seats in the new colleges wasn't easy, and critics focused on the low admissions standards the new schools used to do so. Indeed, a 1909 Carnegie Foundation report suggested that, in their early years, "a large proportion of the agricultural colleges of the country are still engaged in secondary education," meaning they were viewed as functioning more like high schools than colleges.[35]

At the University of Kentucky, president James K. Patterson remembered such opposition very well. "The old established colleges and universities looked askance upon the new intruders into their prescriptive domain," he recalled in a 1910 speech. "'A waste of public land and private fortunes' and 'the dreams of amiable but visionary enthusiasts,' 'another illustration of the following of attempting to make a silk purse out of a sow's ear,' a 'foolish effort to substitute an imitation and a counterfeit article for the genuine coin and currency of the realm,' a 'doctrinaire experiment that would end in failure,' a 'project analogous to the fantastic device to extract gold from sea water'—such were the comments and such the skeptical similitudes upon the lips of the learned."[36]

At Cornell, an agricultural instructor who taught during the 1870s and '80s recalls an educational journal that referred to the institution as "a school where hayseeds and greasy mechanics were taught to hoe potatoes, pitch manure and be dry-nurses to steam engines." The instructor recalled, "We were even dubbed a 'Godless, fresh-water college planted in Ezra Cornell's potato patch' by the students of one of the older New England colleges. These and many other things of the same sort were hard to bear, for at that time we were not sure that we should laugh last."[37]

Of course, we now know the proponents of the Land-Grant College Act have decisively had the last laugh. Today historians look back on the creation of land-grant colleges as one of the most important innovations in the history of American higher education. Within eight years of Morrill's law taking effect, thirty-seven states had begun work on colleges that would teach agriculture, mechanical arts, and military tactics.[38] A significant subset of America's leading schools, including the Massachusetts Institute of Technology and the Universities of California and Wisconsin, stemmed from Morrill's bill, and many of the Historically Black Colleges and Universities were founded as a result of its progeny legislation. "Practical" fields such as engineering and veterinary medicine—today considered professions—were revolutionized by work done on campuses at land-grant colleges.[39] Military historians say that the training these colleges provided to thousands of men in subsequent decades was an important reason America's military proved so successful over the next century—and played an underappreciated but crucial role in U.S. victories in World Wars I and II. By 1955 more than 20 percent of American college students were enrolled in a university that owed its existence to Justin Smith Morrill and his land-grant legislation. The bill, Eddy writes, "forced education to fit the changing social and economic patterns of an expanding nation. It helped to create equality of educational opportunity offering education at public expense to the industrial classes; it gave some measure of dignity to the vocations provided such class."[40] James Bryant Conant, who presided over Harvard from 1933 to 1953, compared the creation of the land-grant colleges to the opening of public libraries across the country: an important step in democratizing learning and making knowledge available to every American.[41]

Over time, however, the land-grant colleges evolved. Their disruptive power dissipated, and many became part of the establishment. Among the original land-grant colleges are places like Cornell and Berkeley, which have evolved to become just as elite and inaccessible as the ancient, Ivy-covered colleges Morrill took aim at a century and a half ago.

Eventually, the disruptors moved upmarket themselves, succumbing to Harvard Envy—and creating the opportunity for new generations of disruptors, which we'll visit in later chapters.

IT'S IMPOSSIBLE TO examine higher education's upward-is-better problem without acknowledging the role that college rankings play in driving it. Since *U.S. News & World Report* unveiled its inaugural rankings in 1983, universities have become obsessed with their relative status. The limitations of the *U.S. News* rankings have been the subject of a generation-long debate and a thousand op-eds; they've even inspired boycotts and countless alternative ranking systems. While I'm no more a fan of this list than most educators, I'm less interested in the imperfect methods used to create the rankings than the negative effects they've had on colleges. The biggest damage: these rankings drive colleges to focus less on educating their students and more on ploys designed to push colleges a nose ahead in this annual horse race.

One of the most frustrating and futile aspects of this race is that despite all the effort and resources devoted to it, they have little demonstrable effect. In 1991, Clark Kerr, the legendary former president of the University of California and a noted higher education thinker, published an essay titled "The New Race to Be Harvard or Berkeley or Stanford." In it, he compares a 1906 ranking that measured America's top fifteen colleges against a 1982 ranking. "Over the nearly 80 years from 1906 to 1982, only three institutions dropped out from those ranked in the top 15—but, in each case, not by very much—and only three [new schools] were added," he wrote. The point continues to the present.[42] As Robert Frank and my Duke professor Philip J. Cook point out in *The Winner-Take-All Society*, if you examine a list of the eleven institutions ranked as "the best in the nation" in 1940 and compare it to any of the various lists published today, you'll find there's little, if any, difference.[43] As Kerr wrote, "A reputation, once established, is an institution's greatest asset. These listings also imply that, whatever may be the sources of the reputation to begin with, they will mostly continue to support the reputation."

Indeed, the primary reason Harvard Envy can be so dangerous is that it represents a fundamental misallocation of resources. Instead of focusing laser-like on educating more students or better educating the students they already have, leaders of the top few hundred colleges are more likely to "win"— become heroes, get better jobs, have statues erected or buildings named after them—by setting their sights on a more elite group of students. They must spend huge money on big-ticket items designed to increase their institution's prestige, in the hope of gaining new ammunition as they fight over the same small group of high-end students who are already certain to attend college. All too often these battles serve mainly to tip more students from the same pot into their own institutions rather than the one down the road. In this zero-sum game, each school races to get the best students, but there is very little expansion in the overall pool of students who have access to traditional four-year institutions. The top twenty universities in the United States educate around 1 percent of the nation's college students. Their competition reallocates the seats in class, but does not add to them. And that reallocation comes at a staggering cost.

Students and parents who are highly conscious of their own competition to enter elite schools may not fully appreciate the amount of effort schools are making to attract them. The students spend four years of high school racking up high grades and impressive extracurricular activities—and yes, taking SAT preparation courses—to make themselves attractive to schools that themselves are expending enormous resources to make themselves as appealing as possible to the prospective students.

The most obvious signs of Harvard Envy are the cranes and scaffolding that are fixtures on so many college campuses. If you're a Major League Baseball manager, you measure your worth by wins and losses. If you're an investment banker, you keep score by the number of deals done. And if you're a university president today, one important measure of your legacy is the number of new buildings erected on campus during your term of office.

Part of this is driven by fund-raising concerns: any philanthropist who's writing a big check loves to see his name chiseled into the cornerstone of a building that will last for generations. And on some campuses, it often seems that buildings are built merely to justify the fund-raising.

This phenomenon is not new. In fact, I recently came across a book published in 1949 by Harvard University Press titled *Education, Bricks and Mortar: Harvard Buildings and Their Contribution to the Advancement of Learning.* The book opens with two pages of black-and-white aerial photos of Harvard's campus. Most of the rest of the book features black-and-white glamour shots of various Harvard buildings, along with statistics about their construction. There are also inspiring quotes along the lines of this one: "Education to survive must be given form and substance." As best I can tell, this book's sole purpose was to entice alums to put their names on new Harvard buildings.

Higher education's fixation on buildings sometimes reminds me of home renovators' obsession with fancy kitchens. Just because you have a Sub-Zero fridge and a six-burner Wolf stove doesn't mean you're going to be a good cook. As in many things, education is more a function of the software than the hardware. And better buildings don't make a better college. Faculty members, not buildings, teach students.

More than a half century after that Harvard fund-raising book was published, higher education's fascination with bricks and mortar continues. In early 2009, in the wake of the global financial crisis, journalist Nina Munk visited Harvard to find a university in full-blown panic as its rate of spending could no longer be supported by an endowment downsized by the financial crisis. "The university is facing the onerous financial consequences of over-building," she wrote. Between 1980 and 2000, Harvard added nearly 3.2 million square feet of new space, and between 2000 and 2008, it added 6.2 million more, a covered area that's roughly the size of the Pentagon. "All across campus, one after another, new academic buildings have shot up," Munk wrote, putting the total price for this building spree at $4.3 billion.[44] All this construction took place during a period in which the student population at Harvard grew by only about fifteen hundred. It's tempting to think about how many needy, deserving students could have been put through more affordable colleges—or through Harvard itself—with the money Harvard invested in all those new buildings

Harvard's construction campaign is an epic example of how the empire building that goes on at traditional colleges can sap the wherewithal of a university, forcing it to cut back on more vital functions. At the beginning of the 2009/2010 academic year, Harvard president Drew Faust addressed the school community to discuss the impact of the financial crisis on Harvard. The school's renowned endowment, which peaked at $37 billion in 2008, had dropped to $26 billion in just one year's time. "That's an $11 billion drop," Faust said for the benefit of faculty who weren't in the math department. It's particularly troublesome because, unlike a forty-year-old whose 401(k) loses value, Harvard essentially lives off endowment income, which provides one-third of its annual income each year. Universities typically spend 5 percent of their endowment each year, so Harvard's shrinking endowment means the university's operating expenses faced a $500 million shortfall. As if that weren't trouble enough, new donations had dropped around 10 percent in the face of the Great Recession.[45]

In her remarks, Faust discussed the many ways Harvard was seeking to tighten its belt—and in doing so, gave a glimpse of the many ways in which the university's sprawling, duplicative bureaucracy drives up costs. She noted, for instance, that Harvard has seventy different libraries. "Our collections are amazing; our staff is remarkable; but there are aspects of our structures and economic arrangements that don't make sense," she said. (Only at a university could this statement be controversial.) As at many universities, power at Harvard is so dispersed and decentralized that the school operates more like a loose confederation than a single entity. "When each of us has discretion to decide which of thirty different shades of crimson to put on our business cards, we've carried things too far," Faust said. To try to match expenses and revenue, Harvard offered voluntary retirement packages that were accepted by 500 staff, laid off more than 275 employees, and instituted a wage freeze for faculty and staff. Some of these cuts had a direct impact on students. The freeze on new tenure-track hires, combined with staff attrition and retirement, led to cuts in classes including statistical finance, junior economics seminars, and political science. In 2009, the *Harvard Crimson* reported that the Faculty of Arts and Sciences was aiming to stick more closely to an average eighteen-person lecture section (the university's long-standing target—versus the previous thirteen-person section average) by reducing the number of section leaders by 8 to 10 percent.[46] The school faces unique challenges in the years ahead as it tries to recover from overambitious growth that has left even this unimaginably wealthy institution cutting class sections, increasing class sizes, and scrambling to pay its bills.

Pause for a moment and think about the way Harvard uses its vast resources. At its recent peak, Harvard had approximately $37 billion in endowment with a total enrollment of fewer than twenty-two thousand students—or more than $1.5 million per student. At a certain point, shouldn't the discussion shift from how to use this wealth to create new buildings or amenities for this relative paucity of existing students, to how to use this money to educate *more* students, to provide wider access to this educational bounty? Mightn't the university at least try to find a way to permit more students from lesser colleges to take undersubscribed classes at Harvard? Or have Harvard professors teach classes at other schools, or let more students from other institutions have access to Harvard's labs, libraries, and data centers? But because expansion might make Harvard just a sliver less exclusive—thus perhaps narrowing ever so slightly its prestige lead over other institutions—it really doesn't happen.

You don't need to spend much time around campuses to be struck by the scale and scope of the building projects underway—a phenomenon that's particularly surprising in light of the Great Recession. In late 2009, Stanford had eighty-seven different construction projects underway at a total cost of $1.5 billion.[47] The University of Virginia borrowed $250 million the same year to finance nineteen different capital projects.[48] The list goes on at campus after campus. Donors will surely be proud to see their names emblazoned over the doorways, but as the Harvard example illustrates, it's far from clear that this construction will end up improving the education being provided to students.

The fact that so many of these buildings incorporate architectural styles designed to make them look older than they are says much about the fallaciousness of chasing status in higher education. One of the reasons Harvard is Harvard is because it actually *is* old: in academics, longevity is an integral part of prestige, and this serves as a big impediment to college presidents at newer institutions who try to find ways to move upmarket. One of the many downsides of chasing Harvard is that you'll never catch it: 2011 marked Harvard's 375th consecutive year as America's most highly regarded university.

AS COLLEGES PUT up new buildings around campus, administrators need to find something to put inside them. That's one reason why universities seem to be continually creating new academic programs—and rarely eliminating the ones that have outlived their usefulness or relevance. There often appears to be little regard for whether the world actually needs the services of the graduates these programs produce.

One way to get closer to Harvard, to take a step up the food chain, is to add prestigious graduate schools in areas such as law and medicine. Administrators, alumni, and boosters so covet the status that comes with such a school (even better if a hospital comes with it) that they'll sometimes do whatever it takes to make the case for getting it done.

Take Florida. In the mid-2000s it had a problem: not enough doctors to serve its growing and aging population. The trouble wasn't that Florida wasn't creating enough doctors, many observers argued. Indeed, in 2010, the state's existing publicly funded med schools (the University of Florida, Florida State University, and the University of South Florida) graduated 345 doctors collectively. The problem was that half of the students attending Florida medical schools left the state upon graduation and decided to make their careers somewhere else. To some, the most cost-effective solution was obvious: modestly grow the size of the existing public medical schools, while getting local hospitals to create more positions for the postgraduate "residency" training that's a core part of a new doctor's education. If doctors don't need to leave the state to train after medical school, the argument goes, they'll stay and make a career in state. But to some of the state's public universities, this would have been a tragic waste of a good crisis. Supporters of Florida International University, a Miami-based public university that has been steadily moving up the academic food chain, argued that the better solution would be to create a new medical school on its campus. It was joined by the University of Central Florida in Orlando, which contended it should get one, too. Even boosters of these expansions acknowledged that the costs would be high: over ten years, the two schools would consume approximately $500 million in taxpayer resources, along with an expected $20 million each in annual operating costs per year, all to train fewer than 250 new doctors each year.[49]

Lots of observers found the arguments for new medical schools to be unconvincing. "Reject Medical Schools" the *Palm Beach Post* editorialized, calling the planned med school expansion "ludicrous."[50] Officials at competing colleges suggested that the efforts to create new med schools were driven by concerns that went beyond the number of doctors in Florida. "Medical schools and great football teams are things that give your university increased stature," said Dr. Stephen Klasko, dean of the College of Medicine at the University of South Florida. (He would know: freshman applications to USF's undergraduate programs grew by 9 percent in 2009, to a total of 29,629 applicants, due in good measure to both the prominence of USF's medical school and the on-field success of its football team.) "Part of what's driving [this] is the need for more doctors, and part of what's driving it is what they want to achieve for their universities."[51]

Nonetheless, in 2006 the board that oversees the state's university system endorsed the plan to create two new med schools. In 2009, just as the financial crisis was forcing the state to raise tuition, cut class offerings, and lay off staff at its public universities, both UCF and FIU welcomed their first classes of aspiring doctors into what all agree are high-powered new medical schools. And once the train got moving, it was hard to stop: in the fall of 2011, Florida Atlantic University, the second youngest of Florida's state universities, also opened a medical school.

The University of Massachusetts faced an even tougher case

a few years ago in its attempt to add a law school. Though Massachusetts has more lawyers per capita than any place in the United States except for the District of Columbia, New York, or Delaware,[52] it had no public law school—unlike most of its New England neighbors. The glut of lawyers, meantime, was creating a problem for the private Southern New England School of Law, which strained to attract students, and whose grads struggled mightily on the bar exam and in the job market.

This was a match made in heaven. A state with a surplus of lawyers (and a shortage of cash)[53] meets a law school that's hemorrhaging money and can't get accreditation. The obvious solution: merge the law school into State U.

Proponents of the deal argued that if students had the option to attend law school at a state university whose low cost didn't necessitate six-figure student loans, more Massachusetts law grads might be willing to enter public service and give back to society, instead of simply joining corporate firms to earn big salaries and pay back their debts.[54] But, aside from the less costly ways to achieve the same goal, the case against the merger seemed pretty compelling. Thanks to the recession, demand for legal services has fallen steeply: in recent years, newspapers have been filled with stories of law firms resorting to laying off or arranging sabbaticals for law school grads they'd hired but for whom they had no actual work. "From an economic point of view, it's an investment in a profession that we may not need more of," State Treasurer Timothy Cahill told the *Boston Globe*.[55]

Financially, the project seemed dicey, too. Boosters said that while the law program might continue to lose money in the short term, over time, UMass would be able to increase enrollment dramatically, to more than 550 students by 2017, and that increase would bring in $81 million in revenue—enough to increase the quality of the program, win accreditation, and become profitable. Opponents questioned those numbers, however, suggesting that there was a chicken and egg problem with that logic: the existing law school's low quality would be a barrier to accreditation, and the school's continued lack of accreditation would impede efforts to boost enrollment and raise tuition revenue.

In the end, UMass trustees liked the plan, and UMass took over the program. By most accounts, it's off to a solid start: the size of the first-year class more than doubled, to 182.[56] But there's a lot riding on the program actually winning accreditation, and in the long term, the UMass takeover of this failing school may not be such a positive development for the state's taxpayers, or even for the students who are enrolling in a program with such an uneven history. But University of Massachusetts administrators now have a law school—a measure of prestige and another feather in their cap.

Even people inside the academy sometimes look with wonderment at the number of academic programs that exist with no real economic rationale. James B. Twitchell is a professor of English at the University of Florida and a keen observer of American commercial culture. When he looks at the way his academic department operates, he's a little perplexed. He estimates that his university spends about one-third of its departmental money and time teaching graduate students—even though a glut of humanities PhDs means there are very few full-time, tenure-track, college-level teaching jobs available for English doctoral graduates.

"Why don't we contract the program?" Twitchell writes in *Branded Nation*. "In fact, why don't we shutter it until the market for our product improves? No, we expand it, thinking that if we want to be seen as a major university, we have to be bigger. We need more heft, we are told. Plus, we like having [our graduate program]"—in part, Twitchell says, because having a lot of grad students around lets professors outsource more and more of their teaching to them.[57] He notes that the university has no economic justification for taking in the grad students, since most of them are on full scholarships, with their costs being borne largely by taxpayers.

In theory, many of these soon-to-be professors are doing research that makes the world a better place. In reality, too many of them toil away on off-in-the-weeds research projects that give new meaning to the word *obscure*. "The amount of redundant, inconsequential, and outright poor research has swelled in recent decades, filling countless pages in journals and monographs," write Mark Bauerlein, a professor of English at Emory University, and three colleagues in *The Chronicle of Higher Education*.[58] "The avalanche of ignored research has a profoundly damaging effect on the enterprise as a whole. Not only does the uncited work itself require years of field and library or laboratory research. It also requires colleagues to read it and provide feedback, as well as reviewers to evaluate it formally for publication." Once it's published, libraries feel compelled to subscribe to the journals that contain it—even if they're rarely consulted. As those journals pile up, the library will grow crowded, and soon it will be time to commence a Library Expansion Capital Campaign—a process that will send the college president out to woo the donors who will finance the cranes and scaffolding that will soon take up residence outside the "old" library. And so the cycle continues.

THERE'S ANOTHER COMMON way that Harvard Envy manifests itself: by the efforts top colleges go to in attempting to poach star faculty members from competing institutions. Too many colleges think if they can woo just one more A-list professor to their ranks, they'll get a sudden boost in the perception people have of their school.

The practice is not altogether new. As former Harvard president Derek Bok has noted, Harvard was transformed during the presidency of Charles William Eliot (who served from 1869 to 1909), in part because he aggressively recruited stellar faculty members from rival institutions.[59] Competition for the best faculty (and best students) can result in a vibrant intellectual experience; indeed, that is one of the ways the land-grant universities emerged as major players in the post–World War II era. Bringing in an outstanding new faculty member can energize an entire department.

But the effort to bag so-called "trophy professors" has accelerated in the last fifteen years. In the early 2000s, Indiana University and Purdue University estimated they'd spent more than $80 million each to create endowed chairs to lure star faculty members.[60] Writing in the *Boston Globe*, Patrick Healy outlined a fully formed taxonomy of the various kinds of stars who were up for grabs. "Rock Stars" are celebrity professors known for their controversy (e.g., Elie Wiesel at Boston University). "Stature Stars" are more serious academics who start or shore up important programs (e.g., economist Joseph Stiglitz at Columbia). "Department Stars" are less heralded faculty who fill a hole in a department's lineup (e.g., Rohit Deshpande at Harvard). "Sunset Stars" are in their fifties and sixties—their best work may be behind them, but they can still add luster to a school during the final years of their careers (e.g., philosopher Richard Rorty at Stanford). And "Superstars," Healy writes, do it all: "They have crossed over from academia to become stars that average Americans have heard of" (e.g., Henry Louis Gates at Harvard).[61]

Over the last decade, the most successful example of this star faculty recruiting has been at New York University, where president John Sexton has pursued a hypercharged strategy to bring the best and brightest to his Greenwich Village campus. During the 1990s, Sexton succeeded in raising the profile of NYU's law school, of which he was dean, which led to his promotion to lead the entire university in 2002. In that job, he set his sights on creating a world-class economics department. By 2003, he'd embarked on a hiring spree unprecedented in academia, leading to comparisons with the acquisitive late Yankees owner George Steinbrenner. While Sexton typically offered big salaries to established stars at rival schools, he also offered Greenwich Village apartments, guarantees of how many graduate assistants the professors would have, and light teaching loads. Mostly, though, he used his own energy and power of persuasion, flying across the country on short notice to woo a target, and talking up the collaborative environment that person would enjoy when Sexton lured in even more top-flight talent.[62]

And it worked: just as NYU's law school soared from number nine on *U.S. News & World Report*'s rankings when Sexton took over as dean to number five when he was installed as NYU's president in 2002,[63] so, too, have NYU overall ratings improved during his presidency. The Times Higher Education rankings of the top two hundred world universities listed NYU at number forty in 2008, up from number seventy-nine just four years earlier.[64] This has meant an increase in freshman applications to over thirty-eight thousand for fall 2010 admission.[65] The more applications a school receives, the harder it is to get into—and the more prestigious it is considered.

The most obvious criticism of pursuing academic talent the way Hollywood agents steal a rival's clients is that it requires the expenditure of time and money on something that has little impact on a typical undergraduate. It's a view espoused by Ronald Ehrenberg, a higher education researcher at Cornell. "The general quality of undergraduate teaching is not based on the few stars, but on all the faculty of a university," he says.[66] Indeed, one of the ironic side effects of the war for top faculty is that many of these academic stars have even less contact with undergrads than they did in the days when professors tended to spend their entire careers at a single institution. As economists Robert Frank and Philip Cook have pointed out, in the 1970s a typical professor might teach four courses a semester. By the 1990s, that figure had dropped to three courses—and for a top professor, it's likely to be even less.[67] Competitive recruitment of faculty stars may make eminent sense for the university that enhances its reputation with a new luminary, but it tends to be a zero-sum game for society—and maybe even less than zero-sum if it results in less teaching by the best faculty.

Critics who have spent time inside universities see more insidious results of these faculty wars. Writing in the *Boston Globe*, Healy cites James Duderstadt, former president of the University of Michigan, who sees the faculty recruitment wars as a threat to the preeminence of American universities by putting faculty research agendas ahead of the needs of the students. "Universities have become so preoccupied with wealth and status symbols of success that Duderstadt fears elite schools are moving away from their educational mission," Healy writes.[68]

Beyond high salaries, light teaching loads, and offers of university-financed housing, there's another way to help recruit and retain these star professors: by setting up specialized centers, with devoted staff and budgets, to study the subject that happens to be the star's specialty. For a measure of how pervasive this practice is, simply go to the Web directory of any big university and marvel at the number of "Center for the Study of XYZ" or "Institute for Research into ABC" filling the page. Some of these centers sound almost ridiculously removed from the academics that are—or should be—at the center of university life. Consider the Historic Costume and Textiles Collection at Ohio State University, or the University of Chicago's Center for Italian Opera Studies, or the Polish Music Center at the University of Southern California.

I like a good polka as much as the next guy, but it's hard to argue that the average family struggling to pay tuition at these schools would be eager to kick in a few extra hard-earned bucks to fund these institutes, that the taxpayer would feel good about subsidizing them, or, for that matter, that their existence furthers the goal of preparing today's undergraduates to contribute to the fast-changing world economy.

And make no mistake: even against the sprawling cost structure of the modern university, these high-priced faculty members and their staff represent a very real cost driver. At Harvard, personnel expenses represent roughly 50 percent of the annual cost of running the university.[69] Daniel L. Bennett of the Center for College Affordability and Productivity has calculated that between 1997 and 2007, the administrative and support staffs at colleges grew by 4.7 percent a year, double the rate of enrollment growth. "This burgeoning army of college bureaucrats defends this extraordinary growth as necessary to provide consumer-oriented students with an expanded breadth of non-instructional services," Bennett writes. If this growth continues, he figures, by 2014, U.S. colleges will have more administrative support employees than instructors.[70]

At a normal business, the fast growth of overhead costs would raise alarms. But in traditional higher education, three forces act to mute concern over costs. The first is that the vast majority of colleges are run as nonprofits, where there is often little incentive for reducing costs unless the institution itself is at risk. The second is that the economics of higher education are in many ways similar to the economics of health care, in which so many of the costs are borne not by consumers but by third-party payers, so that rising costs don't directly affect demand. (In health care, this money comes from insurance plans or federal health care programs; in higher education, it comes via federal and state subsidies, student loans, and charitable donations, a set of forces that are discussed in more detail in chapter 2.) And the third force muting concern over costs: in one of the more perverse side effects of Harvard Envy, elite colleges have been able to convince consumers that the ever-rising price of attending a top school is actually a sign of quality.

The elite schools are able to get away with this because demand for seats far outpaces supply: for Harvard's Class of 2015, the admissions office fielded nearly 35,000 applications and admitted just 2,158 students, an acceptance rate of 6.2 percent.[71] While elite, endowment-rich schools such as Harvard have tried to mitigate the effects of rising tuition by providing increasingly generous aid packages to middle-class families, the percentage of financially needy students at the country's wealthiest schools hasn't budged in recent years.[72] And when the Ivy League schools bump up tuition, schools a level below them—which often lack the riches to provide generous financial aid packages—often raise their own tuition rates, too.

THERE IS A well-honed counterargument to the criticism that today's universities are losing focus, are behaving too much like conglomerates, or are engaged in costly "mission creep." To wit: that "research universities" aren't in the business simply of teaching undergraduates, but instead should be equally focused on *creating* original knowledge.

Jonathan Cole, a longtime professor and former provost at Columbia University, is among the most articulate and passionate defenders of this broader set of aims. In *The Great American University*, he describes a meeting with Columbia alumni who, despite their education and sophistication, seem unaware of just how much of what goes on at Columbia has little, if anything, to do with teaching undergraduates—which, Cole says, is exactly how it should be. "The laser, magnetic resonance imaging, FM radio, the algorithm for Google searches, Global Positioning Systems, DNA fingerprinting, fetal monitoring, scientific cattle breeding, advanced methods of surveying public opinion, and even Viagra all had their origins in America's research universities, as did tens of thousands of other inventions, devices, medical miracles, and ideas that have transformed the world," Cole writes. In his view, it's this creation of knowledge that makes America's research institutions the best in the world.[73]

I agree with Cole. The research that takes place at America's universities makes a critical difference across much of society. Through these research advances, the American investment in universities has been repaid many times over. But agreeing, even wholeheartedly, as I do, that research universities provide exceptional value does not end the argument over whether America's universities as a group are efficiently delivering on their goal of *educating America's students*, or whether there are better paths for our country's educational investment.

I also think there's a real question as to how many institutions are actually performing this level of research. According to Cole's count, as of 2007 there were roughly 4,300 U.S. institutions of higher learning, most of which offered only undergraduate degrees. Only 260 were classified as "research universities," and Cole parses that number even further, concluding that "only about 125 contribute in meaningful ways to the growth of knowledge."[74] Cole isn't a snob: he gives strong praise to colleges well down the academic food chain, including community colleges. These places aren't curing diseases or inventing the next Google, but Cole says they're "essential to flesh out the opportunity structure that exists in the United States like nowhere else."[75]

The problem, as I see it, is that too many of the four-thousand-plus schools that *aren't* in the same class as Harvard are spending too much time and energy trying to be something they're not. One way to understand this is with a medical analogy. Consider three types of places a patient can go to get medical treatment: a walk-in clinic inside a drugstore staffed by a nurse practitioner (a model being popularized by MinuteClinic), the office of your trusty and beloved internist, and the specialist's practice at a leading academic hospital. Smart consumers understand that there's good reason to go to each of these providers: to the clinic to get a simple prescription for strep throat or an ear infection; to the internist for diagnosis of a more complicated malady and to coordinate care among specialists; to the specialist for surgery or treatment of a serious condition that's beyond a generalist's ability to treat. Many Americans are sophisticated enough to use these different facilities for what they're intended, and we all receive a benefit from this division of labor: lower cost and easier appointments at the walk-in clinic; thoroughness, familiarity, and coordination of care from an excellent primary care physician (like my wife); and the most focused expertise from a specialist when we need it. And since health care reform has been a top political and social issue for so many years now, we're probably all versed in the market dynamics on the supply side of this industry: that America has too few primary care physicians and too many specialists. (I'll leave "Specialist Envy" for another book.)

This smart and efficient division falls apart, however, if the nurse practitioner in a MinuteClinic, wanting a bigger challenge than stitching bagel-slicing cuts, tries to perform angioplasty; the results might not be pretty. The converse is also true: it would be pretty inefficient if a patient went to a cardiologist for her flu shot. Yet too many of these mismatches happen all the time in higher education.

We'd all be better off if consumers of higher education were more attuned to the segmentation that exists in this field—and understood that the gamut of services offered by a research university such as Harvard, a good state university such as Kansas, a small liberal arts college such as Pomona, a commuter college such as Cal State Fullerton, and the local community college are just as distinct. Too often, however, these lines are blurred as too many institutions continually try to move up the food chain. It's as if the new manager at an Applebee's woke up one morning and decided to make it his life's mission to attain a three-star Michelin rating, or the CEO of Kia figured if he added more comfortable leather seating and a top-notch car stereo, his cars could compete with Mercedes.

They're lofty, ambitious goals, but they don't make bottom-line sense.

A simple thought experiment highlights the point. In business, managers typically go after the market segment that seems most likely to deliver profits, and this might require moving upmarket or down-market. To expand the number of potential customers in the 1990s and early 2000s, luxury carmakers like BMW, Mercedes, and Volvo moved down-market by pushing their "entry-level luxury" cars, with sticker prices starting below $30,000. In retailing, the two biggest success stories of my lifetime have been Wal-Mart and Target, both aimed at mass-market consumers who'd prefer to save money rather than shop in a pricey department store.[76]

Now imagine a university president who tries to employ the same strategy. "We're currently ranked in the second quartile of the *U.S. News & World Report* rankings," she tells her board of trustees one day. "But we think there's a better market for us if we drop down to the third quartile. We'll eliminate some programs, some high-priced faculty, and our sports teams, and be able to cut prices and increase enrollment. We'll be able to fill the dorms. We won't have to give as much financial aid. We'll get more revenue, and it's a more sustainable strategy."

Any president who suggested this would be run out of town. The faculty would revolt: they want to teach the best and brightest. The alumni would go crazy: as the ranking of the school fell, so would the perceived value of the degree they'd worked to attain. Alumni donations would plummet. Every stakeholder related to this school would rebel.

There's a reason this scenario never plays out in the real world: Harvard Envy. Colleges have to aspire upward. There's really no alternative.

High-achieving high school students tend to get very caught up in the frenzy of trying to get in to one of the top colleges, but in reality they face little downside risk (other than repaying their loans). They're going to college one way or another, and while it may be important to them whether they go to Princeton or Michigan State or Davidson, it doesn't matter all that much to society. These students are going to get wonderful educations at great institutions, be exposed to new ideas, and are likely to get an entry pass into the club that includes our most esteemed citizens. So when schools incur huge expenses to compete over them, there's no real societal gain. If Amir goes to Oklahoma and Maria goes to Nebraska, or the other way around, it's essentially the same for society. So when Oklahoma and Nebraska start fighting over professors or building new libraries to try to steal each other's applicants, we're just spending more money to send the same pool of kids to college, with the taxpayers subsidizing the competition.

A key part of understanding Harvard Envy and the Ivory Tower Playbook is that the people engaged in this arms race *are acting rationally* within the system in which they reside. In this world, it is the job of the university president to make her school more prestigious, and the rules of what is "more prestigious" are pretty clear: better campus, higher-status faculty, better students, and so on. The president is hired specifically to accomplish those goals. The problem is that the incentives are themselves flawed, because they don't align with society's interests. The race to be more prestigious is an enormously expensive one, and the per-student costs are rising at a time when we should be conserving resources, focusing those that are available on student learning, and radically expanding the number of students who are granted entry.

While the forces that drive Harvard Envy may seem insurmountable, we still need to be conscious of the real costs that Harvard Envy has on all of us. My friend and colleague Peter Smith understands these costs better than most. Smith is a former congressman who has spent a long career in higher education, including stints as founding president of a community college and of a public university. Since 2007, he's worked alongside me at Kaplan as a senior vice president for academic strategies and development. In 2004, he wrote a book called *The Quiet Crisis: How Higher Education Is Failing America*, and much of what he wrote is as applicable now as it was then.

"If the goal of a college is to be well-thought of by other colleges; if the president of a college wants to move up to even more prestigious, high-paying jobs; if the aim is to enroll only the wealthiest, smartest, and most promising students who have already demonstrated their capacity for academic work, [then the existing model of higher education] serves pretty well. It will weed out those not ready. . . . It will teach cutthroat competition. . . . It will produce a few extraordinary alumni," Smith writes. "If the goal of a college, however, is to serve its community and nation by equipping students and graduates to be socially, economically and civilly competitive in a global society, this model must be revamped."[77]

And unlike much of the revamping being done on America's campuses, this one does not require bulldozers, cranes, or another endowed chair for a professor who will rarely step inside a classroom. Instead, it requires college administrators who focus on their core students, and do not obsess over winning the more elite students they wish they had. It requires educators who want to find ways to use the resources they're given to provide opportunities to more students, instead of finding ways to turn away more applicants in a bid for prestige. Some institutions are trying, most notably Arizona State University under its visionary president Michael Crow. But they are too few and far between.

New buildings, star professors, and quasi-academic "improvements" are just one set of techniques the leadership at traditional colleges use to accelerate the musical-chairs-like system in which too many prospective students compete for too few seats. At least most of these approaches are tied to the academic purpose of a university. Star professors and well-stocked labs, after all, may be expensive and ultimately lead to an unsustainable financial model, but they do contribute to the quality of education available to students and create the conditions for true excellence. No one, least of all I, doubts that the students at America's top universities have access to the most well equipped, learning-ready environments available anywhere. But as colleges seek ways to compete, they've found that one of their most effective tools to lure in more applicants is to spend billions on items far afield from the educational or research purpose of the university. As we'll discuss in the next chapter, many of today's universities are successfully attracting students, and thereby moving up the higher education pecking order, by turning their campuses into fun-filled resorts.

Club College

Why So Many Universities Look Like Resorts

Once upon a time there was a college where the students liked to relax by climbing rocks. Wouldn't it be great, the college thought, if students didn't have to trek into the wilderness to climb, but could do it right here on campus? So the college hired a construction team to create a giant wall studded with plastic bumps that, if you were particularly imaginative, resembled rock outcroppings. When the college opened its climbing wall, students loved it, and life was good.

Except life was suddenly not so good at a nearby college where students had nothing to climb. This college considered itself just as good as, if not better than, the first college, but its lack of a climbing wall created a deficiency. Over time, the second college began to feel inadequate. So administrators there decided that it, too, needed a climbing wall. And since the students who attended this college deserved something just as good as, if not better than, the students who attended the first college, the second college decided to make its wall a little bit bigger and a little bit better than the first school's wall. Indeed, when the wall was complete, it stood a few feet higher than the climbing wall at the first school. Now the students at this school could don harnesses and climb up and rappel down the structure—and life was good.

But it wasn't good if you attended a third nearby college, whose students looked at the first two colleges and suddenly felt deprived. When they'd decided to attend this fine institution, they'd expected it to keep pace with its rivals. Its administrators fretted: Shouldn't our students become just as proficient at an important life skill such as rock climbing as students at rival schools? So this third college began building a climbing wall—and in a development that will surprise no one, it made sure its wall was just a little bit taller and a little bit better than its rivals' climbing walls.

This parable of petty rivalry may sound like a group of eleven-year-old girls when the first in their crowd gets a cell phone. But there's nothing fictitious about it. Among higher education officials, this incident is known as the Texas College Climbing Wall War.

The conflict began about a decade ago, when Baylor University decided to build a climbing wall. "Plans called for the wall to extend 41 feet," the *Dallas Morning News* reported. "Then officials learned that Texas A&M University's wall is 44 feet. Baylor adjusted its blueprints for a 52-foot wall. Then the University of Houston built a 53-foot wall."[1]

Baylor's wall remains a focal point on campus tours. Kelli McMahan, Baylor's assistant director for campus recreation, says that at the time of its construction, Baylor's wall was "the tallest free-standing rock wall in Texas," and while other colleges climbing walls have surpassed it in height, she believes it's still the nicest. "Some would say it's more stunning—it's in the middle of the building, free-standing, versus attached to a wall," she says.

Today, Texas State University–San Marcos claims to have the highest collegiate climbing wall in the state. It's an L-shaped structure with arches that can accommodate ten climbers at a time; it opened in 2008. "We're taller than the others," says Glenn Hanley, director of campus recreation at Texas State at San Marcos. "There's some debate over whether we're taller than [the wall at] University of Texas at San Antonio, but we're taller. We have more surfaces to climb on. We have more variation in our surface. We have a larger bouldering section."

Not true, says Eliot Howard, assistant director for outdoor pursuits at the University of Texas at San Antonio. "As I understand it, our wall is a couple of feet taller than theirs," Howard says. He believes San Marcos's wall may have more "vertical square footage" than the San Antonio structure. But when it comes to height, which should be the true measure of what matters, he believes San Antonio comes out on top.

This mine-is-bigger-than-yours debate may seem a little ridiculous, but the people in charge of these structures see them as legitimate tools that help them in their pursuit of a worthy goal: recruiting students. "I think it's attention-getting for students to hear we have the tallest collegiate climbing wall in Texas," Howard says. "I think that in the scheme of things, adding amenities to our campuses to attract and retain students and to build that sense of pride in our campus makes sense. Climbing walls are one piece of that."

THERE ARE 168 hours in a week, and at the average college, an undergraduate student takes 15 credit hours per semester—meaning he or she will be in class for 15 hours a week. (Well, almost: on a college campus, a classroom "hour" is 50 minutes.) This means that 93 percent of his or her time will be spent outside the classroom. Some of those hours will be consumed by studying. Some students may spend time doing research, attending special lectures or performances, or participating in an internship. Many will have part-time jobs, join clubs, or engage in a community service project. But no matter how you account for the remaining time, it still leaves plenty of time for fun.

You don't have to rely on hypothetical math to conclude that today's college students are having plenty of extracurricular enjoyment—there's actual data that prove the point. In 2008, a group called Postsecondary Education Opportunity published a report examining how college students utilize their time, based on the results of the American Time Use Survey, which is administered by the Bureau of Labor Statistics. For full-time college students aged 18 to 24, it found the average student spends 2.9 hours a day on education (defined as attending classes, doing research or homework, or participating in non-sports extracurricular activities such as student government). In contrast, the students spend 4.5 hours per day on "Leisure and Sports."[2] (The education numbers might even be overstated: a 2011 book crunches survey data to indicate that students at four-year traditional colleges spend barely more than twelve hours per week studying.[3])

There's nothing wrong with having fun at college. But if you spend time on campuses today, you can't help but marvel at how much energy and money colleges are spending to help support students' desire to have a good time. Many traditional universities today are morphing into full-blown resorts. They have gyms that are better appointed than most commercial health clubs. They've replaced traditional dining halls with more intimate bistro-style eateries, restaurant-quality facilities, and food courts like those found in a shopping mall. Traveling around campuses, I'm convinced today's college student has better dining options than most business travelers encounter on the road. These schools' theaters and museums rival the cultural offerings in many smaller cities. Modern residence halls—no one calls them "dorms" anymore—offer the comfort and luxury you'd find at a mid-range hotel. In fact, many parents who are too frugal to splurge on a quality weekend getaway for themselves are nonetheless incurring enormous expenses to send their children to these luxurious campuses for four years.

It would be one thing if students and their families could opt out of the non-educational offerings that drive up the costs of attendance. But in most cases, they can't. Like cable companies, higher education institutions typically offer a "bundled product," an all-inclusive package that requires you to pay for a set of amenities whether you like it or not. In the same way that cable customers who never watch a moment of MTV or E! wind up paying for those channels in order to get CNN and ESPN, students at most colleges wind up paying for recreation complexes, lush landscaping, the campus radio station, and the women's lacrosse team regardless of whether they ever swim a lap, admire the lawn, listen to the radio, or watch a game. While there are ways to avoid some of the charges associated with attending a college—commuter students can avoid paying for a high-end dorm, for instance—for the most part, students are held captive by the ways colleges set prices. You can't just buy the education. If you want in, you have to buy the gardens, the café, and the football team as well.

All of this comes at a significant cost. For the 2010/2011 academic year, the average private, not-for-profit four-year institution charged annual tuition of $27,293, according to the College Board. The average four-year state institution charged in-state students $7,605, a number heavily subsidized by state financial support.[4] (The prices don't include room or board.) These numbers don't reflect the burden borne by families who choose to send their children to the nation's highest-priced colleges, whose costs for tuition, room, board, and fees can now routinely top $50,000 per year, a figure that itself doesn't nearly reflect the full cost of attendance.

If you drilled down into an upscale college's finances, you'd be amazed at how much of the money goes to supporting things that have nothing to do with the classroom—and is instead spent on activities that aren't included in any real definition of education or learning. In some ways, this is not surprising. Many universities appear to have concluded there's not much more they can spend on education. At top schools, there is already an ample supply of respected professors, top-notch computers, comfortable classrooms and well-stocked libraries. So as these schools' price tags keep rising, more of the money is going toward making sure one school's climbing wall is at least six inches taller than that of its nearest competitor.

Free market proponents may see nothing wrong with this: it's how our capitalist system works. I may buy a Ford, but if you can afford a Jaguar, go for it. If Google wants to build its Googleplex and transport its employees to work in WiFi-enabled vans, feed them free lunches, and have their dry cleaning picked up, that's its choice—one justified, presumably, by the advantages doing so gives it in recruiting good employees. So why shouldn't universities be able to offer new amenities to accomplish the same thing?

There's a simple answer: universities receive huge funding and subsidies from U.S. and state taxpayers. Some of this money flows directly via government grants. Some flows less directly, via government-subsidized financial aid or the tax deductions offered to colleges by their nonprofit status and the charitable donations they receive. These subsidies and grants amount to some $15,540 per student at four-year public institutions.[5] Colleges tend to sequester some forms of spending so alumni donors pay 100 percent of the bill, particularly if the expenditure involves a new football stadium. But money is fungible, and allocation of funds to one project frees up money for another. And the tax system is still subsidizing the donors writing the checks and the universities that are cashing them. The $1 million donation from a generous alum in the highest tax bracket is costing the federal government as much as $350,000 in foregone federal income tax revenue—money the government could have spent on something else, or returned to taxpayers (or that might have been donated to another cause.)[6]

Economically, there's a powerful case that the government should promote and help fund higher education. Every time a new college graduate walks across the stage at commencement, we all benefit: that person has become better skilled and more productive. Our economy receives the boost of more creative thinking, more sophisticated analysis, or maybe just more avoidance of dumb mistakes. Most grads will silently contribute to the economy; some will create goods or services (or even make breakthrough discoveries or invent new products) that will make a big difference to society. Grads will also pay more in taxes than if they remain uneducated and limited to a lifetime of lower wages: while estimates of the earnings payoff that results from education vary, a widely cited 2002 study by the U.S. Census Bureau figured that a person earning a bachelor's degree enjoyed lifetime earnings of $2.1 million (in 1999 dollars), compared with $1.2 million for a high school graduate and $1 million for a high school dropout.[7] Up to one-third of the productivity growth in the United States from the 1950s to the 1990s was the result of education, according to one study;

another concluded that if America's educational achievement rose to that of top nations such as Finland or Korea, U.S. GDP would have been 9 to 16 percent higher in 2008.[8]

But that argument, so strong insofar as it applies to educational investments, starts to fall apart when it's applied to expenditures that in truth have little or nothing to do with education. What is the societal return on investment in the sorority semiformals, the water polo matches, and the long evenings of beer pong that are very much a focal point of life on many campuses—all of which are, to one extent or another, being subsidized by taxpayers? Why should a guy on a factory line or serving Cokes at Bennigan's be taxed to fund a French restaurant because it happens to be located inside a college's student union? Why should taxpayers be indirectly subsidizing Michigan's quest to defeat Ohio State's football team?

ACROSS THE COUNTRY, examples abound of the luxurious life led by undergraduates.

Consider the once-humble dormitory. My kids think I'm Methuselah when I tell them that my freshman dorm room was a barren, 150-square-foot white rectangle with two twin beds, a linoleum floor, and a single plug on each side of the room, all housed in a simple, unornamented brick building in a distant corner of campus. It wasn't too many years ago that students who wanted microwaves or mini-fridges in their rooms had to bring them to campus themselves. Today, in newer residence halls, these amenities are often built in. Years ago, coin-operated laundry facilities were located in dormitory basements. Today, the nicest dorms feature in-suite washers and dryers, shared by just four roommates and with no need for coins. At First Street Towers, a newer residence hall at

Purdue University (a land-grant college), students enjoy private one-person rooms and bathrooms, kitchens, coffee bars, and "heirloom quality" furniture, some of it built by local Amish craftsmen. During the 2009/2010, academic year, a stay in First Street Towers (including a twelve-meal weekly plan) cost $14,204.[9]

At Boston University, residents in Student Village II, a twenty-six-floor glass-and-steel tower built near the banks of the Charles River, enjoy a spectacular view east toward downtown Boston and its harbor. "Sometimes I miss the elevator because I'm too busy looking out the window," one student told the *Boston Globe*. The spacious suites have walk-in closets. The media room features a plasma-screen television. The downstairs laundry facility features washers and dryers that alert students via computer when they're available. "So luxurious is the 960-bed dorm that parents' jaws dropped in disbelief when they helped their children move in," the *Globe* reported. "The suites of singles and doubles, with elegantly furnished common rooms…resemble nothing like what older generations remember of their college housing—sterile cinder-block boxes with institutional bunk beds and a communal bathroom down the hall." The newspaper quoted one parent who eyed her daughter's new accommodation with a mixture of incredulity and envy: "If there's a martini bar, I'm staying."[10]

At Princeton, a residential college named after former eBay CEO Meg Whitman features triple-glazed mahogany-framed casement windows made of leaded glass, a dining hall with a thirty-five-foot ceiling gabled in oak, and spacious rooms. According to *BusinessWeek*, the hall is part of a ten-building complex that cost Princeton $136 million—or, as the magazine calculated it, $272,000 for each of the five hundred undergraduates it will house.[11] (As a point of comparison, the average price of a single-family house in the United States in mid-2010 was $183,400.)[12]

The *Pittsburgh Post-Gazette* summed up many people's reaction to these overly comfortable residences: "Luxury housing spoils rich kids, divides students by class and encourages conspicuous consumption, none of which colleges are supposed to do."[13]

Building over-the-top residence halls is an expensive undertaking, and one not every school can do. But there's one critical piece of the student experience that's far easier to upgrade: the dining hall. In recent years, many schools have made big strides to improve their food offerings. Organic foods, local produce, and a wide variety of ethnic offerings are now de rigueur. Some schools go even further.

At Virginia Tech, students can choose a live lobster from a tank and have it prepared before their eyes. Each fall, the university's dining services personnel contact the families of incoming freshman to ask about favorite recipes, the *Daily Beast* reports, and then add students' favorites to the regular menus.[14]

At Oregon State, the dining staff flew to Mexico to gain experience with authentic ethnic cuisine in order to recreate it for the student body. When a student wrote a column in the school newspaper complaining about the lack of spicy chicken, the dining services team had it added to the menu in a matter of hours.[15]

At Wheaton College, a former Ritz-Carlton chef oversees menus, which in a typical week might include entrees such as handmade Belgian truffles, sweet chili chicken, pork loin with *dulce picanta* salsa, and wheat berry pilaf.[16]

To work off all these calories, students need exercise. At even an average campus, the athletic complex offers countless ways for them to get it. But based on my informal perusal of college Web sites, few of those options will offer as much fun as an afternoon in the Student Leisure Pool at Texas Tech. Built at a cost of $8.4 million (paid for via student activity fees) and opened in May 2009, the facility features a 645-foot winding Lazy River that students navigate on inner tubes, a 20-person hot tub, a 10-foot drop slide, a Cascading Water Wet Deck, and a Bubble Couch.[17] To be honest, I'm not sure what a Bubble Couch is, but I'm guessing it's hard to pull out the physics textbook when one is lounging on it.

As much as they may make older adults want to go back to college, these examples should also make them wonder: Why do colleges feel the need to provide nineteen-year-olds with Belgian truffles and Cascading Water Wet Decks? When I asked that question to a group of college counselors, I was told that if I truly wanted to understand the "resortification" of colleges, I might want to take a look at High Point University. So I boarded a plane bound for central North Carolina.

THE FIRST THING a visitor sees upon driving through the gates at High Point is a row of prime, reserved parking spaces to the right. In front of each spot is a red LED sign emblazoned with a prospective student's name and his hometown. They remind me of the signs that car rental companies use to guide preferred customers to their cars—and they're the first indication that High Point University's notion of how to woo students is different from that of most institutions.

At typical colleges, campus tours can accommodate a dozen or more students and their families, and they're almost always done on foot. At High Point, campus tours are private affairs—one admissions rep for every one or two families—and they're accomplished via golf cart. Outside the admissions office, a small fleet of golf carts stands ready.

When High Point College was founded in 1924—it traded "College" for "University" in 1991—it had a faculty of nine and was housed in three partially complete buildings. Its Depression-era students sometimes paid their tuition with livestock. Over the years, finances remained a challenge: in 1934, the college declared bankruptcy, but after World War II, its financial situation improved as returning GIs arrived with their federal education funding.[18] Like hundreds of other small, regional private colleges, the school found a reasonable degree of success educating a clientele made up mostly of local students who weren't equipped for more elite schools but whose families could afford to pay more than state university tuition. Chris Dudley, High Point University's vice president of administration, graduated from the school in 1994, and he speaks frankly of the institution's status in that era: "Honestly, it was a sleepy school that was like a lot of other liberal arts schools—well thought of, but not thought of a lot."

This began to change in 2005, when the university appointed a new president. Nido Qubein, a wealthy consultant and motivational speaker, had graduated from High Point in 1970 and served on its board. Upon becoming the school's president, he began raising money and went on a construction binge aimed at giving High Point a world-class campus and a whole new image.

Dudley walks me around the grounds, highlighting the changes. Until a few years ago, a major roadway bisected the campus, but Qubein had the road rerouted to create the "International Promenade." Flags of foreign countries, each representing the homeland of a High Point student, hang from flagpoles lining the walkway. Classical music plays from outdoor speakers as we walk past benches with life-size statues of such great thinkers as Galileo, Aristotle, and Shakespeare.

But the touches that led so many counselors to point me

toward High Point are mostly in the fifteen new buildings that Qubein had the college build in the past few years. (Thirteen more are under construction.) In the new School of Commerce, there's a trading room lined with desks, each with two screens filled with stock charts; a stock ticker runs around the walls of the room, up near the ceiling. Down the hall is a graphic design classroom. Two dozen students sit at large desks, each equipped with a big-screen Mac on the right and a touch-sensitive tablet on the left. Today's assignment: create an album cover for a musical act. Students use styluses to draw on the left, and view the results on the screens at the right. Toward the back of the room, a basketball player wearing a cockeyed baseball cap is working on an image with the rapper Jay-Z as its centerpiece. A professor wanders the room, looking over shoulders and offering pointers.

Just across the street, on the third floor of the recently opened Nido R. Qubein School of Communication building, there's an International Media Wall: eighteen flat-screen TVs of various sizes display a wide array of foreign news channels, including Al Jazeera, the BBC, and various Asian stations. Lining the walls of the hallway are photos of famous speakers who've appeared at High Point University, a group that includes Buzz Aldrin, Cal Ripken, Justice Clarence Thomas, and former presidents George W. Bush and Bill Clinton.

Near the center of the campus, past the large sculptures, three big fountains, and a pond, is University Center, which opened in August of 2009. The building contains 274,000 square feet of space—more than twice the size of your average Wal-Mart—and cost $70 million to construct. I can smell the fresh pastries being prepared at the Great Day Bakery as we go downstairs to The Point, a nonalcoholic sports restaurant with big-screen TVs. The Point serves buffalo wings with all kinds of sauces, ranging from "honey mustard" to "hot," priced at $5.99 a half-dozen. On one wall of the restaurant hangs a full-size replica of a NASCAR racecar, a reminder that in 2009, High Point University sponsored a car in the racing series, with one of its freshman students as the driver. Downstairs from The Point is The Extraordinaire Cinema, a luxurious two-hundred-seat movie theater with plush leather chairs that incline far back. The theater plays free first-run movies and classics.

In a wing toward the back of the complex is a residence hall. The model room, set up to be shown to prospective students on campus tours, contains furniture that looks like it came out of a Pottery Barn catalog. The room contains wide double beds instead of twins, standard for newer High Point dorms. The bathroom and small kitchenette have granite countertops. The bedrooms are carpeted, rather than laid with the cheap tiles found in old-style college dorms.

Back in the lobby, we head to the concierge desk, just past the television screens displaying Happy Birthday messages to all students who are celebrating their big day. The concierge desk is overseen by Roger Clodfelter, whose title is "Director of Wow!" Clodfelter describes his job as dreaming up and implementing things that will impress both current and potential students, and eliminating what he calls the "un-wows" that turn them off. The concierge desk is one such innovation: students can borrow electronic readers there, book appointments with tutors, get help in finding hotel reservations for parents, drop off library books or dry cleaning, obtain basketball or concert tickets, order flowers, and get other help navigating the university. "Putting everything in one place has probably saved money for the university," Clodfelter says.

We head upstairs to 1924 Prime, a full-blown steak house reminiscent of The Capital Grille, with leather banquettes, dark wood paneling, and an open restaurant-style kitchen. Reservations are required, and students can eat there once a week—assuming they're dressed in a collared shirt and aren't wearing sneakers. On the menu: iceberg wedge salad with applewood smoked bacon, cast-iron-seared black angus filet mignon, grilled wild Scottish salmon, and pan-fried chicken parmesan.

There are no prices on the menu at the steakhouse. Like Club Med and Sandals resorts, High Point practices "all-inclusive" pricing. Everywhere you turn on the campus, you're told that things are free: the bottled water being handed out from a kiosk on the Promenade, the ice cream served out of a truck that meanders around campus, the movies, the tandem bike rentals, the Kindles. For the 2010/2011 academic year, High Point's estimated all-inclusive price is $35,400. (Students who live in the nicest residence halls pay a surcharge, which can add $4,400 to the tab.)

On the top floor of University Center we head into the Presidents Club, a spacious suite of rooms with the feel of a private club. There are two large boardrooms with conference tables, several formal seating areas with elegant furniture centered on Oriental rugs, and a large dining room table. Oil paintings line the walls, and on one table an ornate chess set sits ready for play. Just outside the President's Club is a 1,344-square-foot veranda with a commanding view of the campus.

PRESIDING OVER ALL of this is Nido Qubein, a sixty-two-year-old man with graying hair and a broad smile. When I meet him, he's wearing pinstriped pants and a striped shirt with a monogram at the breast. He settles into a chair in the President's Club and tells the story of how he's transforming this college.

The way Qubein sees it, High Point had—and continues to

have—a solid academic program. The trouble was the school is surrounded by too many similar private colleges offering academic programs that were just as good, or better, which made High Point's education undifferentiated. "We didn't really have to do a whole lot to improve the academic process—everything works quite well," Qubein says. "It was clear to me that High Point was a solid academic institution, but it was also clear to me it was a diamond in the rough—it was an institution that didn't know anything about positioning a product."

To differentiate High Point from its competitors, Qubein decided to place his focus not on the academic coursework, but on the campus and the overall college experience. He compares High Point to a fine work of art that has suffered from poor framing and bad lighting. "If you took the Mona Lisa and you crumpled it up and threw it in the corner, even though you might be in a museum, you may not bother to look at it," he says. "On the other hand, if you took the Mona Lisa and frame it in a gorgeous way, put the right lights on it, and maybe even put ropes around it, all of a sudden the Mona Lisa is an exceptional piece of art."

To say that Qubein is different from most university presidents is like saying a Ferrari is different from most cars. Although he now teaches a freshman seminar on "life skills"—public speaking, financial literacy, job-interview techniques—he's never been a full-time college professor. He rarely talks about what goes on in the classroom at High Point; he seems perfectly content to leave those details up to his faculty. Instead, he talks in terms familiar to business consultants—and he looks to businesses, not rival colleges, for some of the ideas he's brought to High Point.

"I don't want anyone here thinking outside the box," he says energetically. "We throw the box outside the window. We did not go around and look at other schools—that's thinking outside the box. We said 'Tell me what Walt Disney thought. Tell me what Howard Schultz at Starbucks tells his people. Tell me about how Ritz-Carlton runs their business day in and day out.'"

Parts of High Point have been directly modeled on these types of businesses. For instance, at most colleges, there are one or two recreation complexes where students can exercise, and a couple of big libraries. While High Point has a main library and a two-story athletic complex with an overhead track, atrium basketball courts and the latest cardio gear, each new residence hall has its own smaller exercise room and its own hotel-style business center. Qubein sees moves like this as common sense. "What is a residence hall? It's a place where a hundred and fifty or two hundred people will live. How is that different from a hotel? It's basically the same concept." High Point's concierge desks are a concept drawn directly from resorts and high-end hotels.

Around the campus, Qubein has tried to add sights and sounds that will appeal to prospective students' emotions, the way savvy retailers try to play just the right mix of music in their stores. "Facts tell, emotions sell," Qubein says. "When you look around High Point, you'll see sculptures. You'll see flags. You'll see water. You'll hear classical music. You'll see benches everywhere. You'll see hammocks. You see abundance. You see generosity. You see a place that's happy and joyful. . . . We believe a student who's happy outside the classroom is much more likely to perform better inside the classroom."

There is more to Qubein's vision than lots of fountains. He believes strongly in a concept he calls "holistic education," which is a fancy way of saying he's trying to produce graduates with emotional intelligence. They're polite. (Every time I try to open a door around campus, some fresh-faced undergrad passing by is there to open it for me.) They're taught how to shake hands firmly. They're supposed to be confident in job interviews, at cocktail parties, and in other professional settings. As Quebein believes, there's little value in being an A+ biology student if Merck will never be able to promote you out of a lab because you lack people skills.

The formula seems to be working. Since Qubein became president in 2005, he's spent a staggering $468 million to improve the school's buildings and grounds. Since then, the number of freshman enrolling at High Point has increased from 370 a year to 1,220 a year. The academic credentials of the average student have increased, with average SAT scores of incoming freshman rising by 100 points. The number of applicants is up three and a half times. In 2009, this school that once had little name recognition outside North Carolina received informational inquiries from 42,000 potential applicants. In its 2009 college rankings, *U.S. News & World Report* ranked High Point University its number one "up-and-coming" baccalaureate college, and in 2010, High Point was ranked number three among regional schools in the South (up from number fifteen four years previously). Those measures make Qubein a spectacular winner by the first rule of running a college today: make your institution more prestigious.

It's striking that, unlike at other institutions, High Point's rise came without the use of lavish financial aid packages. Over the last decade, as many institutions have tried to move up the collegiate food chain, the formula for doing so has often entailed offering bigger scholarships to better students and employing sophisticated enrollment management techniques to optimize the schools' chances of getting the best students possible for every dollar in aid spent. Qubein has seen competing schools play these games; he refers derisively to one nearby private college's tactic of awarding every admitted student a $4,000 scholarship as a feel-good marketing effort. In contrast, he has raised High Point's price from just over $23,000 to over $35,000. And while the school increased its total financial aid budget by 77 percent between the academic years 2006/2007 and 2010/2011, its increased enrollment means that the average undergraduate financial aid package has dropped sharply, from $15,000 to about $10,000. So, under Qubein, High Point has succeeded in raising prices and reducing discounts—a clear sign that there are many families who want to buy the package he's offering. "If you did this in a for-profit business, they'd be throwing stock options at you left and right," he says.

An hour into our conversation in the President's Club, we move from a couch to a dining table set with fine china. The waitstaff brings in lunch: chicken with shrimp and asparagus, followed by strawberry shortcake. Toward the end of the conversation, I mention some criticism I've heard about High Point from college counselors. Some of them say the excessive focus on things such as ice-cream trucks, steak houses, and lavish dorms makes them suspicious about the school's academics. High Point appeals mainly to unexceptional students from nouveau riche families, I've been told, and while nearly every student who visits comes away "Wowed" by High Point's amenities, the more substantive, serious ones usually wind up migrating toward schools with better academic reputations.

"What you've described is a very natural response," Qubein replies evenly. "It's part of our humanness that if one thing is really great, the other thing must be not as great—that's just the way we think." So these people must be misinterpreting the nice campus to mean subpar academics, he says—a judgment that may be easy to make, since it's very hard to get a good feel for an intangible like a school's academic strength during the course of a standard campus tour. Qubein says part of the problem may stem from his own admonition that tour guides not spend too much time talking about academics, lest they seem defensive. Over time, he says, people will come to understand that High Point offers a great campus *and* a great education. "People thought Howard Schultz was an idiot for trying to sell four-dollar cups of coffee," he says. "All innovation begins with a degree of skepticism. I don't mind skepticism—skepticism is very healthy."

I ask Qubein if the rising cost of High Point is a problem, since it makes the education he's offering less accessible to middle-class families. He dismisses this concern. High Point's costs are comparable to those of most other North Carolina private colleges and are, in fact, much lower than nearby schools such as Wake Forest and Duke. For families who can't afford the price, he says, the state university system offers a great education for around $15,000 a year.

After lunch, Qubein heads off to a meeting, and I head to the Slane Student Life and Wellness Center, a newer building at the center of campus. It's a sunny afternoon, and the centrally located outdoor pool is surrounded by nearly three dozen students. The female-to-male ratio (at the pool) is about five to one, and the percentage of females in bikinis holds steady at 100 percent. Inside the gleaming two-story glass atrium, a few students shoot baskets at the six-hoop basketball court, while others use brand-new cardio machines in a nearby alcove or run on the indoor track. Adjacent to the basketball court is a food court and a seating area.

Andrea Deal, nineteen, is finishing her lunch there. A freshman, she says she is delighted with her decision to come to High Point, and particularly loves the amenities that make living on campus enjoyable. "Here everyone respects the campus and treats it like their home," she says. She sees the first-class facilities as similar to the way an NBA team justifies its investment in a top-notch locker room and fitness facility: it's an environment that supports achievement. "If they treat us right, we're going to do our best in college." Indeed, Qubein cites this logic, albeit using a different formulation: students know that if they spend too much time at the campus movie theater or in the sports restaurant, their grades won't allow them to come back next semester.

At another table, two seniors recall how drastically High Point has changed during their time here. None of the new buildings were open when they arrived as freshman, and classes were smaller. "People think it's evolved into a country club," says Kara Boatman. "When I came in, everyone was driving Chevys and Hondas. Now it's 'For my Sweet Sixteen, I got a Corvette.'"

All the new buildings and other amenities have come at a cost. These two women began at High Point as part of a group of five close friends, but the big tuition jumps, abetted by the weak economy, drove three of those students to transfer to cheaper schools. When these two students matriculated here, they say, High Point was a school whose population had a lot of economic diversity. But as tuition rose, the more middle class kids slowly disappeared. Now, they say, High Point is mostly a school for rich kids.

FOR A SMALL school, High Point has an extensive athletic program, with sixteen Division I sports, two stadiums, and a basketball arena. As at most schools, the programs improve the quality of life for students and offer an opportunity for athletes to remain involved in a sport beyond high school. When I spoke to the star guard on the High Point basketball team, however, he made clear he wasn't there just to keep in shape. He wants to make the NCAA Tournament, and then—who knows?

Even if you believe in High Point's model of holistic education, I consider it a stretch to think of the average college's sports program as a vital piece of the education the school offers. On many campuses, intercollegiate athletic programs receive an enormous amount of money and attention—both of which would be much better allocated to issues of education and access.

I'm on dangerous ground with this view, for a couple of reasons. College football games remain wildly popular among alumni and the wider public, and March Madness has been catapulted into a national institution, with even non-sports fans now hooked on the excitement generated by penny-ante bets on those ubiquitous brackets. College sports aren't just a passion for the wider public; they're a passion of mine, too. It's been nearly thirty years since I graduated from Duke, but you will not be able to reach me by phone, text, or email when a Duke basketball game is on television. I travel a couple of times each year to watch the team play. So in criticizing the excesses of college sports, I'm not just criticizing a very popular institution, I'm also opening myself up to the charge of hypocrisy.

So be it. The fact that I (and many others) enjoy something doesn't mean taxpayers should be footing so much of the bill for it, which is what happens every time a college football team runs onto the field.

This concern is not new. Since 1989, the Knight Commission on Intercollegiate Athletics has been studying the conflicting priorities of collegiate sports. While the group's early work focused on the lack of academic success shown by NCAA athletes, much of its recent focus has been on the budget-busting effects of college sports.

One of the most significant studies on this issue came in the form of a 2008 report. Daniel Fulks, an accounting professor at Transylvania University, analyzed the revenue and expenses of NCAA Division I athletic programs for the 2004, 2005, and 2006 fiscal years. Although the huge crowds of free-spending alumni at a football game lead many observers to think that college sports are a cash cow, in fact just the opposite is true: for the vast majority of universities, athletic programs drain cash. In 2006, Fulks calculated, only nineteen schools among those with the biggest football programs—the so-called Football Bowl Subdivision (FBS), a group of more than one hundred colleges—generated revenues in excess of expenses. The others lost, on average, $8.9 million on their sports programs. The report also calculated that the average head football coach at FBS schools earned $855,000 a year.[19]

These figures seem small when compared to the huge sums spent to support some of the top programs. The University of Texas, which spent $90 million to upgrade its football stadium in 1999, did another $150 million remodel less than a decade later. Around the same time, the University of Michigan spent $226 million on its football stadium, which seats well over 100,000 fans. (I've taken my son to the "Big House," and I have to say they did a nice job.) Oklahoma State spent more than $100 million on its stadium at mid-decade.[20] The revolving cast of coaches hired to pace the sidelines can create enormous costs, too. In 2010, Bloomberg News found that severance packages to fired coaches in the six largest athletic conferences resulted in payments of more than $79.5 million over a three-year period. "The only thing worse than being in the arms race is not being in the arms race, because then you won't have the best people coaching for you," said Stanford University athletic director Bob Bowlsby.[21]

In early 2010, *USA Today* produced a sophisticated analysis that went beyond simple profit-and-loss figures to try to figure out how much the general funds of each university went toward subsidizing the operating deficits of its sports programs. It found that for ninety-nine Football Bowl Subdivision schools, a total of $826 million flowed from the general coffers into the athletic programs.[22]

Schools justify these expenses in a variety of ways. One of the more convincing ways involves the so-called Flutie Effect, a term used to describe the phenomenon in which applications at Boston College surged in the years following quarterback Doug Flutie's miraculous 1984 "Hail Mary" pass to beat Miami. It's not an uncommon occurrence. According to researchers at Virginia Tech and the Wharton School, a school that wins the NCAA football or men's basketball championship sees applications jump by 7 to 8 percent. Simply making the NCAA field typically yields a 1 percent boost, and making it through to the Sweet 16 nets a 3 percent jump, on average.[23]

Schools also justify the costs because athletics provide a key venue for alumni to maintain ties to their alma mater, which encourages them to continue making donations.

In other words, at most colleges, athletics are part of the school's marketing efforts. However, this does not justify the financial shell game that is modern-day collegiate athletics. As *New York Times* columnist Joe Nocera wrote in 2007, "Big-time college football is now so divorced from what actually goes on at a university as to be a kind of subsidiary, not even tangentially related to education." Nocera quotes Sheldon Steinbach, former general counsel of the American Council on Education, asking a question so simple that it becomes profound: "The most basic question of all is who decided to get higher education into the intercollegiate athletic business?"[24] It's an apt question, particularly when you consider the recurring scandals caused by athletes who break the law, schools that violate rules to recruit star players, and issues such as steroids and abysmal student-athlete graduation rates. A recent analysis found that in the last decade, the NCAA punished nearly half of all big-time college sports programs for major rules violations.[25]

To their credit, many college presidents do express concerns about these problems. In 2009, the Knight Commission conducted a survey of more than one hundred presidents at schools with major football programs. Less than 25 percent believed that the rate of spending on college athletics is sustainable at most Football Bowl Subdivision schools nationally. Eighty-five percent believe that college football and basketball coaches' compensations are excessive.[26] The trouble is that few of them have been willing to abandon the arms race unilaterally.

The fact that so much of the money that supports sports programs, particularly on big-ticket items like stadium construction, comes in the form of donations from alumni doesn't mean students aren't hurt by the practice. Presumably if alums couldn't get great football seats by funding fancy scoreboards and turf fields, some of that money would flow into the general university coffers. Some of the rest of it might go toward traditional charities doing cancer research or providing disaster relief. And what donors didn't give away they'd pay taxes on.

Reformers have focused on the tax code as one way to try to stop the arms race in spending that drives college athletics. John Colombo, a professor at the University of Illinois, has suggested that the IRS begin examining college athletic departments' finances the same way it regulates other charities, and attach conditions to their spending in order to continue the schools' tax-exempt status.[27] Some have gone even further, suggesting that due to the huge money and excessive salaries that are becoming widespread, intercollegiate sports should lose their nonprofit status altogether.

For my part, I'm at least slightly encouraged by the courage shown by several college presidents who have been willing to risk angering alumni by shutting down athletic programs that had become too much of a drain on their universities. Usually, though, the programs that get the axe are less popular and don't have any chance to draw revenue. At MIT in 2009, for instance, administrators cut Alpine skiing, competitive pistol, golf, wrestling, ice hockey and gymnastics, saving the university $1.5 million.[28]

But some schools aren't afraid to kill off even the most popular sports. In the fall of 2009, Northeastern University discontinued its football program after seventy-four seasons (the final six of them playing below .500), saving the school more than $3 million a year. "I'm sure that people are going to be angry, and disappointed, and confused," athletic director Peter Roby told the *Boston Globe* as the decision was announced.[29] In its final game, Northeastern beat Hofstra University's team—and soon afterward, Hofstra also decided to abandon the gridiron, saving $4.5 million, which the school planned to devote instead to academic initiatives.[30]

That's the kind of win every fan should feel good about—but it happens all too rarely. According to a *Chronicle of Higher Education* article, five colleges launched new football programs in 2009, six more took the field in 2010, and eleven have announced plans to start a new team during the 2011, 2012, and 2013 seasons.[31]

IF MONEY-LOSING ATHLETIC programs and over-the-top noneducational amenities were being paid for exclusively by alumni boosters and families who were consciously choosing to spend more to send a child to Luxury U, these excesses might not be so troubling. But in fact, we're all footing the bill. Along with health care, higher education is one of the most heavily subsidized sectors of the U.S. economy. Every time a college puts a shovel in the ground to build something that will entice more applicants, someone has to pay for it. And the odds are overwhelming that taxpayers are directly or indirectly doing at least part of the funding.

According to the College Board, the federal government provided $146.5 billion in aid to colleges in the 2009/2010 academic year. This money comes in a variety of forms: Pell Grants and other direct aid programs, subsidized loan programs, tax credits such as the Hope and Life Time Learning Educational credits, and federal work-study benefits. Over the last ten years, federal aid to education has grown by 136 percent, according to College Board calculations.[32] States also provide significant direct subsidies to higher education. In the 2009/2010 academic year, state appropriations for public colleges and universities totaled $79 billion.[33]

Beyond direct federal and state subsidies, localities wind up carrying part of the bill for higher education. Next time you visit a bucolic college campus, ask yourself a simple question: How much do you think this land and all these stone buildings are worth? Ordinarily that's a question for municipal tax assessors, who are charged with estimating the value of real estate so its owners can pay their fair share of property taxes. Traditional universities, however, are nonprofits, so they're excused from paying property taxes. If they had to pay ordinary property tax bills, the total amount owed would run into the tens of billions of dollars.

Consider one small snapshot. Joshua Humphreys, a senior associate at the Tellus Institute, authored a 2010 study on how the financial crisis had affected six New England colleges. He examined the finances of Boston College, Boston University, Brandeis University, Dartmouth, Harvard, and MIT. Humphreys puts the value of the six campuses' real estate at $10.6 billion, and figures the combined property tax bill facing these colleges would be $235 million a year if not for their tax-exempt status.[34] (Colleges sometimes make far smaller "payments in lieu of taxes," which in the case of these schools, the report notes, collectively equaled less than 5 percent of the tax bill they would have owed. And, as Humphreys notes, some schools skip these payments altogether.)

Philanthropy accounts for a large part of the subsidy. In 2009, the recession and a moribund stock market created a tough year for university fund-raisers, but they still managed to receive donations worth $27.9 billion from alumni, corporations, foundations, and other donors. (That's off 11.9 percent from the $31.6 billion they raised the year before.)[35] As is nearly always true in higher education, the distribution of this wealth was hardly equal, with the vast majority of it flowing to schools that were already blessed with oversize endowments. In 2009, Stanford's donations totaled $640 million, Harvard pulled in $600 million, and Columbia, Cornell, Johns Hopkins, and Penn each received gifts in excess of $400 million. While there's nothing wrong with rich folks writing checks to their alma maters, it's important to recognize that because of the tax deductibility of these gifts (assuming donors are in the highest tax bracket), taxpayers are indirectly subsidizing each contribution—to the aggregate tune of some $10 billion a year.

Despite these immense subsidies, many families still spend extraordinary amounts of money to send their children to college. This is not a new phenomenon. Measured in constant dollars (based on the June 2003 Consumer Price Index), Americans spent $5,008 per college student in 1929/1930, a figure that rose to $18,396 by 1999/2000, and has continued to sky-rocket since.[36] By some accounts, college pricing has grown at four times the rate of general consumer prices since the early 1980s.[37] What's most striking about that inflation rate is that those eye-popping price tags account for only a portion (and in some cases, a small portion) of the overall costs of attendance.

According to calculations by the Delta Project, a think tank that studies higher education costs and productivity, after you account for the "discounting" that's provided by college financial aid offices, the average student at a public research university (such as the University of Wisconsin) pays just 51 percent of the costs of her education. The rest is paid by subsidies from taxpayers and donors. At a private university (such as the University of Chicago), students and their families foot between 56 and 84 percent of the bill.[38] The fact that families can pay more than $50,000 a year for a child to attend an elite college and still require hefty subsidies is a testament to the inefficiency that lies within the average university cost structure.

The exploding cost of traditional higher education, combined with stagnant learning outcomes (or worse), has raised concerns of a higher education "bubble."[39] If legislators start questioning the rationale for funding the ever-higher costs of traditional higher education and pull in the purse strings—or if the costs to students start to exceed the anticipated financial return on their education—the financial model on which most traditional colleges are based could collapse. Most in danger would be the expensive mid-tier traditional universities, which would be the first to lose students to less expensive alternatives, and which don't have the endowments to shield them from the wrenching cost reductions that would become necessary. As Glenn Reynolds, University of Tennessee law professor and author of the influential *Instapundit* blog, puts it, "Something that can't go on forever, won't. And the past decades' history of tuition growing much faster than the rate of inflation, with students and parents making up the difference via easy credit, is something that can't go on forever."[40]

It's impossible to say how much of the average college budget is devoted to noneducational frills such as fajita restaurants and luxury dorms. There is no line item in colleges' financial reports labeled "Excessive Luxury Items." Nor can almost any of the expenses we've discussed in this chapter be found in schools' marketing budgets, marketing being the most accurate way to describe these expenses' underlying purpose. But research into college financing has provided evidence that in recent years a smaller piece of college budgets is being devoted to actual teaching. The Delta Project concluded that the share of educational and research spending dedicated to instruction declined at all types of institutions from 2002 to 2006.[41] Researchers who have examined university budgets describe colleges as employing larger and better-paid staff, yet not producing measurably more or better graduates. "While it takes far less time for workers to make a ton of steel, type a letter, or harvest a bushel of corn than it did a generation ago, it takes *more* professors and college administrators to educate a given number of students," says college finance expert Richard Vedder, author of *Going Broke by Degree* and perhaps the most insightful writer on inefficiency in the modern university.[42] "However measured, the enterprise of higher education takes immensely more resources to operate than it did a generation or two ago, [and] over time, a larger percentage of university resources has gone for research and administration, and less has gone for instruction."[43]

In 2010, the Delta Project released another massive set of data on college spending for the period 1998–2008. The numbers provided unmistakable evidence that colleges are becoming less focused on what happens inside the classroom. "Share of College Spending for Recreation Is Rising," ran a headline in the *New York Times*.[44] Reacting to the data, Vedder concluded, "The cost inflation of higher education has little to do with the financing of learning, and a lot to do with the blob of assorted other activities schools take on, ranging from unsponsored research to the country club-like student services provided."[45]

The numbers are particularly troubling when you begin comparing U.S. higher educational expenses against those for the rest of the world. According to a 2010 study by the Organisation for Economic Co-operation and Development, in 2007 the United States spent 3.1 percent of its gross domestic product on postsecondary education. That's more than twice the 1.5 percent average spent by the other OECD countries, many of which are producing more college graduates per capita than America.[46] The numbers are particularly irritating when you look at a list of the countries where college students and their families pay either zero tuition or a very nominal fee—a list that includes Brazil, Denmark, France, Norway, Scotland, and Sweden.[47] People are paying less in taxes toward higher education, students and their families are paying little, and the schools are still graduating a higher proportion of students than we are. There's something wrong with this picture.

Where is all the money going? Ronald Ehrenberg is a Cornell economics professor and an expert on higher education financing, a field in which he gained firsthand expertise during a stint working in Cornell's administration in the mid-and late 1990s. He recounts his experience working the numbers in *Tuition Rising*, a book that provides a vivid picture of just how many noneducational expenses university administrators are forced to obsess over. It contains an entire *chapter* on Cornell's air-conditioning system, an immense expense that's required, in part, to maintain optimal humidity levels to preserve the millions of books in the university libraries.[48]

Ehrenberg relates how, in the late 1990s, Cornell's dining services needed to close one central facility near most of the school's classrooms to conduct temporary renovations. The campus still had plenty of cafeteria space, but it was concentrated around residence halls, not the classrooms, where students prefer to eat lunch. Ehrenberg proposed a solution any economist would love: Why not offer any student who eats lunch in the distant cafeteria a two-dollar-per-day rebate? Administrators rejected this idea, and certainly a "lunch truck" that served sandwiches for those truly in a hurry wasn't viewed as acceptable. Instead, the university spent $9 million to build a new facility. "Higher dining rates increased the total costs of attending the university," Ehrenberg writes. "For students receiving grant aid from the university, every dollar increase in dining costs automatically increases their grant aid by a dollar... [which means] that less money will be available to spend on the academic functions of the university."[49]

During Ehrenberg's tenure, the university also decided to create more upscale residence halls in an attempt to lure students who would ordinarily move off campus to instead live on campus during their entire stay at Cornell. As an economist, Ehrenberg sees valuable life lessons from living off campus: learning to negotiate a lease, shop for groceries, and cook for oneself. Again, the economic arguments fell short, and Cornell's development office rushed to find donors to fund the $100 million dorm improvement project—money that otherwise might have gone to further strengthen Cornell's academic offerings or open its doors to more students.[50]

DESPITE THE CRITICISMS I've offered, I continue to believe that if you measure colleges on the achievements of their top graduates, America's universities remain the best in the world. It's a belief supported by international rankings, and anecdotally by reports such as the 2007 survey showing that nearly six hundred thousand foreign students enrolled were in colleges and universities in the United States—seeking to get the best education they could.[51]

Still, American higher education is losing strength as an engine of U.S. economic growth. It's failing to produce as many graduates as it can or should, it's consuming far too many resources to produce the graduates it does manage to get through to completion, and there's a real question as to whether students are learning as much today as they did before campuses turned into resorts.

In their 2011 book, *Academically Adrift: Limited Learning on College Campuses*, authors Richard Arum and Josipa Roksa write that too many students at traditional institutions are learning little and "drifting through college without a clear sense of purpose."[52] Based on their analysis of Collegiate Learning Assessment data, close to half of traditional college-age students showed no improvement in critical thinking, complex reasoning, or writing skills in their first two years of college, and more than a third showed no improvement over four years. "They might graduate," the authors report, "but they are failing to develop the higher-order cognitive skills that it is widely assumed college students should master."[53] One of the reasons may be academic rigor: many students are taking courses that do not require significant amounts of reading (defined as forty or more pages per week) or writing (defined as twenty or more pages per semester). Top students may still be getting exceptional learning experiences, but there's a real question as to whether the average student is.

Part of the challenge is that the leadership at traditional colleges has come to understand, sometimes reluctantly, that the most efficient way to increase the prestige of an institution often has nothing to do with improving the quality of its education. The competitive environment is pushing these institutions to shift their focus from what has driven American innovation— the education they offer—to the college "experience," heavily sweetened with ancillary and ultimately unimportant offerings that impress students but don't ultimately improve them. In fact, these ancillary offerings may serve to make students more materialistic and entitled, while actually undermining the focus on learning.

As I discuss in chapter 6, our higher education funding system is equally generous to universities that do not deliver strong educational outcomes and to those that do—and as a result serves to encourage spending unrelated to the educational purpose of universities. The country would be well served to craft that funding mechanism to encourage learning, access, and other national education priorities. (I believe most college presidents would agree, by the way.) In the meantime, higher education will undermine its hard-earned and well-deserved long-term public support by asking taxpayers to contribute to non-essential costs, and by using their resources to focus on what's fun, instead of what's fundamental. Students needn't sleep in barracks to get a good education, but they don't need to live in resorts, either.

The increase in cost is necessarily reducing access to higher education, one of the main reasons why the United States has sunk to twelfth in educational attainment in the world. There's only so much money to go around, and we're spending it on luxurious frills rather than on classrooms for less advantaged students, including working adults. What our country needs are schools that efficiently focus on a practical approach to delivering real learning outcomes to a broad range of citizens. That's what will drive our economy and deliver a powerful return on our taxpayer investment in higher education.

In theory, these places already exist. They're called community colleges. But as we'll explore in the next chapter, they're being asked to do so many things, with such a muddled funding model, that they have a hard time fully delivering on our aspiration of being America's efficient and effective educator of the masses.

||||||||||||||||||||||||||||||||||||||||||||| 3

The (Theoretically) Perfect Solution

The Challenge of Community Colleges

Six months into his presidency, Barack Obama was in trouble. The U.S. economy was sagging. Since January, when he'd taken the oath of office, the unemployment rate had jumped by more than two points, to 9.5 percent. The stimulus package he'd pushed through Congress in the first weeks of his administration didn't seem to be helping, and popular anger was rising. As is often the case in the White House, his advisors felt pressure to do *something*. So on July 14, 2009, they boarded Air Force One and told the pilot to fly west, toward the heart of the nation's unemployment crisis: Michigan.

That afternoon, Obama stood at a lectern at Macomb Community College in Warren, a working-class suburb that is home to General Motors' sprawling Technical Center. Macomb County became famous in the 1980s as the home of the so-called Reagan Democrats, those working-class voters whose parents voted for FDR but who were themselves beginning to favor a conservative message of self-reliance and optimism during tough economic times. Macomb Community College, home to fifty-nine thousand students, is a place where that self-reliance is exercised—a fact Obama acknowledged in his speech.

"This is a place where anyone—anyone with a desire to learn and to grow, to take their career to a new level or start a new career altogether—has the opportunity to pursue their dream, right here in Macomb," he said. "This is a place where people of all ages and all backgrounds—even in the face of obstacles, even in the face of very difficult personal challenges—can take a chance on a brighter future for themselves and their families."

Obama, jacketless and with his sleeves rolled up, singled out two of the college's success stories: Joe, a laid-off worker who had gone back to school, earned a degree, and found a job as a maintenance mechanic at a local hospital; and Kellie, a downsized forklift driver who'd been retrained at the college as a pipefitter. "Joe and Kellie's stories make clear what all of you know: Community colleges are an essential part of our recovery in the present—and our prosperity in the future."

Obama came to this campus bearing more than words: he was also bringing the prospect of money. In his speech, the president outlined an ambitious program called the American Graduation Initiative (AGI). That program promised $12 billion in new funding to help community colleges create five million additional graduates over the next decade, though only $2 billion was ultimately approved. "Time and again, when we placed our bet for the future on education, we have prospered as a result—by tapping the incredible innovative and generative potential of a skilled American workforce," Obama said, citing the Land-Grant College Act and the GI Bill as past examples. For nearly a half hour, he talked about using these federal funds to create more nurses, high-tech workers, and people to fill clean energy jobs. He talked about how the new funding would let community colleges study ways to help more students actually graduate—and to do a better job of tracking outcomes, to figure out which programs achieved results and which didn't. "All too often, community colleges are treated like the stepchild of the higher education system; they're an afterthought, if they're thought of at all,"[1] the president said. And he intended to change this.

In recent years, the U.S. presidency has been an office reserved for men with elite educations. The last four presidents have graduated from at least one Ivy League institution; the last two presidents have each had a pair of Ivy League degrees. But despite that high-class education and regardless of their party, when they talk about the future of the U.S. economy, these presidents have something in common: they see community colleges playing a vital role. President George W. Bush regularly spoke at community college commencement ceremonies, lauding the schools as a gateway to the middle class, particularly for immigrants. President Clinton routinely spoke about making the thirteenth and fourteenth years of schooling—the first two years of college—a universal part of the American education regimen, and his administration enacted $1,500 HOPE Scholarships to help fund it. Obama isn't even the first president to give a speech at Macomb Community College; in fact, every president since Ronald Reagan has visited the campus.

Politicians love to embrace community colleges because they're seen as the potential answer to the complex problem I've described in earlier chapters: that America has fallen behind when it comes to producing the college graduates we need to fill the skilled jobs being created by our modern economy, and that the prestige-driven traditional colleges, which are being managed according to the Ivory Tower Playbook, have become too costly, too exclusive, and too inaccessible to the average person in need of additional education and training. Community colleges, in contrast, are the anti-Harvard. They're practical, flexible, inexpensive (at least if you consider only tuition, and don't factor in the cost to taxpayers), and attuned to the real needs of employers. The leaders of community colleges ignore the dictates of the Ivory Tower Playbook. Instead, they run their institutions based on a very different set of conventions—one I think of as the All-Access Playbook: They see their mission as providing an opportunity for everyone. They offer an extremely wide (some might say absurdly wide) gamut of training and services. If you spend time on community college campuses, you'll find that many faculty and administrators have a missionary zeal for their work, which they see as boosting Americans in a lower socioeconomic class upward on a path toward middle-class prosperity.

That's the theory, at least. The problem is one of performance. Beneath this gauzy ideal celebrated whenever a politician shows up to shower resources on community colleges is a track record reflecting deep challenges. In 2008, for example, Macomb Community College had a graduation rate of 13.1 percent,[2] a number that's not atypical. To be sure, the graduation rate measurements that the government uses are deeply flawed instruments, built around assumptions more suitable for four-year colleges. And community colleges serve low-income students with many more risks of not graduating—meaning that their student population would be significantly less likely to graduate regardless of the institution they attended. But even if you gauge these institutions using broader measures, there's no disputing what MIT economist Paul Osterman concluded in a recent paper on community college performance: "The majority of students who enter community college do not succeed, and this failure comes at great cost to them and to society."[3]

Part of the problem with community colleges is the wide variety of goals and missions they are attempting to tackle. "If you visit a four-year college, you can predict what sort of student you are going to bump into," writes *New York Times* columnist David Brooks. "If you visit a community college, you have no idea. You might see an immigrant kid hoping eventually to get a PhD, or another kid who messed up in high school and is looking for a second chance. You might meet a 35-year-old former meth addict trying to get some job training or a 50-year-old taking classes for fun."[4]

Brooks is right to applaud community colleges for "tackling some of the country's biggest problems." But in light of the challenges these schools face in moving students through to graduation, it's understandable that many observers have raised questions about whether community colleges' attempt to be all things to all people is a fundamental problem with their model. A wrench is a fantastic tool for tightening a bolt, but if you try to use it as a hammer it's not very good—and if you try to use it as a screwdriver, it's useless. Likewise, colleges that are trying to educate nurses, teach Thai cooking, train auto mechanics, and deliver a course on digital photography are being used for more purposes than they were designed for. It's hardly surprising if they don't perform as well as we'd like.

The challenges with community colleges aren't just performance-driven. These schools are operating with a financial model that's fundamentally broken. They are highly dependent on (widely variable) state budgets for most of their funding, and are often deeply reluctant to ask students to contribute much money to their own education. For students, perhaps the biggest appeal of community colleges is their low tuition price: the average annual tuition and fees were just $2,544 in 2009/2010.[5] Very low price, however, does not mean very low cost. Delta Project data find that the average community college spends

$9,184 to educate each full-time student. State legislatures and local governments—i.e., taxpayers—make up most of the $6,640 difference. As state legislatures became painfully aware during the Great Recession, however, taxpayer resources aren't unlimited. In fact, they typically decline when the economy turns down. Unfortunately, that's precisely when more people decide to return to school because of poor job opportunities. And sure enough, that's what has happened at community colleges over the last few years: a crush of new students has entered while taxpayer subsidies have declined, leading to a calamitous mismatch of supply and demand. It's a profound example of how the All-Access Playbook by which the leaders of community colleges operate works far better in theory than in day-to-day reality.

NO ONE DISPUTES that America needs institutions of the type that community colleges represent. That's true for a few simple reasons: not every student is ready for college three months after graduating from high school, not every student wants (or can afford) the residential, full-time experience that traditional colleges were built to provide, and the traditional four-year residential system cannot come close to accommodating every prospective college student.

There are many ways to look at a typical high school class. People refer to jocks and cheerleaders, preps and geeks, band members and "stoners." But when I look at high school students, I focus on a group I call the Automatics. The Automatics are the kids everyone knows will go to college. They may not be straight-A students, but they've learned how to study. They know how to sign up for the SATs and ask a teacher for a letter of recommendation. Their parents, many of them college graduates themselves, are not only supportive of their children going to college, but many are also willing to pay some (or even all) of the bill.

At a top private high school, the entire graduating class may be Automatics. In an affluent suburb, more than 90 percent of the students may go straight to college. On elite college campuses, you may have a hard time getting people to understand the concept of Automatics, since the students there rarely encounter anyone else. "Of the hundreds of students I taught at Harvard and Dartmouth, I'm relatively sure it never occurred to a single one of them not to go to college," writes Zachary Karabell, an economist. "For these students, college is just what one does."[6]

Nationally, the ranks of the Automatics are far smaller. According to research by Anthony Carnevale, Jeff Strohl, and Nicole Smith of the Georgetown University Center on Education and the Workforce, more than two-thirds of Americans attend college or vocational training after graduating high school, but just 34 percent of students who are tracked from eighth grade onward will wind up with a degree from a two-year or four-year school.[7]

What happens to the non-Automatics, those who missed the first window to go to college right out of high school? It's an important issue, because our economy has changed dramatically over the years. Since the early 1970s, the share of employed Americans who work in office, health care, education, and technology jobs has increased dramatically—and the vast percentage of these workers have at least some college. The growth of these sectors has come at the expense of jobs in factories, mines, farms, and fisheries—jobs that generally don't require college degrees.

The financial returns they obtain from those extra years of study are substantial. Between 1983 and 2007, the number of prime-age workers with a bachelor's degree saw their average real wages (in 2007 dollars) grow from $33,000 to $48,000, while prime-age workers with a master's degree or higher saw real earnings grow from $45,000 to $72,000.[8] According to other research, a student with an associate's degree can expect lifetime earnings of about $400,000 more than someone with only a high school diploma.[9] And the children of college graduates—and even college attendees—face vastly better educational and economic prospects than those whose parents didn't attend college.[10]

The data back up a point that is probably self-evident to anyone who pays attention to economic news: America needs more people attending and finishing college in order for the country to remain competitive. According to the Lumina Foundation for Education, an organization that advocates for increasing access to higher education, preliminary research shows that the United States needs to push the percentage of its population that holds "high-quality degrees and credentials" upward to 60 percent to fill the types of jobs being created by our knowledge-driven economy. We also need to produce more college graduates to compete with other nations, where the attainment rates of young adults with college degrees now routinely outpaces ours. To meet Lumina's goal of 60 percent of the workforce having a degree by 2025, the nation needs to create roughly twenty-three million more college graduates—meaning twenty-three million more than are expected at present college attainment rates.[11]

Today's economic challenges are very different from those of a century ago—but even back then, a group of farsighted educators could see that the traditional colleges had become increasingly inaccessible to a growing pool of people who needed more schooling. Compared with traditional residential colleges or the land-grant universities that rose up to complement them, community colleges are a relatively recent addition to the higher education landscape. The first private, two-year school was founded a little more than a century ago by a reverend named Frank Gunsaulus, with funding from Philip Danforth Armour, wealthy scion of the Armour meatpacking company. Their Armour Institute, opened in Chicago in 1893, later became the Illinois Institute of Technology. Most historians, however, point to Joliet Junior College, spun off from the University of Chicago in 1901 and set up adjacent to a suburban high school, as the first real example of a community college, since it was created under public auspices.[12] By 1917, the North Central Association of Colleges and Schools had begun accrediting two-year institutions, and by 1918, junior colleges had their own national honor society.[13]

The two-year college remained a minor feature in American education until midcentury, however. At that point, with the end of World War II, Congress tried to do something to help smooth the reentry of sixteen million returning soldiers into the U.S. economy. They had a compelling reason to do so: After World War I, returning servicemen had been given little more than a sixty-dollar bonus and a train ticket home. Many had trouble returning to work, and during the Great Depression these unemployment woes became profound. In 1932, veterans marched on Washington and engaged in a standoff with U.S. troops, an incident that historians at the U.S. Department of Veterans Affairs remember as "one of the greatest periods of unrest our nation's capital had ever known."[14]

As Congress considered the aftermath of World War II, it did not want a repeat of young men marching on the capital—particularly not the young men it had just spent several years teaching how to shoot. Accordingly, in 1944, Congress began work on a piece of legislation known as the Servicemen's Readjustment Act, which became famous as the GI Bill. Its key provision allowed veterans to attend college tuition-free and to receive monthly living allowances during their period of study—thereby staging the returning soldiers' reintroduction into the workforce until the economy was ready to absorb them.

After FDR signed it into law in 1944, the bill became a transformational government act. "Thanks to the GI Bill, millions who would have flooded the job market instead opted for education," write officials at the U.S. Department of Veterans Affairs. "In the peak year of 1947, veterans accounted for 49 percent of college admissions. By the time the original GI Bill ended on July 25, 1956, 7.8 million of 16 million World War II veterans had participated in an education or training program."[15]

Among legislators, there was skepticism that many returning soldiers would be enthusiastic about going back to school, and universities were unprepared for the onslaught of new students. "Campus life was transformed by their presence," writes educational commentator Diane Ravitch. "Quonset huts sprouted to house the students and, in some cases, their spouses. Many colleges doubled their usual enrollment to make room for veterans. . . . Inexperienced teachers, some of them graduate students, were pressed into duty to teach the bumper crop of undergraduates."[16]

Soon the glut of soldiers turned students became a full-blown crisis for higher education—one that its lobbyists were inclined to exploit. At the urging of the American Council on Education, President Truman—the only twentieth-century U.S. president who didn't graduate from college himself[17]—appointed the President's Commission on Higher Education to study the best ways to meet the needs of the growing population of college students.

While the GI Bill served as the impetus for the commission's work, the time was right for the United States to rethink the role of college in American society. Higher education, once a privilege reserved for an elite few, was on its way to becoming an experience to be enjoyed by a large swath of the population. Over the preceding fifty years, the average American's education had changed dramatically. In 1900, about 11 percent of the school-age population was attending high school, but by 1940 that had jumped to 73 percent. When it came to college, however, the rise was more gradual: in 1900, about 4 percent of high school graduates attended college, and by 1940 the share had risen to 16 percent.[18]

To help boost that number and accommodate the growing population of adult college students, the Truman Commission called for an expansion of two-year institutions, which it called "community colleges." By higher education standards, the commission's impact was rapid: by 1960, America had 390 community colleges. Between 1960 and 1975, as the civil rights and women's movements gained ground and helped a broader cross-section of the population aspire to college, the number of institutions rose to more than one thousand, and the number of students enrolled jumped from around one million to just under four million.[19]

As with past acts of educational innovation such as the Land-Grant College Act, the advent and fast expansion of community colleges were controversial: not everyone saw the people attending these new schools as college material. One former university professor called the new community colleges "inferior institutions whose faculty will be composed of high school teachers, because no first-class scholar will teach in a junior college when he can secure employment in a first-class college or university, and whose courses of study will not prepare anyone to enter the University or fit him for life solving any of our problems." This critic continued: "What is needed is for parents to send their boys and girls who have failed in high schools back to school to make up their deficiencies."[20]

As historians Steven Brint and Jerome Karabel have observed, some of the antagonism came from administrators at less-than-stellar four-year colleges who could see that their own market position might be weakened by the new entrants, who could become disruptive innovators. "It copies the liberal arts college in a cheap way and promises more than it delivers," complained the president of Baldwin-Wallace College in Ohio.[21]

These early critics also complained that community colleges were trying to embrace a sort of faux academic atmosphere that was inappropriate for places that attracted working-class students who were as likely to study automotive repair as Milton or Sophocles. "Community colleges, in trying to legitimize their status in American education, are taking on the trappings— liberal arts courses, academic rank, faculty senates, etc.,—of traditional colleges without really understanding the meaning of 'liberal education,'" wrote W. B. Devall.[22]

One of the most remarkable and underappreciated aspects of the GI Bill is that it gave its beneficiaries the power to choose where they wanted to study. The benefits weren't awarded only to existing universities (which lobbied hard for direct grants). Similarly, the soldiers weren't corralled off into specialized "GI schools." Instead, their benefits were portable, like a voucher that can be used at virtually any school. This approach, later incorporated into the primary student funding mechanism, forced schools to compete for funding student by student—and became the basis both for the type of competition among traditional schools described in chapters 1 and 2, and for the new types of institutions I'll describe later that offer different value propositions for students who don't prefer a traditional approach.

Today there are about twelve hundred community colleges, which together enroll more than eleven million students. Those numbers are an astonishing testament to how, at the most basic level, the leadership of these schools has succeeded according to the rules of the All-Access Playbook: the schools now account for a full 43 percent of all U.S. undergraduates.

In keeping with the goals set out by the Truman Commission more than a half century ago, there's now a community college within driving distance of the vast majority of Americans. The average age of those students is twenty-eight. Some 80 percent of full-time community college students work part time or full time. Forty percent are minorities, and 42 percent are first-generation college students. Many of the graduates of these schools go on to earn degrees from four-year colleges; many more become nurses, law enforcement officers, or radiology technicians, earning solid middle-class wages. A few of them even become famous: among the nation's community college graduates are astronaut Eileen Collins, poet Gwendolyn Brooks, New York television anchor Chuck Scarborough, and Secretary of Transportation Ray LaHood.[23]

TO GET A glimpse of how a strong community college can change lives, I went to Miami Dade College, located in an urban neighborhood in the western part of downtown Miami. Altogether, Miami Dade has eight campuses and 170,000 students, making it one of the largest colleges of any kind in the United States.

The downtown campus consists of seven buildings, including a parking garage. When I visited, across the street from the parking garage, a crane was working on a new campus structure. None of Miami Dade's buildings feature Gothic architecture or crawling ivy: the central complex, Building One, is made from utilitarian concrete, with an open-air atrium, murals, and escalators running up the center of the building.

On a Friday afternoon at the start of a semester, a microbiology lab is crowded with students. Thirteen women and three men, all clad in lab coats, sit on stools in front of Leica microscopes. Dianelys Diaz, a twenty-two-year-old wearing big hoop earrings and an L-O-V-E necklace, emigrated from Cuba five years ago when her father won an immigration lottery. Her father currently works at the local gas company; her mother is a housekeeper. Dianelys hopes to be a nurse. Today she's working with *E. coli* bacteria, using a cotton swab to wipe it into petri dishes and examining it under a microscope.

Like many local students from working-class families, Dianelys didn't do an exhaustive college search. If it hadn't been for Miami Dade College, she doubts she'd have pursued higher education at all. "I guess I'd be working as a salesperson, making eight dollars an hour," she says. If she succeeds in completing her studies and becomes a nurse, she'll do far better than that: the median annual income for a registered nurse in Florida is around $60,000 a year.[24]

Across the street, on the second floor of Building Two, the Computer Courtyard—a large room filled with PCs—is half full. During the prime hours of 9:00 AM and 1:00 PM on weekdays, it's hard to find a free seat here. That's because, unlike the undergrads at many universities, a lot of the students at Miami Dade can't afford their own laptops and are dependent on the school to provide computer resources—and even if they have a computer of their own, many of their homes lack broadband Internet service.

In yet another building, a three-dozen-piece orchestra plays a movement from *Romeo and Juliet* by Tchaikovsky. You wouldn't guess it from the pitch-perfect quality of the performance, but these students are still in high school. They're members of a program called the New World School of the Arts, which allows talented high school students who aspire to artistic careers to study on the Miami Dade campus for eight years, emerging with both a high school diploma and a bachelor of fine arts from the University of Florida. Graduates of the program currently work on Broadway, on television shows, and with the Alvin Ailey American Dance Theater.

Measured by acreage or the number of buildings, Miami Dade's downtown campus can't compare with a typical residential college. The place even lacks a cafeteria: on the day I visited, the only places to grab a bite were at outdoor food stands or the McDonald's across the street. (A food court under construction in Building Two on the day of my visit has since opened.) Still, if you measure the institution's impact not by its physical facilities but by its effect on the community, Miami Dade is a force to be reckoned with. The local fire chief is a graduate. So is the Miami-Dade County mayor, and the public defender and the state attorney, most of the county commissioners, the heads of the big hospitals, the managing partners of the city's biggest accounting firms. . . . The list seems to go on and on.

Consider just one example of a life changed on this unflashy downtown campus: that of Eduardo Padrón. Padrón was born in Cuba. He came to the United States when he was fifteen years old with a brother, leaving his parents behind. "My father finished high school, but my mother only finished third grade," Padrón says. When he left for America, his mother made him swear he'd get a college degree. "Even if I had to go hungry at night, that was okay," he says. "I knew I had to do that; I would never let her down."

It's obvious, perhaps, that Padrón was not an Automatic, and so when he sat down with his high school guidance counselor to discuss his future, he was told what so many other non-Automatics are told: "You are not college material." He'd be better off going to a vocational school to learn a trade, the counselor said. But Padrón began looking at colleges anyway. "Miami Dade was the only place that welcomed me with open arms, gave me all the support in the world, and gave me a chance," he recalls.

There is a difference between being welcomed into a school like Miami Dade and actually succeeding there, but Padrón managed to succeed. After two years at Miami Dade, where he earned an associate's degree in business administration, he went on to a four-year college, then graduate school, and eventually earned a PhD in economics from the University of Florida. Upon graduation, he went back to Miami Dade—this time as an assistant professor. By 1995, he'd become president of the college.

Today Padrón is one of America's most recognized educators: *Time* magazine has named him one of the country's ten best college presidents, *People* magazine has named him one of the world's most influential Hispanics, and his résumé boasts membership on so many national education committees that it's a wonder he's able to perform his day job. In late 2010, President Obama named him chairman of a presidential advisory commission on Hispanic education.

I spoke with Padrón in a large boardroom adjacent to his suite of offices in Building One on Miami Dade's downtown campus. He sat at the head of a long table, beneath a pair of abstract paintings, with late-afternoon sun streaming through the windows. Padrón wore a blue suit, a green tie, Armani glasses, and a gold Miami Dade pin on his lapel. His soft Cuban accent was a reminder of his roots.

He is justifiably proud of the work his college does. Miami Dade currently has students who come from 178 different countries and speak eighty-six different languages.

More than half are nonnative English speakers, and more than half are first-generation college students. Three-quarters of the school's incoming students are deficient in some basic skills, and need to take remedial courses before they're able to complete college-level work.[25] Despite those handicaps, Padrón boasts that his graduates who go on to four-year universities perform just as well—and often even better—than the traditional undergrads who began there as freshmen. "Why?" he asks. "The answer is simple: they're hungry. I mean hungry in the big sense—the sense that they are really motivated, that their only real passport to a better life is higher education."

I ADMIRE PADRÓN'S passion, and I admire how successful his institution is in creating opportunities and tapping the talent of so many working-class Miamians. There's a reason Miami Dade is so frequently singled out as a world-class community college, one that's become a routine stop for politicians who want to show their commitment to education. (It has had three presidents—Clinton, George W. Bush and Obama—as commencement speakers in the last four years.) And there's a reason so many of Miami's leading citizens are Miami Dade grads. The school is doing what everyone hopes a community college will do: provide a launchpad for those who need it, at a reasonable tuition price.

But Miami Dade is not perfect. Even this model college has deficiencies that, in one way or another, affect nearly every community college. According to government data, Miami Dade College's graduation rate is 26 percent.[26] While that's roughly on par with the average graduation rate for two-year colleges—which stood at 27.8 percent for students who entered in 2004 and should have completed degrees by 2007—it still means that nearly three-quarters of students do not progress to graduation.[27]

Beyond that, by Padrón's own admission, the system he presides over is showing serious signs of strain. Simply put, its funding model is broken. That's forcing Miami Dade to exclude many of the students it's meant to be serving.

For a literal look at this phenomenon, you'd need to gain access to the college's IT department at midnight on the day in late June when the school's online registration system allows students to begin registering for fall classes. At precisely 12:01 AM, torrents of students log in to try to register for classes the moment the registration system opens, knowing there are far too many students clambering for too few seats in classes. It's become common for the rush of students to overload the technology, leading to a crash of the computer registration system.

The problem is one any Econ 101 student can understand: supply and demand. Enrollment at Miami Dade, as at most community colleges, has soared in recent years, while its primary source of funding, taxpayer dollars, has shrunk. To cope with the funding shortage, in 2008, Miami Dade reduced the number of course sections it offered by some twelve hundred. In 2009, according to the *Miami Herald*, the school laid off employees and cut academic programs, including courses in hospitality and oceanographic engineering.[28]

For students, the result is that getting a seat in a class at Miami Dade has become a bit like musical chairs, a reality that its president acknowledges is a big problem.

"This year we have about thirty thousand students who couldn't take all the classes they needed," Padrón says. "We had over five thousand who could not take the remedial classes they needed. In my opinion, that's the worst thing that can happen to a community. Every time we fail to admit one student, what options do they have? They don't have the resources to pay for another college. [Many of them] can't get admitted to another college. They don't have the money to go out of town [to study at a distant institution]. It's a waste of human talent and causes tremendous potential for social unrest."

The funding problems, common to community colleges across the nation, are a function of the colleges' financial model. According to the American Association of Community Colleges, public community colleges receive 38 percent of their revenue from state appropriations. Another 17 percent comes from local appropriations. Five percent comes from federal grants and contracts. Those tax subsidies, which make up well over half of the colleges' revenue, are the key reason community colleges are able to keep tuition so low: tuition and fees account for just 20 percent of the money coming in.[29]

When you talk to community college officials about the funding problems, they reiterate the "forgotten stepchild" status that Obama referred to in his speech at Macomb. They complain about how little per-student funding they receive when compared with K–12 and four-year university education. As they see it, because the majority of voters send children through public elementary and secondary schools, elected officials have every incentive to shower dollars on those schools. And when it comes to postsecondary education, the State U's have big advantages: often a sizable percentage of any state's legislature is made up of alumni, and even politicians who didn't attend State U are often fans of its athletic programs.

As Thomas Bailey, a Columbia University professor and the nation's leading researcher on community colleges, and James Jacobs, president of Macomb Community College, have noted, "In Michigan, the entire state appropriation to all 28 community colleges [which have combined enrollment of some 254,000] is about equal to the state support for Michigan State University [with an enrollment of more than 47,000]."[30]

"The community colleges are getting squeezed in the middle,"

Padrón says, noting that Miami Dade College gets about a quarter of the per-student funding received by students at Florida's state universities. "You cannot blame it on the recession—the recession compounded the problem, but it's been a problem in the making," Padrón says.

My own take on the politics of community colleges is slightly different than the analysis offered by educators such as Padrón. Politicians like to give speeches and voice support for community colleges because they like the spirit of the All-Access Playbook under which such schools operate. These schools represent a democratic ideal, and supporting them is considered "politically correct." At the same time, the legislators who write the checks are aware of the struggles students have at these schools to reach graduation, and even today some wonder if the ideal of universal postsecondary education is realistic—whether all students should be considered "college material." They'll fund community colleges to the extent that it's politically necessary, but no further. Even those legislators who strongly believe in access and who have taken time to understand the challenges of graduating low-income, higher-risk students such as those at community colleges can't help themselves from comparing graduation rates with the four-year universities with which most are intimately familiar. As with the debate over the poor performance of many public K–12 schools, educators have spent so many years constantly clamoring for more money to fix problems that never seem to get fixed that legislators have become quietly contemptuous, fearful that throwing more money into what they see as poorly performing schools is a bad investment.

There are potential solutions, of course. Padrón is an economist, but you don't need a PhD to understand how raising tuition might help fill the gap. During my visit to campus, I pressed Padrón on this: with more than 170,000 students, even an extra $100 per student per year—$8.33 per month—would go a long way toward easing the shortfall. Padrón rejects this idea out of hand. "Do you realize that for many of our students, raising tuition by five dollars is the difference between putting food on the table and going to school?"

As someone who has worked with low-income students for years, I'm highly sympathetic to his point. But in my view he's sticking too closely to the All-Access Playbook, which dictates that paying for education is primarily the responsibility of taxpayers, with students to be shielded from cost to the maximum extent possible. Inevitably, community college backers feel, raising tuition would be a form of price rationing, and would go against the community college mission of keeping the door open for everyone. Still, while they wait for taxpayers to kick in more money, community colleges are forced to deny access to thousands of students who want to take the courses that can change their lives. One way or another, unfortunately, they're rationing. In fact, nearly all of the students are eligible for student loans, which they may not prefer to incur but would be able to pay off if they succeed in graduating and getting the higher-paying jobs accessible to someone with a college degree.

Padrón is unconvinced. "The fact of the matter is if we [raise prices], we're going to be depriving education of people who need it the most, who are vulnerable and can't afford to pay more than what we're charging now."

No matter how much you admire the people running Miami Dade College, they face immense challenges because their economic model simply doesn't work. They're charging tuition that's far below the actual costs, they're attempting to close that gap by depending on funding sources that don't increase as student demand increases, and they're unwilling (or unable) to raise prices to cover the difference. In Silicon Valley parlance, the community college model simply doesn't "scale." These schools are able to service a fixed or slow-growing number of students, so long as the growth of their enrollment doesn't exceed legislators' and taxpayers' willingness to subsidize the education the schools provide.

Yet, in recent years, enrollment growth has accelerated, and to keep up, the community colleges require subsidies that are larger than legislators and taxpayers appear willing to offer. Absent a shift in sentiment in cash-strapped state capitals, there's simply no way to ramp up the community college system to create the millions of new graduates America requires. It's akin to Jeff Bezos building Amazon.com thinking it will never have to serve more than ten thousand customers a day, and configuring his warehouses, inventory levels, and logistics to work at that capacity. At a certain point his company would become a victim of its own success—which is exactly what's happening to community colleges as too many Americans follow President Obama's advice and look to them as a place to retool for the New Economy.

EVEN IF COMMUNITY colleges didn't suffer from a strained financial model, they'd still face the problem that their students are failing to graduate at a rate comparable with rates at other types of colleges. To be clear, this isn't too surprising—in fact, it's almost intuitive. Think back to the phenomenon of the Automatics that I described earlier in this chapter. The Automatics are typically the better students in a high school class, and they're mostly headed to four-year schools. It makes sense that community colleges, which practice open enrollment and accept anyone who wishes to enter, would typically enroll academically weaker students, and that weaker students aren't as likely to graduate. Add in the fact that many of these students are returning to academics after years out of the classroom, and that most of them are juggling jobs, families, and financial struggles, and the odds are stacked against this population right from the start.

But with community colleges being asked to educate so many Americans—and receiving so much tax money to accomplish it—understanding the reasons why so many students fail to graduate has become an important matter of public policy. One of the most comprehensive studies of the phenomenon dates from 1992, in a journal article by Kevin J. Dougherty. He cites three different national surveys that found, on average, that "70 percent of four-year college entrants received a baccalaureate degree when followed up four to fourteen years later, whereas only 26 percent of public two-year college entrants reached the same destination."[31]

Dougherty cites three different obstacles that community college students encounter en route to a bachelor's degree: surviving in a community college, transferring to a four-year college, and persisting in a four-year college. In his 1994 book *The Contradictory College*, he notes that even when you control for student characteristics—massaging the data to account for the fact that community college students are more likely to come from lower socioeconomic classes or to have fewer academic qualifications—research still found that male and female two-year college students were 10 to 18 percent, respectively, more likely to drop out than their four-year-college counterparts. Even those who did well in community college suffered from inadequate advice and encouragement when they tried to transfer to a four-year school. (That's not unexpected either: as Thomas Bailey and James Jacobs have pointed out, "Most [community colleges] have one counselor serving thousands of students."[32]) And even among those who successfully make the leap to a four-year college, after three to five years, about a third of them have dropped out.[33]

More recent studies have drawn similar conclusions. A 2003 paper by Michael D. Summers, for example, says that the existence of high attrition rates at community colleges "largely remains an unsolved problem." The paper examines studies that took place from 1960 to 2003 that found fewer than half of community college freshmen successfully completing a degree.[34]

When presented with these sorts of criticisms, community college professors typically offer a series of responses. First, they point to the risk characteristics and low academic quality of the incoming students and the inherent challenges in educating a disadvantaged population. They make the legitimate argument that it's inherently unfair to compare the graduation rates of a community college with those of a traditional college, since the traditional college is getting the cream of the educational crop.

Second, they argue, defining success solely by measuring the graduation rate is shortsighted, and the way these measurements are done is patently unfair.

I agree: the "graduation rate" measurement, like so many of the conventions of higher education, is based upon the norms of traditional colleges and doesn't necessarily translate to institutions that educate a broader range of students. For instance, the graduation rate measurement is designed to track first-time, full-time students who complete their studies quickly; even part-time students who might eventually earn a degree are counted as "failures" if they fail to earn an associate's degree in three years or a bachelor's degree in six years, or if they get their degrees from a different institution from the one at which they started. That's descriptive of a lot of non-Automatics.

Community college backers also argue that students can benefit greatly from the study they do there even if they don't earn a degree. Consider a student who reads at an eighth-grade level and enrolls in "developmental" classes at a community college. A year later he may read at a twelfth-grade level. Even if he hasn't earned a degree, isn't he far more employable as a result of his studies? The same goes for an immigrant who learns to speak English by taking community college classes. His employment options and ability to navigate society are far better than before, even without a degree. By focusing on only the graduation rate, community college advocates argue, researchers are taking students whose achievements should be seen as a success, because their lives have been improved by their studies, and misclassifying them as failures because the students didn't complete a degree.

Third, they argue that community colleges serve such a wide spectrum of needs that many of their programs aren't even intended to create graduates. Indeed, many students enroll in a community college in order to learn a discrete skill, such as using PowerPoint, learning to swim, or acquiring hobbies like cake decorating. The fact that these students don't earn a degree should be irrelevant to the debate over community college effectiveness, they say. Some even argue that this wide array of missions creates inherent challenges not just for measuring community college success, but for helping students to be successful in the first place. As researcher Vanessa Smith Morest frames the problem: "The potential problem of offering so many educational services is it is impossible to do any of them well."[35]

It's hard to overstate this problem. Some community colleges have even begun offering four-year college degrees, a move that puts them in direct competition with traditional colleges and, some would argue, is at odds with their original mission. (Some might even see the distant glimmer of Harvard Envy.) In Florida alone, more than nineteen community colleges—including

Miami Dade College, which, like so many others, has decided to drop the word *community* from its name to reflect its move upmarket—are authorized to offer bachelor's degrees; nationwide, seventeen states now have four-year community college programs.[36] One higher education expert has called this innovation "a solution in search of a problem,"[37] and at a minimum it may represent an example of the "overshooting" that's led so many colleges astray.

In their book *Minding the Dream: The Process and Practice of the American Community College*, Gail O. Mellow and Cynthia Heelan articulate the community college counterargument with unusual clarity: "On average, community college students are poorer, more likely to be [studying] part-time and working, and more likely to be the first member of their family in college than students at four-year universities. [Criticisms about their success rates] come from a commonly adopted perspective that makes elite four-year colleges the normative model against which all other colleges are judged. In effect, it asks, 'Why don't community college students look, behave and achieve more like students who enter a four-year college?'"[38]

Mellow and Heelan go on to argue that the community college population is so different from that of traditional schools that talking about what constitutes success requires an entirely new frame of reference. "No attempt has been made to articulate what the nation expects of its community colleges," they write. "Is a 50 percent pass rate in developmental education great or problematic? Is it acceptable that almost 70 percent of students do not graduate with a degree, or is it a miracle if a community college can get its graduation rate up to 30 percent in four years? Is 90 percent passage on the national nursing certification exam terrific, or is that wasting a community's precious resources on the 10 percent who failed?"[39]

It's stunning that there are so few clear standards or bench-marks in the world of community colleges—a set of institutions responsible for educating 43 percent of all American undergrads, and which together are consuming billions in taxpayer funding. It's at least somewhat encouraging that this lack of clarity is now clearly recognized as a problem, and there's a growing debate over how to assess the performance of community colleges.

There are some possible answers. The core issue of compar-ing institutions with vastly different student populations could be solved by creating a common yardstick that compared in-stitutions with similar demographics. The data exist: the U.S. Department of Education has identified seven specific "risk fac-tors" that make students less likely to graduate—factors such as delayed enrollment, single parenthood, and full-time employ-ment.[40] Institutions whose students average fewer than two of the department's risk factors should be compared with other "low-risk" institutions; those with students averaging between two and four of the risk factors should be compared with other "medium-risk" institutions; and those with more than four, with "high-risk" cohorts. Comparisons within these risk cohorts on a range of metrics—graduation, placement, default, income change, etc.—would be appropriate, and would enable us to see which institutions were succeeding with a given type of stu-dent population, and which were not. These comparisons would highlight best practices and let institutions know where they need to do better, based on measurement against institutions with common challenges.

Nearly thirty years after *A Nation at Risk* focused Ameri-ca's attention on the poor results of the country's K–12 educa-tional system, there's been a growing interest in accountability, metrics, and outcomes at all levels of our educational system. There's an old saying on business school campuses: "What gets measured gets managed." Measurement permits comparison—and competition. Higher education has begun receiving more attention from managerially minded philanthropists such as Bill and Melinda Gates and the Lumina Foundation, who are championing an influential new "Completion Agenda" for community colleges that seeks to inject a focus on degree completion into the All-Access Playbook. (Valencia Community College in Orlando, for example, has generated graduation rates well above those of its peers by focusing less on attracting additional students and more on getting those they have to finish.[41])

Some of the most exciting work in this area is being done by a nonprofit group called Achieving the Dream: Community Colleges Count. The organization states its goal simply: "Achieving the Dream is dedicated to making the student success agenda a priority at community colleges and with state and national policymakers and stakeholders."[42] So far, the group has found it difficult to achieve meaningful, measurable changes in student outcomes, but in helping build a culture of data, it may be creating a foundation for future improvements.[43] This effort represents an acknowledgement that community college students shouldn't be measured in exactly the same ways we measure students at Penn or UCLA—but they should be measured. Achieving the Dream is applying approaches that businesses have used for years: experiment with small samples, try a variety of approaches, test to see which works best, and then try to roll out the most successful approaches on a broad scale.

WHEN I VISITED Miami Dade College, I was carrying a blue folder emblazoned with the Kaplan University logo. When I shook hands with a group of Miami Dade administrators upon arriving, one of them pointed to it and joked tensely about their willingness to let the competition inside their gates for a tour.

It was a lighthearted comment, but behind it was a very real sentiment. For years community colleges were the only place for students who weren't part of the Automatics, but this has changed. Now a new generation of for-profit institutions is providing an alternative—more expensive to students, but less expensive for taxpayers and more successful at graduating students and getting them jobs. Indeed, inside community colleges today, many people see Kaplan University and its for-profit siblings as a new form of competition—and not everyone views the rivalry as friendly.

I see things a little differently. I'm full of admiration for community colleges and the work they do. In fact, when I spend time with community college administrators, I'm struck by how similar our worldviews are: we share a deep passion for identifying and nurturing the talent in people who might have once been dismissed as "not college material." Like Eduardo Padrón and the people leading the rest of America's community colleges, I'm convinced that if we continue to think about college as a place for only eighteen-year-olds with high SAT scores—as a place for only the Automatics—America will be in big trouble in the years ahead.

At the same time, as much as I respect the community college mission, I don't think they alone can get us far enough when it comes to turning out enough college graduates and successful members of the workforce. They lack the capacity and the funding to meet demand, and their historic struggles in getting their students through to graduation will inhibit taxpayers' willingness to put even more money into a system that's already spending tens of billions of dollars a year. Further, until their leaders are willing to bring focus to their mission—to choose whether they are primarily associate's degree providers, four-year college feeders, workforce trainers, adult general-interest educators, or any of the many other roles they often take on—community colleges will be trying to do too many things, and be destined to do too few of them excellently. Breaking up community colleges into smaller, more narrowly tailored schools may be part of the solution; the Completion Agenda, Achieving the Dream, and other new approaches that emphasize data, transparency, and graduation over head counts offer additional promise. Certainly, the focus of the Obama administration and major foundations on finding models to assist these schools in succeeding can only help. Ultimately, though, it is the responsibility of states to demand excellence from their community colleges. They are the majority investors in the system and primary beneficiaries of its output. They need to hold themselves, the institutions, and the students accountable for achieving results. When they do, I believe they can find willing allies in the faculty and administration of the colleges themselves.

Community colleges have an arduous path to travel to deliver consistently on student success and taxpayer efficiency. The focus on common data and measurement is an important move in the right direction. Even so, it's clear that more is needed to address the crucial educational and workforce needs of our economy.

The way I see it, the taxpayer-funded community colleges are complemented by a new breed of colleges that have risen up in the last decade. These new colleges are using a different financial model to achieve many of the same goals. They're data driven, outcome oriented, and—perhaps most important—designed to be scalable.

In the next chapter, I tell their story.

4

A Crucial Part of
the Solution

How a New Kind of University Serves
a New Kind of Student

From a seat high in the upper level, the events taking place on the floor of this arena in downtown Miami look like a typical college commencement ceremony. The Miami Brass Quintet plays "Pomp and Circumstance" as a long line of students in black robes file toward their seats. In the stands, families clutch cameras, smile, and wave excitedly at the graduates. Professors, clad in the colorful academic hoods that signify the universities where they earned their advanced degrees, fill in the rows behind the grads. A military color guard carries in the American flag, and a baritone sings the national anthem.

But as Kaplan University's 2010 winter graduation ceremony unfolds, there are not-so-subtle indications that the people who will be accepting degrees today aren't typical college seniors.

After the national anthem, for instance, the college president asks graduates who are members of the military to stand and be recognized—and nearly 10 percent of the class rises. Even more are watching live on the Internet from their overseas postings.

Aside from the colors on their hoods, it's hard to tell the grads from the professors, since the average student is nearing middle age herself.

There are none of the ubiquitous "Thanks, Mom and Dad" signs taped to the top of the mortarboards. In fact, when the students start filing across the stage to accept their degrees, the most frequent cry going up from the spectators is "Yay, Mom!" It's a sign that at this graduation, it's often the parents who are the graduates, and their children are the ones cheering them on.

Carlos Negron is seated with the School of Criminal Justice, from which he's receiving a master's degree this morning. Negron, thirty-two, was born in Puerto Rico and moved to Florida when he was twenty. He briefly enrolled at the University of Central Florida, but it didn't fit his schedule. "Juggling three jobs and college didn't work for me," he says. So Negron enlisted in the Coast Guard, and soon after enrolled in an online degree program at Excelsior College. In 2006, at age twenty-nine, he earned his bachelor's degree. Then he enrolled in Kaplan University's master's program, which he also completed online. "I believe in online education—period," Negron says. "It allows people like me who don't have the time to go to a brick-and-mortar college to get the same level of education." With his master's degree in hand, on his graduation day Negron had a provisional offer of employment from the Federal Bureau of Investigation; if he passed the background check and fitness test, he planned to take a job there that paid an extra $20,000 a year over his current earnings. If he didn't get into the FBI, his degree would make him a competitive applicant to attend the Coast Guard's Officer Candidate School, which would also mean a significant pay increase. "I'm certain my education will play a big part in my future," Negron says.

Lisa Evert is sitting on the stage this morning, waiting to take the podium as the ceremony's student speaker. Evert, forty-five, earned her associate's degree at a community college. Family illnesses and her own medical problems made it difficult for her to continue attending traditional night-school classes. So in 2008, while recovering from surgery for a heart condition, she decided to try online classes. "I heard about Kaplan, I did tons of due diligence, and I was really impressed with what I saw and read," Evert says. She finished her bachelor's degree in psychology in eighteen months, and became very involved in mentoring other students and in leading the Golden Key National Honor Society. She's already begun studying for a master's degree, and soon after today's ceremony she expects to start hunting for a job in corporate training and development.

Patricia Feggins, fifty-three, is also one of today's graduates. Feggins spent twenty-eight years working at a McDonald's franchise, where, as a scheduling manager, she saw firsthand how hard it was for working families to juggle jobs and childcare. "It was so hard for me to run the shift," Feggins recalls, because workers were constantly calling in sick due to lack of child care. So in 2004, Feggins opened Patricia's Child Care Center in Brodnax, Virginia. Today her center cares for sixty children and has a staff of ten.

Feggins was impressed by the academic rigor of the Kaplan classes—even if, at times, she was slightly overwhelmed by the number of research papers and essays her professors required her to write. "Because I was enrolled in two to three classes each [term], there were many times in which research papers were due at the same time, which resulted in a strain," she says. "However, I understood that these classes needed to be intense in order [for me] to get all the relevant information." She was also able to work efficiently: instead of commuting, fighting over parking spaces, or waiting for professors to show up in a lecture hall, she could invest all of that time in actually studying.

Feggins also felt that the faculty were more supportive than those she encountered in the community college she once attended. For instance, even though most of her professors weren't in Virginia, they knew Patricia operated a child care center there, so when she asked questions about regulations that were specific to her state, several professors were willing to do extra research to provide her with the answers. "They went to the extra mile to assist me," she says.

In eighteen months, Feggins earned an associate's degree in interdisciplinary studies with a focus on child development, and she's spread the lessons she has learned throughout the staff at her child care center. "When I learn something, I make sure to come back and share it with the group," she says. She also advises the working-class parents who are her customers that they need to continue their schooling, too. "Get as much education as you can," she says.

Another participant has clearly seen the advantages education can bring. From the lectern on stage, Colin Powell tells the assembled students at the commencement exercises that by virtue of his résumé—four-star U.S. Army general, chairman of the Joint Chiefs of Staff, secretary of state—many people mistakenly believe he's a West Pointer or a Rhodes scholar. The truth is less glamorous: as an undergraduate he attended City College of New York, where he was a C student who might not have graduated if not for the As he'd earned in ROTC. After college, Powell joined the army, where he learned that continuing education was the key to advancing, in both the military and in life. Powell earned a graduate degree while he was married with children, and he knows that in today's economy, these students will have to continue to advance their educations to stay ahead. "Today, celebrate your achievement," Powell said. "Tomorrow, get back online and see what you are going to do next, because you can never stop. You can never stop."

IN THE FIRST half of this book, I examined the evolution of traditional higher education and the ways it has developed its own internal incentive system that leads to continued investment in the educational "haves," even when that incremental investment leads to only marginal educational returns—or, in many cases, has nothing whatsoever to do with education. I've suggested that using some of that investment to increase access for "have nots" would lead to greater returns for students, our economy, and our society. In chapter 3, I discussed how community colleges, despite their challenges, offer practical, lower-cost access to millions of students—and could do more with a better funding model.

In the second half of this book, I want to explore how a different kind of institution—the for-profit, or "private-sector" college—has emerged to play a valuable complementary role in the higher education landscape. There's no disputing that we need more Americans earning college degrees, and there's no way to get the necessary number of graduates out into the workplace without the added capacity and innovative techniques offered by these new institutions. Many private-sector colleges are offering effective, cost-efficient education to millions of working adults, helping them advance to better, higher-paying jobs and lead better lives. Like the land-grant and community colleges before them, private-sector colleges are often met with skepticism, concern, and even derision by some academics and other traditionalists—a subject that will be the focus of chapter 5. For-profit colleges are far from perfect. While some wariness is justified, however, a lot of it isn't. But it is a predictable price one pays for innovating in a sector of the economy that's long been unusually resistant to change.

Despite the criticism, in the last decade a lot of students have decided that private-sector colleges are the right choice for them. Data for 2008 (released in 2010) show that 2.75 million students were enrolled in degree-granting, proprietary colleges—a proportion that accounts for roughly one in ten Americans studying at a postsecondary, degree-granting institution.[1] Over the last thirty years, the private sector has been adding students at an average annual rate of 11.6 percent, compared with only 1.8 percent average annual increase at traditional degree-granting institutions.[2]

The largest of the private-sector schools, the University of Phoenix, counted more than four hundred thousand students in 2010, an enrollment larger than the undergraduate enrollment of the entire Big Ten. While many of its students pursued their degrees online, University of Phoenix also has more than two hundred physical campuses and learning centers in thirty-nine states plus the District of Columbia and Puerto Rico.[3]

Students are choosing these schools for many reasons. As the stories of Carlos Negron, Lisa Evert, and Patricia Feggins all indicate, convenience is part of it. Unlike traditional colleges, which typically offer semester-long classes each fall and spring, many of the private-sector colleges start new classes every few weeks, and run year round. While students at community colleges fight over scarce seats in required classes, most student-focused private-sector colleges will do what it takes to get students into the courses they need to progress quickly toward their degree. While the majority of classes at traditional colleges take place during the daytime, when most Americans are at work, private-sector colleges offer classes at night—or, for online students, often in an "asynchronous" setting that allows them to participate in class at any hour they choose. It's not just these innovative practices that are leading more students to private-sector colleges, however: the financial problems and capacity shortfalls that are becoming apparent at traditional schools are also a key driver. "At a time when American public higher education is cutting budgets, laying off people, and turning away students, the rise of for-profit universities has been meteoric," concludes *The Chronicle of Higher Education*.[4]

Still, convenience and capacity alone are not responsible for students' enrolling in private-sector colleges: this enrollment growth stems from the perception of many students that these colleges better meet their needs. Private-sector schools tend to align their curriculum around those skills that are most needed in the workforce. Many of these institutions have advisory boards that consult with employers to get feedback on what employers want from prospective employees in a given area, and they regularly update their curricula to teach to those skills. Private-sector colleges use technology to deliver those portions of the education that technology can do best. The best of them measure and assess teacher quality, curricular issues, and student readiness in ways that often surpass the methods used by traditional colleges. They make use of practitioners in the given field of study to teach classes, rather than (or in addition to) pure academics. They invest heavily in career centers to help their graduates find jobs. They provide a suite of advising and support services and help centers to address the kinds of problems that can knock students off track in other institutions, ranging from financial challenges to math phobias. In short, private-sector educators are able to tailor their education to specific, identified learning outcomes and measure performance against those outcomes.

Many observers believe that private-sector colleges are a new phenomenon. They're not. For much of human history, education was a business like any other, with students paying fees to their teachers, in much the same way they'd pay for any practical tool. "The earliest universities in late medieval times were profit-making corporate associations, and the black gowns that professors still wear at graduations and special events have deep pockets into which students in the thirteenth and fourteenth centuries deposited their fees," writes George Keller, an educational historian. Even today, Keller writes, America has more for-profit postsecondary schools than nonprofit ones, most of them focused on training vocational workers such as secretaries, welders, massage therapists, and truck drivers.[5]

Over the last one hundred years, however, the for-profit model receded in prominence among American colleges, largely because government-funded schools rose up to dominate the industry. "Higher education during the twentieth century underwent drastic changes as reformers forcefully argued education was the business of the state, and society could be improved by strong, publicly backed schools," write scholars James Coleman and Richard Vedder.[6] Indeed, instead of thinking of private-sector colleges as newcomers trying to steal market share from established colleges, it's more historically correct to look at the last century as an anomalous period during which a massive infusion of taxpayer money led the subsidized public university and community college to become the dominant models. With legislatures showering money on state universities, driving annual tuition down to below $5,000 a year at some taxpayer-funded colleges, it's no surprise that those low-priced institutions gained market share at the expense of schools where students paid their own way. "It is safe to say for the period 1890–1972, for-profit colleges were increasingly marginalized by the growth of highly subsidized public institutions," Coleman and Vedder write.[7]

Viewed in this light, the surge of private-sector colleges over the last generation can be seen less as a new phenomenon taking hold, and more as a long-standing and successful educational model enjoying a renaissance—largely as a result of the unsustainable funding model relied upon by the public institutions that became dominant over the last century.

I've played a small role in this course correction over the years myself, including several years as president of Kaplan University. In that role, I presided over commencement exercises just like the one described earlier. As you'd expect, I think very highly of the group of institutions known as Kaplan Higher Education, and it's tempting for me to devote much of this chapter to describing all the great work that my colleagues do to enable success for our students. But given my position, there's no way for me to be objective about my own company's institutions.

So in order to explore how private-sector colleges are reworking the standard formula for how higher education is supposed to serve students, I decided to spend time inside the headquarters of a competing for-profit institution. To do so, I headed to Arlington, Virginia.

ROBERT SILBERMAN WORKS in a corner office on the twenty-fifth floor of a high-rise building a few miles outside Washington, D.C. His simple suite of offices looks more like an accounting firm than a university: the architecture is nondescript, and the space has none of the grandeur of the President's Club at High Point University where Nido Qubein receives visitors. When

Silberman invites a visitor like me to lunch, there is no need for fine china or a waitstaff: his assistant simply orders out for turkey sandwiches and Diet Cokes.

Silberman is himself the product of an elite education, with an undergraduate degree from Dartmouth and a graduate degree from Johns Hopkins. After serving as an officer in the U.S. Navy, he entered finance, working to raise money to fund alternative energy projects; the first company he helped create converted municipal waste into energy. In 1999, Silberman was living in Omaha, Nebraska, helping to run a natural gas company, which he and his partners sold (that same year) to Warren Buffett's Berkshire Hathaway, for whom Silberman worked for a time. By 2000, he'd grown restless. Some of his old colleagues had launched a private equity firm, and they called him about a job. They wanted to buy a company called Strayer, which operated a for-profit university in Washington, D.C., and they wanted Silberman to run it.

For the next few months, Silberman continued working for the natural gas company, but he began an intensive study of both Strayer and its industry. He liked what he found.

Strayer's Business College was founded in Baltimore in 1892 by a schoolteacher named Irving Strayer. The school provided a nuts-and-bolts business education—heavy on concepts such as accounting and office management—aimed at working adults, many of them moving from agricultural jobs and into the burgeoning world of white-collar office work. "Proprietary institutions were much more prevalent in this country at the end of the nineteenth century than they are now," Silberman says. "There were a lot of schools like Strayer that were started in the 1880s and the 1890s, particularly along the Eastern seaboard." In 1904, Irving Strayer expanded the institution to Washington, where the school operated from a building a few blocks from the White House. Many of its students aspired to obtain civil service jobs in the federal government, and the kind of training Strayer provided gave them a leg up in doing so.

Irving Strayer died in 1910, but subsequent generations of the Strayer family continued running the college into the 1980s. Over the years, it expanded to offer bachelor's and master's degrees, and eventually changed its name to Strayer University. These decades of family ownership are a crucial part of Strayer's ongoing competitive advantage, in Silberman's view. "It had a culture as a family-owned proprietorship, one that believes that the quality of the education is ultimately going to drive the value of the enterprise," he says. "Somebody whose family name wasn't on it wouldn't have come [to believe that] as easily."

By the late 1980s, however, Strayer ran into a problem that's common among family businesses: there was no family member interested in taking it over. So in 1989, the school was purchased by Ron Bailey. Bailey was born in the coal mining region of West Virginia, served in the U.S. Army, and went on to be a key professor and administrator at Strayer. To purchase the school, he mortgaged his house. After the sale, Bailey began opening new Strayer campuses outside of the nation's capital. His aspirations were strictly regional, however: his goal was to be able to drive to every Strayer campus in a single day. By the late 1990s he had ten locations, each within an hour of the Washington headquarters, and an enrollment of around eight thousand.

As Silberman studied up on both the industry and the company, he was impressed. He could tell it was a quality institution that cared about the long-term success of its students. "It was a great business—it was just small, [and] it wasn't growing," he recalls. "My strategy was if we could do this right, Strayer could be a nationwide university, but it would have the same cultural feel [that it had] when I took it over." Silberman toured the D.C.-area campuses with Bailey, attended some classes, and considered the possibilities.

He wasn't the only one with growing ambitions in the world of for-profit higher ed. During the 1990s, established, publicly traded companies such as DeVry and ITT had already begun rolling out a national network of campuses. Silberman read annual reports and studied their success. Companies such as Kaplan were getting involved, too: in 1998 it launched the Concord School of Law, and in 2000, then-CEO Jonathan Grayer led the acquisition of a group of for-profit colleges, one of which was a school in Davenport, Iowa, that was the foundation for what would become Kaplan University. Much of the interest in the sector, however, was being driven by the University of Phoenix, which had been launched in the mid-1970s by a Cambridge-educated historian named John Sperling.

Sperling, who served on the faculty at Berkeley and San Jose State, got interested in private-sector education while working on alternative programs that offered college degrees to policemen and teachers. He met considerable resistance from college administrators, who saw the population that Sperling was serving as "not college material." Frustrated, he decided to set out on his own to create a new kind of college—a quixotic endeavor that led to years of battles with the accrediting bodies. "We violated much that was sacred in the groves of academia," Sperling writes in his memoir. "[We used] an untenured faculty composed of working professionals who taught at night what they worked at during the day; programs developed in cooperation with employers, curricula developed by expert consultants, editors and instructional designers; [and] classes held at places and times convenient to the students."[8]

By 1976, he'd fled California and set up shop in Arizona.

During the 1980s, the venture grew. Its parent company, Apollo Group, went public in 1994, and its stock soared. Apollo's financial success led ambitious businesspeople to rediscover the private-sector school model, which had been overshadowed by the growth of public universities for more than a century. Against the backdrop of the overall economic boom of the 1990s, private-sector education began experiencing record growth—a track record that was largely uninterrupted until regulatory changes arose in 2010.

These new and growing institutions were met with more than a few raised eyebrows. James Traub's profile of the University of Phoenix, which ran in the *New Yorker* in 1997, captures the heavy skepticism these schools have frequently encountered.[9] The headline alone, "Drive-Thru U.," tells much of what you need to know about the treatment. Traub's description of this fast-growing university, which at the time had forty thousand students, drips with derision. It's a "para-university," he writes, a "franchise operation" with campuses "just off a highway exit ramp," whose library exists only online. "It has the operational core of higher-education—students, teachers, classrooms, exams, degree-granting programs—without a campus life, or even an intellectual life," he writes, describing an administrator whose office bookshelf contains just three books, all of them lowbrow human resources guides.

If you can overlook the down-your-nose, elitist view of a school aimed at striving middle managers and the aspirational working class—the type of people who don't subscribe to the *New Yorker*—you'd see clear signs, even back in 1997, that the University of Phoenix might turn out to be a world beater. Already it was becoming evident that the demand for college degrees among people who weren't eighteen years old, who couldn't study full time, and who didn't want (or weren't willing to pay for) climbing walls and dorms was growing sharply. At the same time, the attitude of this group of consumers toward higher education was undergoing a shift. Traub cites research by Arthur Levine, then president of Columbia University's Teachers College, that suggests that a growing number of students were looking at a college degree more pragmatically. "They wanted the kind of relationship with a college that they had with their bank, their supermarket, and their gas company," Levine says. "They say, 'I want terrific service, I want convenience, I want quality control. Give me classes twenty-four hours a day, and give me in-class parking, if possible.' These are students who want stripped-down classes. They don't want to buy anything they're not using." Another telling detail: Traub reports that one stock broker told him that many of the people who'd been bidding up Apollo Group stock were, in fact, professors at Arizona State University. They were investing in the University of Phoenix model, Traub says, because they had "concluded that the U of P delivered pretty much the same product they did, only more efficiently."

Silberman reached the same conclusion about Strayer, so in 2000 he and his partners purchased the school from Ron Bailey and began a nationwide expansion. Today, on the wall of his conference room, Silberman keeps a map of the United States, with colored pushpins representing existing Strayer locations, which currently number eighty-four campuses in nineteen states (plus Washington, D.C.). Today the school enrolls fifty-six thousand students, who earn degrees in fields ranging from information technology to health care administration to criminal justice.

While Silberman teaches an occasional class at Strayer, he's a businessman, not an academic. To oversee the academic operations, he's brought in people such as Sondra Stallard, Strayer's president since 2007. Before joining Strayer, Stallard spent thirty-two years at the University of Virginia. Like John Sperling before her, Stallard became interested in working with nontraditional, older adult students who wanted to return to college to earn a degree. She, too, met resistance, in her case from some of her UVA colleagues, which frustrated her. "I really began to understand that there was this tremendous need for learning for people who had the desire and capacity to earn a degree but no hope of entering what's arguably one of the best institutions in the country," she recalls. "It seemed like the antithesis of what Jefferson believed, that an educated citizenry is essential for the preservation of democracy. I kept thinking, if Mr. Jefferson was here, he would have opened the door."

Over time, with the support of the university's then-president John Casteen, Stallard was able to create a School of Continuing and Professional Studies, which took its place alongside the law, business, and other schools as UVA's tenth school. Its first graduating class featured three women, all in their forties. Over time, Stallard helped nontraditional students go on to medical school, law school, and even UVA's prestigious business school. "What I saw there was transformational, but I was doing it on such a small scale, it was such a drop in the bucket." At Strayer, she gets to do it on a huge scale, and she couldn't be more pleased.

"This is an opportunity to help those who'd been shut out," she says. "We're not an institution of last resort; we're a university of second chances." She describes a student body made up of former military personnel, women who had children at a young age and had to forego college, people who suffered health problems, or "late bloomers" who weren't ready for college at the age of eighteen.

Stallard believes so strongly in this cause partly because she's seen how profoundly education can change a cohort of non-

Automatics. She grew up in Hugheston, West Virginia, in an era when almost no one went to college. "Everybody went to the mines," she says. Then a couple of pioneering students began attending a commuter college nearby. Then a couple more. Fairly quickly, a social epidemic ensued: over the course of just a few years, this community where no one went to college became a place where it was expected. "All of a sudden the mines, or working in the convenience store, or waiting tables, or getting married, weren't the only options," she says. "I saw this little community literally be transformed by education." Now she's trying to replicate that transformation in dozens of new communities.

If you spend time with Stallard, you can't help but be impressed by her enthusiasm for the mission they've undertaken at Strayer; she has what's referred to in religious parlance as the zeal of a convert. But she's hardly the only one. Richard Ruch spent twenty years as an administrator at a private university, a land-grant university, and a liberal arts college before taking a job at DeVry University. "Until a few years ago I thought that all proprietary institutions were the scum of the academic earth," he writes in *Higher Ed, Inc.*, his book on the industry. "I could not see how the profit motive could properly co-exist with an educational mission."[10] But once inside a for-profit institution, he found that his new colleagues lacked horns or tails—and many of them were even more focused on the best interests of their students than his former colleagues at traditional universities. "What many of us have discovered," he writes, "is that the for-profit way of doing education is not so much better or worse than the non-profit way; it is just a different approach."[11]

I'M NOT SURE I fully agree with Ruch on that point. While each model has its strengths, I believe there are at least two significant ways in which the proprietary college model isn't just different, but superior.

The first advantage lies in its financial model. Traditional colleges take in revenue from a wide variety of sources. There are direct subsidies from federal and state governments. There's research money. There are charitable gifts from alumni and other donors. There's investment income from the endowment, a huge source of revenue for older, elite institutions such as the Ivies. Last—and in some cases least—there's tuition. By contrast, in the for-profit model, the vast majority of the money comes from a single source: tuition and fees paid by students—whether it comes directly out of their pockets or via financial aid (in the form of grants and loans, many of them provided by the federal government)—so students are free to choose where to spend it.

When I explain these drastically different models to people, I often use two quasi-mathematical formulas to drive home the point.

For private-sector colleges, the business model is fairly simple:

$$T > E$$

where T is tuition revenue and E is expenses. For private-sector colleges to be successful, their leaders need to be sure that tuition exceeds expenses. For private-sector colleges to grow, they need to focus on increasing the T, and the surest way to do that is to provide a high-quality education that creates successful graduates and positive word-of-mouth among alumni and employers, and to make sure the E piece of the equation is being spent wisely, on things that enhance educational quality. Any other expenses, including marketing expenses to attract students or compensation, must fall within the basic

T > E formula. It's a straightforward model, and there's no confusion over the most important duty of the people leading these institutions: to satisfy the tuition-paying students in order to attract more people just like them. For most students, that means enabling the skills that can help them advance in their careers.

The formula is a lot more complicated at traditional universities. Their model looks more like this:

$$T + A + G + R + I + C + S + M > E$$

where T is tuition, A is appropriations from state legislatures, G is direct government grants, R is research grants, I is investment (or endowment) income, C is charitable contributions, S is revenue from sports teams, and M is miscellaneous revenue (which would include money received for housing students in dorms and feeding them in dining facilities, the school bookstore, parking permits, hospital revenue at some schools and potentially hundreds of other items). The sum of all of those revenue streams must exceed expenses for the university to be financially viable, at least over time.

In theory, it can be good to have a diversified revenue stream. General Electric is a stronger company because the earnings from its diverse collection of businesses help to insulate it from the ups and downs of any particular industry. So, on the surface, the traditional university financial model might seem like a source of security.

In practice, however, the fact that traditional universities depend on such a wide range of revenues causes problems. The biggest conflict is that students pay so little of the actual money that flows into a college that it's possible for them to slip from being the central focus of the leadership. While virtually all of the revenue at most for-profit colleges comes from tuition, at private, nonprofit colleges, tuition makes up just 29 percent of total revenue. At public universities, where taxpayers bear most of the costs, money from students can account for only 13 percent of the revenue.[12]

Stop and consider those numbers for a second. Can you think of any product or service you purchase where the money you're paying is equal to just 13 percent of the total cost? For most of us, the only comparable example is health care, a troubled sector whose economics have been considered a national crisis for most of the last two decades. When customers are paying only 13 percent of the real cost, all kinds of inefficient things start to happen.

That complicated income statement also subjects traditional universities to forces largely outside their control. A university that depends on endowment income—that's letter I in the equation just given—for a large portion of its operating expenses, as the most elite schools do, will see that income plunge during periods when the returns from its investments drop, which is exactly what happened at many schools in recent years.

Consider Dartmouth, which relies on endowment income for 35 percent of its annual revenue. Its endowment lost 23 percent of its value in fiscal 2009, and during his first year on the job, new president Jim Yong Kim had to figure out how to cut the school's budget by $50 million. "I thought I was going to take the first year just to learn about Dartmouth and ask a lot of questions," Kim told the *Wall Street Journal*. "I had never been involved in investments. I had no idea what a hedge fund is."[13]

Needless to say, he had to learn fast. Though his own professional background was in medicine, Kim spent much of his first year as Dartmouth's president closely examining expenses in an effort to balance the school's budget. While Kim was able to

make the numbers work (including cuts in financial aid), he rec-
ognizes the inherent long-term problems in how colleges such
as Dartmouth fund operations. "The larger question is: How
are we going to sustain this model among elite institutions?"
he says. "The actual cost of educating a single undergraduate
student is $100,000 a year, so the cost is more than we charge.
[In 2010/2011, Dartmouth charged $52,275 for tuition, room,
board, and fees, before scholarships or other discounts.] That
is a very difficult model to sustain. You have to make up the
rest from donations and payouts from the endowment. We're all
struggling with this."[14]

This unsustainable model is directly connected with the excesses I described in chapters 1 and 2 of this book. Do the
actual classes at Dartmouth cost $100,000 per student to pro-
vide? Realistically, professors and lecture halls simply don't cost
that much money. Instead, this number may be so large because
of the fully loaded, bundled-product aspect that traditional colleges use to compete: all those food courts, four-star residence
halls, and star faculty lured away from rival institutions carry
very real costs for traditional colleges.

The same issue is true at public universities, where the big
source of funds is grants from state coffers. When the economy
turns down, state tax revenues go down. Because most states are
forced to balance budgets each year (they can't run deficits in the
same way the federal government can), they're inevitably forced
to cut aid to state universities and community colleges, putting
the leaders at those institutions in the same situation as Dartmouth's president. In California in 2009/2010, public college enrollment was pared by 165,000, even as applications surged (and
bigger cuts appeared to be ahead for the state system).[15]

While the funding sources are different, there's a common
problem with relying on stock market returns or taxpayers for

your operating budget: when the economy weakens, funding inevitably drops. That's a particular problem for higher education institutions, because demand for their services is countercyclical. During a recession, when the job market weakens, more people want to go back to school. So here you have institutions whose budgets go down at the precise moment when more students want to attend and expenses go up. In economic terms, these institutions have a pro-cyclical supply model and a countercyclical demand model. Imagine a sports stadium that has sixty thousand seats during years the home team is lousy, but where capacity shrinks to forty thousand in any year when the team is playing for a championship. That's roughly how the supply-demand dynamic works in traditional higher education.

Besides the diverging supply and demand curves, there's another big problem with the complicated funding models used by traditional institutions: these schools' diverse revenue streams makes them servant to too many masters. A traditional college president spends her time focusing as much on I (investment income) or R (research grants) or G (direct grants) or S (sports revenue) or M (miscellaneous)—none of which has much, if anything, to do with the educational proposition the school is offering its students—as on T (tuition from students). For private-sector college leaders, life is much simpler: it's *all about* T, which is ultimately all about keeping students (and their eventual employers) satisfied.

The best evidence of the muddied focus this complicated equation has on traditional college leaders can be found in the daily activities of any university president. At private colleges, she inevitably must spend a huge chunk of time wooing donors to get C (contributions). The next time you're on a private college campus, visit the development or alumni relations department and marvel at how large it is and how many people work in it—then compare it to the "academic affairs" or "dean of students" offices. At public colleges, the president (and her lobbying team) must spend comparable time schmoozing legislators and playing politics, trying to protect their budgets. The argument some have sought to make—discussed in more detail in chapter 5—that for-profit college leaders spend inordinately more time on marketing and nonacademic matters have it exactly backward: their business model incents for-profits to focus almost exclusively on students (both recruiting and educating) while their traditional counterparts are stretched across myriad constituencies. (In a well-run for-profit, shareholders or other owners don't require much attention; they know their interests are best served if leadership is highly focused on student results.)

In theory, students are the customers of these institutions, and the university leadership should have no higher priority than serving them. In reality, the students at a traditional university are only quasi-customers. Since legislators and donors are paying most of the bills, the leadership is pushed to spend much of its time thinking about these other, arguably more important constituencies.

Richard Ruch, who spent decades in traditional universities before landing at DeVry, tells a story that epitomizes how the funding mechanisms of traditional higher education skew sensibilities. Ruch recalls that while he was an administrator at a private college, the school's leadership hired an outside consultant to work with faculty to implement the then-trendy concept of Total Quality Management. The consultant began the engagement by asking the faculty a simple question: Who is your customer? The ensuing drama was anything but simple. Some faculty members objected to the exercise because they found the word *customer* offensive. "The provost came out with a white paper on the subject that said basically everyone was our customer," Ruch recalls. "Two of the deans said that the faculty was their main customer, and it was suggested that the president considered the trustees his primary customers. In the end, it was decided that the principles of Total Quality Management did not apply to an institution of higher education. The consultant was fired."[16]

The difference in the sectors' business models also explains a lot about their relative incentives to grow. In the private sector model, tuition revenue must exceed expenses—but for that to be true, on average tuition revenue *per student* must exceed the cost of delivery of the education for that student. As we've discussed, in a traditional university, frequently the *tuition* revenue per student is *less* that the expenses associated with that student.

Accordingly, for-profits have an incentive to add more students, as each incremental student adds profitability. In the traditional model, if each incremental student *loses* money, there is no incentive to grow. And indeed, private-sector colleges have grown far more rapidly than the rest of higher education over the last few decades. Traditional colleges have recast their business-model-driven disincentive to grow into a virtue: not growing, while seeking better and better students for the scarce available seats, is viewed as the path to prestige and success.

Part of the reason the model works for private-sector colleges is they do a good job of managing their E—partly by focusing on education, instead of fancy gym equipment or soccer teams. As a businessman, Rob Silberman instantly recognized the appeal of this financial model when he began studying the sector more than a decade ago. "We're serving a working adult for whom the physical costs of a large residential university don't matter. So that all we're [spending money on] is the direct investment in the faculty, sufficient classrooms, and technology so they can access the education. The fact that we don't have football teams, several-hundred-acre campuses, or buildings that are used very sparsely—that just speaks to the costs that we don't have to invest in, in order to achieve the educational mission that we've chosen."

In terms of these two different funding models, critics of private-sector education tend to focus on two facts of life. First, they'll assert that the tuition rates at private-sector colleges are, on average, higher than those at a public or nonprofit college. (In fact, for 2010/2011, the average annual tuition at a private-sector college was $13,935, far less than many elite universities, but more than at community colleges.)[17] And they'll also point out that unlike nonprofits, whose name implies there is no profit, private-sector colleges are designed to reward investors by making sure there's something left over after paying expenses. Neither of these arguments is very surprising, but they both miss the point in important ways.

When you look at the funding formulas, it's pretty obvious that, other things being equal, tuition will be higher, on average, for a private-sector college, since the tuition is the only source of revenue. The students who attend colleges such as Strayer, Phoenix, and DeVry do receive federal financial aid (which becomes part of the T they pay the schools), and for-profits typically work to help students navigate the complicated student loan system. But beyond the federal loans and grants that students can use at any eligible institution, for the most part, for-profits don't get additional help from state legislators, donors, or stock market returns. So, yes, a freshman English class at the University of Phoenix will cost the student more than freshman English at Maricopa Community College or Arizona State, but that's mostly because Arizona taxpayers are paying a huge chunk of the bill for students at the latter two institutions. In fact, data show that the underlying cost to deliver the education (the E) is lower at private-sector institutions versus at traditional four-year institutions. But in public institutions the taxpayer is directly picking up much of the tab, whereas in private-sector schools the student is paying. (I'll talk more about the impact on the taxpayer of student loan defaults, which tend to be higher for students in private-sector institutions, in chapter 5.)

The second criticism—that private-sector colleges are suspect because they make a profit—is one that comes down partly to semantics. Just because traditional colleges are classified by the IRS as nonprofits doesn't mean that their revenue must equal their expenses. In fact, over time most traditional nonprofit colleges do earn a "profit" in a traditional accounting sense. "At the end of the day, regardless of how an organization or company or church or university is funded, your revenues better exceed your costs, or you won't be around very long," says Daniel Hamburger, CEO of DeVry Inc. Hamburger, an alumnus of Harvard Business School, points to that institution as an example: In 2008, HBS had revenues of $451 million and expenses of $423 million. In a company, that difference is a profit; nonprofits refer to it as "surplus," or "excess revenues over costs." But no matter what you call it, Harvard Business School took in more than it paid out by a measure of $28 million in 2008, $30 million in 2007, and $23 million in 2006. Indeed, one of the most important distinctions between the for-profit and nonprofit institutions is that unlike HBS, institutions such as Strayer, Phoenix, and DeVry pay taxes when their revenues exceed expenses. In 2008, for-profit universities paid about $1 billion in taxes, according to researchers Robert J. Shapiro and Nam D. Pham—an amount equal to $549 for every student enrolled.[18] That's one reason some have suggested that rather than classify colleges as for-profit and nonprofit, it might be more accurate to classify them as tax-paying and tax-receiving.

Silberman offers an additional insight on why the private-sector model remains controversial. Any time an industry shifts from a publicly funded or nonprofit model to a privately funded model, he says, it's inevitably met with criticism and skepticism. In the 1980s, for instance, hospitals began making this shift, which caused an initial outcry. Twenty years later, for-profit health care isn't controversial anymore. If you've been to a hospital lately, you probably don't even know or care if it's for-profit or nonprofit. If someday you need a serious medical procedure, such as open-heart surgery, you'll probably do extensive research on which hospitals have the best long-term outcomes for a case like yours. But you probably won't give much thought to whether the hospital turns a profit, or whether it pays taxes. You'll focus on the outcome of your surgery, the same way students at Strayer aren't concerned with the school's profit margin, and are instead focused on value: how the cost of their degree relates to how much it helps them advance in their careers. If the price tag rises too high, or the career advancement drops too low, students will choose to avail themselves of one of the many other possible options.

The simple funding method used by proprietary colleges comes with an ancillary benefit for students: because institutions are receiving the full cost of attendance during the years a student is actually enrolled, that student won't spend the rest of her life being interrupted during dinnertime by calls from the alumni development office. While colleges such as Strayer do work to keep their alumni engaged—particularly so they can provide mentoring and job opportunities to future students—they aren't particularly interested in getting them to write checks. If you go to Strayer's alumni Web site, you won't find a mention of "donation." A few weeks after my visit with Silberman, just for kicks, I called Strayer's toll-free number. "Do you accept donations from alumni?" I asked innocently. "Um, hold on a moment please," the rep answered before transferring my call. Her supervisor came on the line: "This is Lauren from student support. How can I help you?" I asked again: "Do you accept donations from alumni?" There was a long pause. "Donations from alumni?" Lauren said, as if she'd never heard of this concept before. "I'm not sure. I can find out for you." Lauren put me on hold for four minutes. When she came back, she apologized. She said she'd asked around, but she couldn't find anyone at Strayer who knew anything about accepting money from alumni.

In my view, relying on today's customers to pay the costs of the services they consume, rather than relying on yesterday's customers, taxpayers, and others to contribute to make ends meet, is a more sustainable way to fund an institution.

THERE IS A second way in which private-sector colleges have the potential to outperform traditional institutions: they're incented to focus more on student outcomes.

If you spend time in traditional higher education, much of the talk focuses on inputs. Administrators will say that the incoming freshman class has average SAT scores of 2100, that the student-to-faculty ratio is seventeen to one, or that the library contains seven million books. There's no question these are all good things. The problem is that traditional institutions don't do nearly as much as one might expect to measure and publish how much learning actually takes place in these resource-rich settings. To be sure, America's traditional higher education system offers some of the world's most energizing and spectacular teaching. However, it can subject its students to plenty of uninspiring learning environments. The ratio of spectacular to mediocre varies considerably by campus, of course, and on many campuses that ratio is very good. But while there are well-honed *reputations* for academic excellence (or not), it's hard to get at *data* to determine which institutions excel in enabling students to achieve learning outcomes.

There are several reasons why actual information about learning is in such short supply. A big factor is the governance structure. Most universities have a relatively decentralized system in which the administration has little control over (or even knowledge about) what goes on in the classroom. Way back when I was in college, I was assigned to a history course taught by a Marxist who spent most of his time lecturing on the evils of capitalism. The good news is the experience broadened me; the bad news was I had to teach myself all the history the other sections were learning in order to have a chance at succeeding in the next sequential class. If you sign up for freshman English at a traditional school, what books you read, what papers you write, and how many exams you take can vary radically based on which professor is teaching the class. Measuring learning in any common way in this kind of environment, while high on the wish list of accreditors and many universities, is very tough to accomplish.

Those of us who attended traditional colleges know how much variability there can be between classes. Every college has its prized professors who make real connections with students and change the way they think forever. At the other extreme, pretty much every school also has its less stellar professors who are protected by the tenure system and its "gut" classes—the ones favored by athletes looking to skip by, or by the GPA-conscious grinds in search of guaranteed As in order to pad out their averages. Many campuses have professors who are known to use the same exam year after year, a practice that virtually guarantees students will know exactly what's on the test and be able to skimp on real learning. Even at the most elite and selective schools, the ones that turn away thousands of applicants each year, a student who shows up determined to skate through doing as little work as possible can probably do just that, by choosing the least taxing courses possible. This student was placed in a combustible setting, but there was no good way to answer a simple question: Did the fire actually ignite?

The business model of proprietary colleges, when executed well, can incent a much greater focus on learning outcomes. While different schools use different procedures (and clearly some perform better than others), generally speaking, private-sector schools operate in a far more centralized fashion, with more standardization and more accountability. Consider Accounting 101. Instead of letting multiple professors design their own versions of the course, proprietary colleges usually have a single syllabus designed by specialized faculty course designers working in coordination with teaching faculty members. The readings will be the same from class to class. The written assignments, quizzes, and exams will assess common content, too. Faculty is supervised more closely, all in an effort to provide a uniform level of quality. Each course has designated learning outcomes that come together into a set of program-level outcomes across all courses in a given major. In the better private-sector schools, there is very close assessment of whether students have actually learned what they're supposed to know before they move on to the next course.

Here's how Sondra Stallard describes the process at Strayer: "If you're teaching for me in Birmingham, Alabama, and somebody else is teaching the same course in Newark, New Jersey, and somebody else is teaching online, they're using the same course guides and doing the same activities every day. It doesn't stifle creativity—you can bring in a lot of your own professional abilities as a teacher, and your own world experience—but we need to be able to measure across the university that everybody that took Accounting 101 and passed it should be able to go into Accounting 105."

Unlike at a traditional university, administrators at private-sector schools will typically look at course assessments, such as exams, in a granular way, in much the same way a pharmaceutical company will look at the before and after data in a clinical trial to see if a prospective drug has its desired effect. If students in one particular section of Accounting 101 don't correctly understand a concept, administrators know they need to help the professor become more adept at teaching that chapter—or, as a last resort, replace the professor altogether. If students across multiple sections don't understand a concept or are showing up in Accounting 105 without sufficient knowledge in a particular area, course designers will revise Accounting 101 to better deliver those concepts. If just a certain subset of students is struggling, it's possible to evaluate what in those students' backgrounds might have predicted this—and remediate it for future students *before* they start struggling. In traditional universities, where little such cross-checking goes on and where the course outcomes may vary by section depending on who is teaching the class, these processes rarely take place. To be sure, the last several years have seen the rise of a movement to bolster the measurement of learning outcomes on traditional campuses, but without common curricula or outcome measures, it's a tough climb.[19]

Some traditional academics would be appalled at the measurement of learning and the comparison of professors—and especially the standardization of curriculum—that I've described. They would view it as removing the freedom of individual professors to teach what and how they choose, and removing some of the "lightning strikes" that take place when students get exposed to something unexpected. And they have an argument. But for students (and their employers) who are looking for assurance that they'll gain the learning outcomes they sought when they enrolled in a school, a standardized, closely evaluated process is more likely to hit the mark consistently. More important, by standardizing the curriculum, it is possible to measure outcomes and make continuous improvements that will ensure that each term of students is getting a better learning experience than the term before it. Over time, the compounding effect of these steady improvements will be enormous.

Let's reflect for a moment on how differently the learning-testing cycle plays out in a traditional university setting than it does in the real world. Consider the process that allowed you to become licensed to drive a car. You may have studied the basic laws and rules of the road in a classroom course, or studied the written material online or via a printed brochure by yourself at home. You probably took some on-the-road lessons from a high school teacher or a private company, or went out with your parent—as I did with my dad, and my daughter did with me. But when it came time actually to test whether you were up to the task of driving, you almost certainly went to a state office, where someone else—someone who wasn't your teacher, someone you'd never met before—administered the test and decided whether you were qualified to be behind the wheel. The system didn't rely on inputs, such as how many hours of on-the-road training you'd received. Nor did it rely solely on your teacher to check a box saying you knew the material. The process was based on outcomes: it required an outsider to determine if you could drive safely. Many professions operate with similar models. Lawyers need to pass state-administered bar exams, and doctors become board certified. Granted, it becomes exceptionally difficult to create standardized measures of learning across thousands of disciplines, but that is not an excuse to shun common measurement altogether. At a minimum, measurement and comparison should be encouraged in the practical, career-oriented kinds of educational programs that private-sector schools tend to focus on.

While proprietary colleges typically don't go so far as to have outsiders administering grades, they do go much farther than traditional colleges to standardize the assessment process and to pay close attention to the results to ensure that students are actually learning. They believe it's not enough to create the right environment for combustion: they require proof that actual flames were produced. By refusing to cede complete control of course design and learning assessments to each individual faculty member, it's possible for proprietary colleges to be better able to make sure learning actually happens. This may not be the right approach for all students and all situations, but it clearly seems to be an appropriate alternative for some students and programs.

Another advantage some private-sector schools have in managing and measuring outcomes stems from their teaching modality. Many proprietary colleges use online education, and as this delivery system has matured, the world is becoming more aware of how many advantages there are to using technology to help measure what students learn. Indeed, online teaching works especially well with the standardized curricula that most private-sector colleges use: because professors can't see the students' reactions, it forces them to more carefully evaluate how the course is structured, in order to shape it for maximum impact.

For-profit colleges are closely associated with online course-work in part because Internet-enabled educational technology has come of age over the same period that proprietary colleges have enjoyed their renaissance. So, in some ways, the funding model and the teaching modality have evolved together. Schools that rely on online education are better able to track and assess student outcomes for much the same reason a company like Amazon is better able to track customer purchases and make use of other sophisticated analytics: the data are already online and ready to be used. For instance, in many traditional class-room environments, relatively few professors feel the need to take attendance to see who's actually coming to classes. In an online course, instructors and administrators can precisely track the frequency with which students are logging in, how long they're staying, and whether they're navigating through all the parts of an online course. Brief quizzes can assess whether students have completed and understood the reading; if not, the system can route them back to review before permitting progression in the course or attendance in class. In a traditional lecture course, it can be hard for professors to get students to participate; in a typical fifty-minute class, most students won't have a chance to make a comment, and as a result, a professor may have no idea if a particular student understands the mate-rial until that student takes an exam. In an online course, how-ever, student participation can be mandatory; it's fairly typical for professors to require every student to post a short comment or ask a question based on that week's reading. This more fre-quent feedback provides evidence as to whether a student com-prehends the material. In a live, "synchronous" class, a professor can require replies to her in-class questions from all students, and post for all to see only those that further the point she's trying to make—or only those that are missing the point in a way that permits further exploration.

In some ways, the methods that private-sector colleges have used to track and improve learning outcomes are evocative of the methods that Michael Lewis describes in *Moneyball*, in which statistical gurus have revolutionized the game of baseball by closely tracking data. In the same way that Major League managers are now obsessed with "on-base percentages" and "runs created," some private-sector colleges are obsessed with tracking and encouraging learning outcomes.

Over the last decade, traditional colleges have begun to recognize the advantages of online coursework. In a 2009 report, researchers at the Department of Education's Center for Technology in Learning examined more than a thousand empirical studies of online education conducted from 1996 to mid-2008 to determine how online programs compared with traditional instruction. Oftentimes studies like this hedge or qualify their findings. In this case, the conclusion was direct: "on average, students in online learning conditions performed modestly *better* than those receiving face-to-face instruction."[20] That's one reason traditional colleges have begun to accelerate their embrace of the practice. According to a December 2008 study that tried to quantify the number of students taking online courses for the full twelve-month 2006/2007 school year, two- and four-year colleges recorded more than twelve million enrollments in online, hybrid/blended online, or other distance education courses. For-profit schools accounted for nearly two million of those enrollments, but the vast majority were at public and nonprofit schools, particularly two-year public schools such as community colleges.

There's another reason why private-sector colleges may be

better equipped to enhance learning outcomes: by virtue of their mission, these institutions keep in much closer touch with the companies that employ their graduates. This close relationship makes these schools quite responsive to the needs of employers. Students attend an elite, residential college for a variety of reasons: to get an education and obtain a job, sure, but also to make their parents happy, to meet members of the opposite sex, to live away from home for the first time, to gain exposure to new ideas, and because it's the expected thing to do. In contrast, almost all students who enroll in a private-sector college are focused on enhancing their careers, and because that goal is more uniform, it makes sense for the schools to do a good job of tracking how well they do in helping students achieve it.

For evidence of this, click over to the Web site for DeVry University. Near the bottom of the home page is the following statement: "Since 1975, 252,127 undergraduate students system-wide have graduated from DeVry University. Of graduates in the active job market, 90.1% were employed in career-related positions within six months of graduation." While most colleges have career placement offices, few of them are as focused on tracking the career outcomes of graduates—where they obtained jobs and how much they earned—as many proprietary colleges are.

Consider one program run by DeVry to create learning outcomes that will translate into employable graduates. DeVry works with ninety different Industry Advisory Councils, which meet twice a year, as well as six regional councils. At these meetings, employers are invited to go over DeVry's curriculum, offer a critique, and discuss what students actually need to know. They can talk candidly about how well DeVry is meeting their needs in producing high-caliber workers. And they can address how world trends are changing business, and how schools need to adjust the curriculum to respond to those trends. "A recent session involved how green technology might affect the curriculum and the nature of work of DeVry graduates," according to Ben Wildavsky, Kevin Carey, and Andrew R. Kelly, a trio of researchers who've studied the DeVry program.[21] Conversations such as these help proprietary schools remain tightly focused on what should be a primary output of any institution of learning: capable, employable graduates.

IN THE FIRST half of this book, I offered an assessment of the incentives that drive traditional higher education. These incentives, whether codified in the Ivory Tower Playbook at four-year colleges or the All-Access Playbook at community colleges, can distort the behavior of the leadership of these institutions and often push them away from focusing on the student learning that should be at their institutions' core. In this chapter, I've begun to outline the Private-Sector Playbook, a set of rules and incentives that drive the proprietary colleges. I believe that the Private-Sector Playbook actually can create better alignment between the interests of the people running these institutions and the long-term interests of the students who are (or should be) the primary focus of every school.

Rob Silberman understands these incentives better than most. He's leading a college that's been around for nearly 120 years, which for most of its history was owned by a single family. "The whole idea of a family-owned proprietorship over four generations is you build a rather long-term viewpoint," he says. "If you're handing it off to your kids, what you care about is what it's worth thirty years from now."

Today, however, Strayer is publicly traded. Executives such as Silberman continue to focus on long-term outcomes, knowing that the best way to ensure that Strayer's stock keeps rising is for the school to keep offering a solid education that will pay off for students (and their employers) for many years. But that's not necessarily how everyone would manage such an enterprise, and that represents a weakness in the for-profit model—one that Silberman acknowledges.

"If the source of capital is a publicly traded security that someone can get rich on in the short term, independent of the performance of your institution, that's a risk," he says. In other words, if the top executives at a company like his decided to shortchange the educational offering in order to minimize costs and maximize short-term profits, they might make a lot of money over that short term, even if, over time, the institution declined. Silberman admits he's faced pressure like this from shareholders. Some have urged him to increase student-to-faculty ratios to cut costs, or to close campuses to reduce overhead. Silberman says he's repeatedly had to resist such pressures. "It's easy to make these businesses look great in the short term," he says. Instead, he stays focused on the long term. Investors who expect Strayer's management to focus on short-term profits usually wind up selling the stock and taking their investment dollars elsewhere—a phenomenon that makes Silberman happy. "One of the beauties of public companies is you get the shareholders you deserve over time because of the way you communicate," he says. "We have a set of shareholders who understand exactly what our intentions are here."

Like Silberman, I believe that the Private-Sector Playbook provides strong incentives for the people managing proprietary colleges to do the right thing, and to focus on producing measureable learning for students that helps them obtain and flourish in satisfying and well-paying careers. I agree, however, that people can exploit the short-term opportunity for profits that's inherent in this model, in a way that hurts students, taxpayers, and the entire industry. There are examples of this happening (which I'll touch on in the next chapter), and these examples create good reasons for smart regulation to ensure that private-sector colleges act in ways that are beneficial to their students.

Over the last decade—and particularly since early 2010—criticism of private-sector higher education has become loud and profoundly overblown. The sector has become the subject of withering criticism, much of it based on misconceptions, poorly designed statistics, or a basic misunderstanding of its mission and methods.

I'll explore these criticisms in chapter 5.

5

The Case Against Private-Sector Higher Education

Facts That Critics Overlook

On a resplendent morning in late June of 2010, a crowd milled around the gallery of room 124 in the Dirksen Senate Office Building before Senator Tom Harkin banged his gavel. The hearing was now under way.

Harkin, the Iowa senator and onetime presidential hopeful, chairs the U.S. Senate Committee on Health, Education, Labor, and Pensions, a group that Beltway types know by its acronym, HELP. On any given week, the HELP senators convene to listen to testimony and ask pointed questions on a wide range of issues. The week before this particular hearing, they were investigating the BP oil spill, and the following week, they would meet to discuss the lingering health problems affecting 9/11 emergency responders.

On this morning, however, their inquiry was focused on private-sector colleges.

"For more than fifty years, the federal government has provided students with grants and loans to help pay for college," Senator Harkin said in his opening remarks. "It is an investment premised on the idea that a higher education will improve life for the borrower, and also will strengthen our society by giving more Americans the knowledge and skills to get good jobs and give back to their communities."

Lately, however, more of that federal aid has been flowing to newer, fast-growing, for-profit colleges, Harkin explained, pointing to this sector's 225 percent growth in enrollments over the past ten years. Compared with other students, people who enroll in for-profit colleges are much more likely to take out student loans: 98 percent of private-sector college graduates leave school with debt, Harkin said, versus 38 percent of community college graduates. Students at these newer, private-sector institutions also tend to drop out without a degree in greater numbers.

"There is much that we don't know," Harkin said, about this new form of education.

In a way, the fact that this panel didn't feel it knew enough about private-sector schools is not surprising. Harkin is an Iowa State grad who started college during the Eisenhower years. Now-retired senator Judd Gregg, who at the time was the second-ranking Republican on the committee, is the son of a New Hampshire governor, a graduate of Phillips Exeter boarding school and Columbia University, and the holder of two graduate degrees from Boston University. Senator Al Franken, the most recognizable face on the dais (thanks to his time on *Saturday Night Live*), is a Harvard graduate who married a Harvard classmate; they sent their two children to Harvard and Princeton. In short, nearly every senator on this panel was an Automatic, and each of them had a college degree by the age of twenty-five.

Harkin explained that in light of the growth of private-sector schools and the growing criticisms of the way such schools operated, the government felt compelled to take action. "Given the number of students enrolled in for-profit colleges, the dollars in federal aid that these institutions receive, and the lack of clear data on student outcomes," Harkin said, "I believe Congress must devote more attention to this sector and its impact on our postsecondary education system."[1]

Over the next three hours, the senators heard from a lineup of witnesses chosen to represent various criticisms of private-sector colleges. One of them was Yasmine Issa. In 2005, when Issa was a twenty-four-year-old divorced mother of twins, she enrolled in the Sanford-Brown Institute near her home in Yonkers, New York. Her goal: to become an ultrasound sonographer. In her testimony, Issa described being pressured to sign up for the courses and borrowing $15,000 for the one-year, $32,000 program, which she completed in June of 2008. For months after graduating, however, she failed to find a job. After several unsuccessful application attempts, she says, the supervising ultrasound tech at a hospital to which she had applied gave her a reason: Sanford-Brown's ultrasound program isn't accredited by the American Registry for Diagnostic Medical Sonography, a credential that many employers in this field demand. "I felt like I wasted my time and money on a phony school, and fell for their false promises," Issa told the senators. Not only didn't her degree help her, she said, but she was worse off now, because of her debts, than she was before she enrolled.

Next up was Margaret Reiter, a former supervising deputy attorney general from California. She described her investigation of Corinthian Colleges, Inc., which ended in 2007. Reiter said that Corinthian falsified data on the employment records of its graduates in an attempt to comply with a California law that requires schools to demonstrate that 70 percent of their graduates are successfully employed. She reported that investigators pretending to be students were handed Web site printouts by recruiters suggesting that they would earn $72,000 a year after graduating, when in fact the average graduate's earnings ranged from just over $14,000 to about $22,000. "In my opinion, the consumer abuses in the proprietary school industry are among the most persistent, egregious, and widespread of any industry," Reiter concluded.

For the grand finale, the senators heard from Steve Eisman, the celebrated hedge fund manager. Eisman is a central character in Michael Lewis's bestseller *The Big Short*, which recounts how Eisman and his then-colleagues at FrontPoint Partners made more than $1 billion by betting against subprime lending institutions. Eisman had been giving a presentation comparing private-sector colleges to the subprime industry, a performance he reprised for the HELP senators. Eisman said that federal funding of private-sector colleges had increased 450 percent in the past decade, and that its students accounted for a disproportionate percentage of defaulters on federal loans. Some private-sector college presidents, he said, earned twenty-five times the compensation of the president of Harvard, and some had profit margins higher than those of Apple. "These companies are marketing machines masquerading as universities," Eisman said. "If nothing is done, then we are on the cusp of a new social disaster."

As the CEO of a big player in private-sector higher education, I don't find listening to testimony like this much fun—and that morning in June wasn't the only time I've had to do it. For the last several years, regulators, both in Congress and in the Obama administration, have been asking hard questions about the practices of private-sector higher education. They've promulgated new forms of regulation, some of which might dramatically undercut private-sector colleges' ability to enroll students.

Some of this scrutiny is warranted. The industry has had its issues. And as Robert Silberman pointed out, when private-sector colleges issue publicly traded stocks, they face new pressures—and, in some cases, temptations. While the Ivory Tower Playbook creates incentives for leaders at traditional colleges to limit enrollment and maintain exclusivity, private-sector colleges are closely watched by Wall Street analysts and investors, who like to see a steady upward march in enrollment. In addition to the pressure to keep T growing (tuition, using the formula I introduced in the previous chapter), there's also the temptation to boost short-term profits by being overzealous in minimizing E (expenses) in a way that hurts the educational strength and the long-term value of the service that schools offer their graduates.

There's no doubt that effective regulation of private-sector education is appropriate and necessary. I'm convinced, however, that the vast majority of the players in for-profit higher education work very hard to avoid succumbing to these short-term temptations. Most of them seek to do the right thing: enroll students who have reasonable prospects of benefiting, support those students through to graduation, and invest the proper resources to make sure the students receive a high-quality education. That's not just the right thing to do; it's also the path that will lead to long-run success for their institutions and profitability for their owners. Still, there are exceptions to this rule, and that's one of the reasons companies like ours have faced tough questions from Senator Harkin and many other politicians and regulators.

While some of their concerns have merit, many of these inquiries have one thing in common: they rely on a flawed set of assumptions and basic misconceptions about how the majority of private-sector colleges actually work. They judge an entire industry with millions of students based on occasional examples of wrongdoing, and then compare them to idealized assumptions about how effectively and efficiently traditional universities and community colleges operate, without exploration of whether those assumptions match reality.

THE ATTACKS ARE surprising given the problems in our higher education system and in our economy, problems that private-sector higher education seems tailor-made to address.

Just a month after the Senate hearing, President Obama visited the University of Texas at Austin to reiterate how important it was for America to increase the percentage of college graduates among its population. "I want us to produce eight million more college graduates by 2020, because America has to have the highest share of graduates compared to every other nation," he said. Lately we've been coming up short. "In a single generation, we've fallen from first place to twelfth place in college graduation rates for young adults," the president said. "That's unacceptable, but it's not irreversible. We can retake the lead."[2]

The reality is, though, that we can't possibly retake that lead without private-sector colleges. Around the country, both community colleges and state universities are cutting enrollments due to budget constraints. Meanwhile, the private-sector colleges have added capacity: between 2006 and 2008 the proprietary sector invested $2.4 billion in estimated capital expenditures, primarily to drive innovation and support capacity expansion.[3] The fact that private-sector colleges are stepping up while traditional colleges step back has been especially important over the last few years, as unemployment, underemployment, and the threat of layoffs have pushed more individuals to rethink their educational goals.

Beyond simply adding more chairs to classrooms, the private-sector colleges have emerged as primary engines of innovation in higher education. From online education to blended academic programs, from the use of data analysis to support student retention to new methods for measuring student learning, some private-sector institutions are redefining higher education in the United States.[4] The private sector is making its educational programs available and convenient to nontraditional students, and it is experimenting with new pedagogies and technologies that improve student learning. Given time, some of these private-sector institutions will raise the bar for education in this country and around the world.

Further, private-sector colleges are starting to embrace an opportunity underleveraged by traditional colleges: by expanding overseas, they're turning higher education into a viable U.S. export at a time when the American economy desperately needs to find ways to get foreigners to consume more U.S. goods and services. In fact, in that same speech in Austin, President Obama called for a doubling of exports within the next five years. American higher education is widely viewed as the best in the world, so it's an export strategy that makes sense.

At least as important, the private sector is accomplishing all this at a dramatically lower taxpayer cost per student than the public system. Perhaps the biggest fallacy in the debate over proprietary schools is the argument that the private sector is "wasting" taxpayer money because most of its students make use of federal financial aid programs. In fact, the truth is precisely the reverse: analyses show that private-sector colleges use substantially fewer taxpayer dollars per student than traditional institutions, a gap that widens even further when you measure them apples to apples based on the number of demographically comparable students who actually make it through to graduation. Only by comparing use of federal Title IV student aid dollars in isolation, and ignoring all other governmental contributions to higher education, can one plausibly make the case that private-sector colleges overconsume taxpayer dollars. (I'll have more to say about this analysis later in this chapter.) The taxpayer cost of meeting President Obama's goal of retaking the world lead in educational attainment over ten years would be hundreds of billions of dollars *lower* if the growth in capacity came from the private sector rather than the traditional system. While critics depict private-sector colleges as tax drains, in fact, they are easily the most taxpayer-efficient institutions in higher education.[5]

One would think that an industry that advances all of these policy objectives—putting more Americans through college, at lower taxpayer cost, and creating a viable American export— would be embraced as an important partner in meeting the nation's educational goals, not the subject of hearings and negative media accounts.

However, this is a movie we've seen before.

As we saw with the rise of land-grant colleges and then community colleges, new approaches to higher education have always been received with skepticism. For many observers, any college experience that is not like their own—and for a large percentage of the nation's elite, that means Gothic buildings, Frisbee on the quad, and Saturday football games—is automatically suspect. The notion of college delivered in fifteen-thousand-square-foot office park "campuses" along the highway is difficult to fathom. Delivery of an education entirely online is harder still. Those who still get misty-eyed at the singing of their alma mater have an instinctive aversion to these new approaches and assume they must be substandard.

The earlier attacks on land-grant schools and, later, community colleges demonstrated people's fear that the new institutions would reduce quality and expand access to populations that were viewed as not ready for higher education. Back then, many people simply opposed schools designed to service students who "weren't college material." A century and a half later this fear has obviously been misplaced—which can be proven, in part, by the fact that so many of America's leaders, in business, government, academia, and the arts, graduated from land-grant colleges, including senators Tom Harkin, Patty Murray, Tom Coburn, and others. Yet the challenges to private-sector schools incorporate strikingly similar themes, and sometimes even the same language, as the earlier assaults on the emerging land-grant and community colleges.

As in previous waves, incumbent institutions have concerns about the competitive threat that new types of institutions pose, at least over the long run. Many community colleges and small private institutions worry that private-sector schools may siphon off those new students who value what these newer institutions do best, just as smaller, less established private institutions in the nineteenth century feared the emerging public universities even while they belittled them.

One new line of attack in the current debate over private-sector education, however—one that does not simply replay ancient battles over expansion of access in higher education—involves the profit motive. In this charge, the existence of a profit margin is said to suggest that the goals of the institutions are predatory, not educational.

An attack on profit-seeking institutions is an ironic one in a country like the United States, where most major functions are provided by private companies. The food we eat, the homes we live in, the cars, trains, planes, and buses we take to work or to go on vacation, are produced by for-profit companies. Today most Americans are born in private-sector hospitals, spend their careers working in private-sector businesses, and are buried by private-sector funeral companies. Even functions that were once the exclusive responsibility of the government have been outsourced to more efficient, private-sector companies. For instance, many of those who have served overseas in Iraq and Afghanistan are private citizens working for companies to whom the Pentagon has outsourced contracts.

In fact, other than religious institutions, education is one of the last bastions in which for-profit companies are viewed with such suspicion. And even there, the criticism is selective. It's fully accepted that the curriculum in most schools—elementary, secondary, and postsecondary—comes from for-profit textbook publishing companies. The classrooms are built by profit-making construction companies. In most cases, the food in the cafeteria is cooked and served by outside catering companies. The trash is removed by private haulers. The Internet networks are normally maintained by private telecom companies, while the classroom computers and the software running on them are created by private technology companies. In fact, in some schools, just about the only service that's not ultimately the responsibility of a for-profit company is the teacher standing in front of the classroom. The notion that some private companies might provide that service as well to those who choose it is but a small step, but one that looms large for for-profit opponents.

It's true that, as Senator Harkin stated in his opening remarks at the 2010 hearing on private-sector education, for-profit universities have been growing rapidly over the last decade. To some, that's evidence of their vitality and responsiveness to student demands; to this group, a student's choice to pursue these schools, instead of the often less expensive community colleges or local public institutions, is evidence of that strength. To others, the growth of for-profits is Exhibit A in the case being made that these institutions are too focused on growth rather than on education. To grow that fast, critics contend, these schools must be misleading students with false claims, or otherwise luring them into debt and misery.

To make the case that something is fundamentally flawed in for-profit education, critics have to land the equivalent of the triple Lindy dive that Rodney Dangerfield attempts in *Back to School*. They have to make the case that private-sector education is simultaneously low quality, high priced, and growing too fast. As any economist will observe, these are three conditions that rarely come together in a market, suggesting that maybe one or more of them isn't true.

IT'S RARE FOR anyone to lay out a clear case as to exactly what the problem is with private-sector higher education. The case usually emanates from a discordant feeling generated by pairing the words *for-profit* and *education*. Because that's not a satisfactory argument to make in opinion journals and public hearings, claims tend to shift around a series of arguments against for-profit institutions, which can be roughly summarized as follows:

1. They Don't Really Educate.

Most private-sector higher education institutions are built around career advancement. Accordingly, the most powerful indictment of private-sector higher education would be that students don't really emerge having achieved learning outcomes that enable them to succeed in the workplace.

Invariably, this argument is made by implication or anecdote. In March 2010 the *New York Times* ran a front-page article expressing concern over for-profit schools delivering "dubious benefits to students." Its evidence? Three students—from among the 2.75 million attending for-profit, degree-granting institutions—were struggling to find jobs after completing their educations.[6]

Or consider a December 2009 article from Bloomberg.[7] It revolved around a Marine Corps corporal who'd suffered a brain injury in Iraq. After his return to the United States, he enrolled in a private-sector college. Due to his injury, the story alleged, the Marine couldn't recall what course he had enrolled in—a symptom, the story suggested, of the overly aggressive recruiting tactics private-sector colleges use to lure in veterans, who receive federal aid to pay their tuition, whether they're "college material" or not. While the memory-impaired student is an attention-grabbing anecdote, it's no coincidence that some of the heaviest criticism of the private-sector colleges in this article comes from a representative of the University of Maryland's University College, a branch of a traditional college that specializes in serving military students. If you read a story about a new product from the Coca-Cola Company in the newspaper, you don't often read snide commentary from a Pepsi official who's somehow positioned as an objective, uninterested observer. Yet when business reporters write negative stories about for-profit colleges, they often rely on commentary from competing traditional colleges.

News media articles about the sector often follow the model exemplified by these two articles: find a few examples of students who entered a private-sector institution with high hopes and dreams, and then trace their route to dropout and burdensome student loan debt. To be sure, this simple-to-write (I'd call it lazy) formula can be found in news stories across education sectors, describing the dropouts and disappointments that inevitably exist even at the nation's top universities. But it is more compelling when the recipient of the student loan dollars is a for-profit company. Indeed, because the arguments are usually based on implication rather than data, many of the critics offer mutually exclusive claims. For instance, some articles argue that private-sector schools suffer from astronomical dropout rates, meaning too few students graduate; other articles maintain that for-profit schools are "diploma mills," meaning that it's too *easy* to graduate.

So what is the real story? The data that exist on the topic are reasonably clear. Private-sector institutions tend to graduate their students at rates that exceed the rates of traditional institutions, both two-year and four-year, serving comparable populations.

The National Center for Education Statistics (NCES) publishes data on graduation rates by sector and type of institution. The most recent numbers show that among students who started programs of two years or less in 2005, for-profit colleges graduated 59.7 percent of students by 2008, compared with 51.4 for private nonprofits and 22 percent for public two-year schools.[8] That's a striking gap.

For students in four-year degree programs, the industry-wide picture is more complicated—and more susceptible to facile but misleading appraisals. If you compare figures for all students, private-sector schools lag: they graduate 38.1 percent of students, compared with 53.3 percent at public institutions and 64.4 percent at private nonprofits.[9] But that's not a fair comparison. Many of the students at the public and private nonprofit schools are Automatics, who've headed straight to college after high school. These students are more likely to be relying on their parents for financial support, which reduces the odds that they'll fail to graduate because of financial problems. They're also less likely to have kids, or full-time jobs, or be very poor. Is it really reasonable to compare the odds that a nineteen-year-old Northwestern undergrad from Winnetka will make it through to commencement with the odds that a working mother taking part-time, online courses at the University of Phoenix will persevere? These numbers are an apples-to-oranges comparison.

Several academic papers have tried to create a more meaningful comparison by adjusting for student demographics and quality. Frederick M. Hess and three other scholars used Barron's rankings of college selectivity to try to segment graduation rates based on the admissions selectivity of various colleges, a reasonable proxy for the quality of students they enroll. They found that "non-competitive schools"—the category most comparable to private-sector colleges, which are more likely to have open enrollment and, by design, aren't about prestige or exclusivity—graduate about 34.7 percent of students, on average. This compares to the 38.1 percent graduation rate of students at private-sector schools. Even "less competitive" schools graduate just 39.6 percent of students, a number that is also very much in line with the private-sector college averages.[10]

A more direct way of comparing institutions is to assess how their students perform with comparable student populations. The U.S. Department of Education promulgates a list of "risk factors" that, its research indicates, make it more likely that a student will drop out. The factors include: delayed enrollment, the absence of a high school diploma, part-time enrollment, financial independence, the presence of dependents, single parent status, and full-time employment while enrolled.[11]

According to Department of Education NCES data, students across the entire American higher education system who have two or more of these risk factors have only a *17 percent chance of graduating* from an undergraduate program, a powerful indictment of the system's ability to succeed with nontraditional, "riskier" students.[12] By contrast, 24 percent of students with two or more risk factors at for-profit schools graduate.[13] At the best private-sector colleges, the numbers are higher still. I can't access this data for all schools, but, for example, on a fully comparable basis, 32 percent of Kaplan University students graduate, nearly double the national rate.[14] Now, we don't advertise a 32 percent graduation rate among these students, because those who went to elite schools with 90 percent plus graduation rates would scoff. But if all of American higher education had Kaplan University's graduation rates for such students, our country would have eight hundred thousand more graduates each year, and the United States would be well on its way to achieving President Obama's national graduation goals. That's powerful evidence that a for-profit institution can deliver results not just comparable to traditional education, but demonstrably superior.

While no one is ready to celebrate a 24 percent or even a 32 percent graduation rate, these numbers for the nation's higher-risk students show that it is possible to make progress against the most stubborn college completion challenges. Part of the reason for this better performance is that private-sector institutions are built to serve riskier students, and have adapted to their needs. According to an analysis by educational researchers at the Parthenon Group, 54 percent of students at private-sector colleges (excluding four-year schools) fit a "high-risk" classification—three or more risk factors—versus just 36 percent at public and independent colleges.[15] Similarly, four-year private-sector schools are more likely to have students with more risk factors; the average Kaplan University student, for example, has 4 risk factors, versus the national university average of 1.5. Far from the impression left by critics, the fact that private-sector colleges have better graduation rates with a riskier population holds considerable promise as we consider how to extend access to higher education.

Graduation rates, of course, are only part of the story. At least as important: What are the students actually learning? Here, too, to the extent the data exist, they indicate that private-sector institutions do a strong job on delivering learning outcomes relative to comparable traditional institutions.

Unfortunately, the system-wide data on learning are extremely difficult to discern. Given the size of the education sector in the U.S. economy, solid comparative data on learning are surprisingly scant. It's galling that we have far more information about how many bushels of corn we can grow on an acre of farmland, or how many households watched the first ten minutes of *Modern Family* last week, than we do about what students actually learned after attending an institution. That's nearly as true for K–12 education as it is for higher education, and it's one reason why much of the last two decades of education policy debate in Washington has focused on creating and enforcing "standards" based on the commonsense notion that we want people who graduate—whether it is from sixth grade, twelfth grade, or college—to be able to prove they have a universal set of skills and knowledge.

One measure that two-year private-sector schools use is job placement rates—which, while certainly not the same as learning outcomes, is something of a proxy. (These data are also required by some accrediting bodies, which helps ensure common standards.) On that front, private-sector colleges measure up well, as indicated by data from accreditors with large numbers of for-profit schools. "While comparability data is hard to come by for most traditional schools (and regionally accredited schools of all types), about three quarters of degree-seeking students who graduate from schools accredited by the Accrediting Council for Independent Colleges and Schools obtain positions requiring either direct or indirect use of the skills taught in their programs of study."[16] Measured by earnings, too, private-sector colleges look good. According to researchers at the Parthenon Group, the average income for graduates of two-year public colleges increased by 36 percent after they'd earned their degree, while the average income for graduates of two-year and less programs at private-sector colleges increased by 54 percent.[17] Regulators may puzzle over why so many students are flocking to private-sector colleges, but numbers like this are part of the explanation.

Too much of the debate about the value of higher education, and the for-profit sector in particular, has been driven by superficial assumptions made possible by the paucity of solid data. All of higher education would be better served if data on student performance were standardized and published. If we really want our higher education institutions to compete with one another for academic outcomes, the entire higher education establishment should agree on and require publication of standard calculations for:

- what constitutes a matriculating student for purposes of calculating graduation;
- what the demographics and "risk factors" of those students are;
- how institutions measure learning outcomes;
- how students perform on learning outcome measurements;
- what proportion graduate;
- what they've learned;
- what jobs they get; and
- how they perform over the course of their careers.

When judging institutions, we should look at how they're doing with comparable students, accounting for risk factors and demographics. That way, institutions would compete to excel with higher-risk populations, not just Automatics. The current system, which permits facile comparisons of institutions serving very different student populations, only encourages institutions to stop serving higher-risk students in order to improve their own metrics.

It may be surprising that we don't already collect this kind of information, particularly given the taxpayer investment in higher education. What may be more surprising is that as reasonable as it seems for the government and accrediting agencies to collect and measure this kind of data, it's far from clear that it will ever happen. That's true for one simple reason: if real data on these metrics were collected, it would show some colleges dramatically outperforming other institutions with comparable populations—meaning some others would be revealed as low performers. That's a scary prospect. So it should come as no surprise that when a commission formed by former U.S. Secretary of Education Margaret Spellings proposed that much more detailed data be collected in some of these areas in 2006, the idea was quickly shot down. It's time to try again: we should be encouraging information transparency so those institutions that provide better outcomes attract more students, while those that don't provide those outcomes feel pressure to up their game.

Based on what data there are, however, it's fairly clear that when it comes to educational outcomes, private-sector institutions as a group more than hold their own compared with other types of institutions serving comparable populations.

2. They Charge Too Much.

Absent a strong argument over for-profits' educational quality, some people assert that the private-sector "profiteers" succeed by overcharging on tuition and overloading students with debt they cannot repay, thereby delivering a poor value for the money, for both students and taxpayers.

Unlike data on educational outcomes, the data on pricing are relatively easy to come by. According to the College Board's annual *Trends in College Pricing*, in 2010/2011 for-profit colleges on average charged an estimated $13,935 per year in tuition and fees, an amount that placed them squarely between public two-year ($2,713) and in-state public four-year ($7,605) institutions on the low end and out-of-state public four-year ($19,595) and private nonprofit four-year ($27,293) universities on the high end.[18] While the average student borrower graduating with a bachelor's degree has student loan debt of $23,000, the debt for the average for-profit bachelor's graduate is $33,000.

Is this "too much?" Well, it stands to reason that students in for-profit schools, who tend to have lower incomes, will borrow more to complete their education. And it's also true that there are both less expensive and more expensive alternatives for students. So why are the for-profit prices higher than those of some other institutions?

That answer is simple. As discussed extensively in chapters 2 and 4, public institutions get funding from their states that is simply not available to private institutions, whether for-profit or nonprofit. The vast majority of Dianelys Diaz's costs for attending Miami Dade College are paid for by taxpayers in Florida, just as Californians are picking up most of the tab for Erika Ballesteros to attend Berkeley. Recall the T > E formula I introduced in chapter 4 and compare it with the long string of other funding sources that flow into traditional institutions. Taking that into account, it's hardly surprising that students at private-sector colleges need to pay more than students at some other institutions do. But while the *tuition* of for-profit schools is higher than that at community colleges, traditional colleges (including community colleges) are actually collecting more *revenue* per student, when counting the multiple sources of funds.

Taxpayers and donors are just picking up more of the tab.

Often overlooked in the cost-of-education debate is the role of the federal government as price fixer when it comes to private-sector education. Through the complex interplay of the so-called "90/10" rule (applicable only to for-profits) and loan disbursement regulations, federal law inadvertently induces proprietary institutions serving low-income students to raise prices above government loan limits. A change to that law, enabling institutions to limit how much a student can borrow under the federal loan program, would unleash price competition among the for-profits. This would lead to lower student debt, to the benefit of students and taxpayers alike.

Why would students voluntarily choose a school that charges higher tuition when lower-priced alternatives exist? This question is easy to answer at a certain level: tens of thousands of students apply to Harvard and other elite schools each year, even though their local public university also awards a bachelor's degree. They are willing, even eager, to incur about $80,000 more for their degree from a private institution rather than a public one. Some believe they will get better professors at the private institution; others, a more attractive campus (maybe even a campus concierge or hot tub), more networking opportunities, more prestige, a more intimate environment—any number of reasons.

Students similarly choose private-sector colleges over less

expensive alternatives because they believe they will get something they value in exchange for the increased cost. Many appreciate the more convenient scheduling, the student support infrastructure, the career services, the accessible locations, the access to online help and programs, and the predictability of class availability. Many others like the evening or early morning classes that permit them to work full time and still go to school; at many community colleges or state schools, the hit-or-miss aspect of class availability makes this impossible, substantially raising the effective cost—an increase in the time until graduation—of attending that school. The higher graduation rate for comparable students at private-sector schools also has significant value to a prospective student. There's something patronizing about the assertions some people make that lower-income students should always choose the least expensive option for their education, on the assumption that such students are easily misled and incapable of weighing the relative importance of price versus quality, service, convenience, and other attributes.

Some people have expressed concern over the profit margins of some for-profit providers. To cite one example, the parent company of the University of Phoenix had net income of $598.3 million in 2009.[19] Putting aside the irrelevance of this point—are we suspicious of Facebook, Apple, or our local hospital or restaurant when they are profitable?—the fact is that plenty of "nonprofit" schools have significant "revenues in excess of expenses." If you measure on a per-student basis for the period 2006/2007, the pre-recession era when private nonprofit schools were still enjoying large income flows from their growing endowments, private-sector colleges had a profit per student of $2,035, while private not-for-profits had a profit (or "surplus": revenue in excess of expenses) of $20,532 per student—a more than tenfold difference.[20] That's what led to such sharply rising endowments during that period. (During that same period, even public institutions out-earned private-sector colleges, with a $3,289 per-student revenue in excess of expenses.)[21] Even by 2007/2008, when endowments were shrinking, private not-for-profits had "profits" of $1,919 per student, compared with $2,109 for private-sector colleges—a tiny difference.[22] Beyond that, the private-sector institutions pay taxes on their profits. The parent of the University of Phoenix alone paid over $445 million in taxes in 2009. As a *Forbes* article noted, "that's $445 million in income taxes more than every nonprofit college in America combined."[23]

The notion of highly "profitable" nonprofits isn't unique to the higher education sector. "Some of the most profitable organizations I know are 'nonprofits,'" says Daniel Hamburger, president and CEO of DeVry Inc. "For example, 77 percent of 'nonprofit' hospitals are actually profitable, while the percentage drops to 61 percent for those that are 'for-profit.' The combined net income of the top fifty 'nonprofit' hospitals grew from $0.5 billion in 2001 to $4.3 billion in 2006."[24]

In short, the idea that private-sector colleges overcharge just isn't supported by the data.

3. They Recruit Too Aggressively.

In a world where students have an enormous range of choices of where they can pursue their higher education, it's hard to make the case that certain institutions consistently deliver too little (criticism number 1, above) and charge too much (2), yet at the same time too many students are choosing them (i.e., the private sector is growing too fast). Basic laws of economics would seem to foreclose this combination of outcomes all taking place simultaneously, assuming that students tend to act rationally.

The only way to bridge these arguments is to say that millions of students are acting irrationally. The way to make that case is to say that the private-sector institutions are consistently manipulating students (millions of them) into enrolling through heavy advertising, aggressive recruitment tactics, and outright lying. In fact, this is precisely what critics allege. "In order to boost recruitment, many publicly-traded for-profit schools spend huge sums of Title IV dollars—taxpayer dollars—on TV advertisements, billboards, phone solicitation, and Web marketing," Senator Harkin said at a HELP committee hearing. "An analysis of the eight publicly-traded schools shows that, on average, they spend 31 percent of revenues on recruiting and marketing."

There's no question that for-profit schools tend to spend more on traditional marketing than nonprofit institutions, but there is something of an apples-to-oranges issue here, too: much of the "marketing" spending of traditional institutions tends to fall in non-marketing cost centers, so it's hard to really make a fair comparison. The cost of building the climbing walls discussed in chapter 2 undoubtedly fell into a "student activities" or "student recreation" cost line item for the universities who were building them—but what were those costs if not marketing expenses? No one argues that the climbing walls were educational, or necessary for the safety or security of students. They were designed to attract and retain students, pure and simple. That's marketing.

Indeed, most of the expenses of "Club College" are actually marketing expenses. As discussed in chapter 2, only a handful of universities have athletic programs that make money; the rest maintain their programs at a loss because they are important to building the university's brand, building camaraderie at the school, and maintaining alumni loyalty. That's marketing.

So, do private-sector universities spend more than their non-profit counterparts? Clearly, what publicly traded companies are required to detail as "selling and promotional" expenses are much higher than what would be found in comparable line items in nonprofit universities, and it's likely the case that the underlying marketing expenses of proprietary institutions are in fact higher. That's not entirely surprising: private-sector schools are newer and have less brand recognition. They tend not to have guidance counselors in high schools touting their virtues, nor museums and sports teams to extend their brands. So it makes sense that they spend more on traditional media than their nonprofit counterparts. But how much more they spend on all marketing-related activities is tough to say.

Critics also argue that for-profit institutions lure unqualified students into academic programs for which they are unprepared by promising naïve prospective students access to the good life if they pursue their education and get a degree, even though the majority of students (at least in degree programs) don't make it all the way to graduation. Critics point to the training of admissions advisors and the monitoring of recruitment goals as evidence of overzealous recruiting, and cite cases where students felt they had been promised the world and got very little. They maintain that there is an inherent mismatch between a large company and a low-income prospective student who may not have the sophistication to understand the costs and likely outcomes of pursuing an educational program, particularly when subsidized government loan programs make it easy to shift the costs far into the future. And they argue that private for-profit institutions have every incentive to maximize the number of students who enroll, because while the students are charged with paying off their loans over a period of years, the government funding system will pour tuition dollars into the colleges' coffers immediately, regardless of whether the students succeed.

To be sure, there are cases where overaggressive recruitment has taken place—and it's even happened at Kaplan. A month and a half after the Senate hearing I described at the beginning of this chapter, the Senate HELP committee held a second hearing focused on recruiting tactics. In that session, a representative from the Government Accountability Office recounted an undercover investigation in which four investigators posed as potential students and talked with admissions and financial aid representatives at fifteen private-sector colleges around the country. During one meeting in Florida, where the "student" expressed interest in earning an associate's degree in criminal justice, an admissions rep told the applicant that the college was accredited by the same group that accredited Harvard. (It wasn't.) The applicant was allegedly coached during an admissions exam. When the applicant expressed doubt about taking out loans to pay for the degree, the admissions representatives "used hard-sell marketing techniques, became argumentative, called the applicant afraid, and scolded the applicant for not wanting to take out loans," according to a government report.[25] In later testimony before the committee, it was revealed that this incident happened at a Kaplan campus.

That example, and others like it, whether at Kaplan or at other for-profits, is deplorable and unacceptable—and a complete outlier from normal standards. (Kaplan took immediate and decisive system-wide action to address the issue.)

Other schools have taken strong action when presented with evidence of unethical behavior. According to the *Washington Post*, a week after the GAO report was released, Westwood

College changed the way it compensates its admissions reps, a change that "could neutralize the high pressure sales tactics revealed in the undercover investigation." It also implemented a system of "mystery shopping" done by an outside party to verify that its reps were behaving in line with policies.[26] Several companies (including Kaplan) also changed their admissions compensation system to eliminate any consideration of number of enrollments in advisor pay, so advisors don't have an incentive to oversell.[27]

In a country where less than half of all college students at all institutions graduate within six years, there are millions of examples of students whose expectations of a degree never materialized, regardless of how wonderful their school—for-profit or nonprofit—looked in its brochure. There are cases across sectors where students expected and hoped that going back to college would solve many of their problems, but instead just loaded them up with more debt and left them worse off than before.

Recruitment of unqualified students or misrepresentation of the expected outcomes of education, though, are not just morally inappropriate. They are contrary to the financial interests of most private-sector institutions. Because they spend money on advertising and the administrative process of enrolling students and giving them the counseling and orientation most new students require, most private-sector institutions lose money on students who drop out quickly. The profitable students are the ones who stay and succeed—the ones who continue their studies (and pay tuition) without incurring new recruitment and "onboarding" costs. Other things being equal, a school with a high dropout rate will be much less profitable than one with a low dropout rate, because the school with the poor retention rate will have to keep on incurring more recruitment costs to keep enrollments growing. That's one reason why private-sector schools have higher graduation rates for comparable students: they have an incentive to provide their students with a tremendous amount of personalized support to help them stay on track to successful graduation. Similarly, raising the expectations of students that they can get a high-paying job if they complete their education may help get a student in the door, but it will tarnish the reputation of the school if the promised outcomes aren't realistic. Apple has every incentive to ensure that every new iPhone excites and delights; it's what drives the company's long-term business. Automobile companies pay the price when their new models don't meet expectations. So, too, do for-profit education companies have every reason to excel, and every reason not to disappoint. The market punishes those who fall short.

That doesn't mean over-recruiting doesn't happen, because there is plenty of evidence of instances in which it has. It does mean, however, that schools have a real incentive to recruit only students who can succeed in school and accurately understand what they can expect from their education. The school that systematically misleads students or enrolls those who don't have the capability of succeeding is unlikely to last long. It will have a difficult time making money, and it will build problematic word of mouth in the community in which it operates. Students have to believe they can succeed in order to make the commitment that the pursuit of higher education requires, and if word gets out in the community that a school doesn't lead to good outcomes, students will shun it.

New regulations now bar all institutions from using number of enrollments as part of the compensation of enrollment counselors, and create tight reins around the information a school can deliver to prospective students. While the specific regulations may not have been perfectly drafted, the underlying principle is right: students should have good information about the program they're interested in, and an institution's personnel should have incentives that are aligned with, not contrary to, the needs of their students.

Ultimately, the best way to counteract the temptations schools may face to ply students with unrealistic expectations to get them to enroll is for all schools to do a better job of collecting standardized and transparent information about student success. Ideally, every college—nonprofit or for-profit—would have available on its Web site information on the price of the program, expected loan payments, the academic demands the institution would make on the student, graduation rates, and the average earnings of its graduates, so there would be no way for any individual to fudge the numbers. And as long as they are not compensated based on higher enrollments, admissions advisors won't have the incentive to do so.

At Kaplan, we've gone a step further by making the first weeks of school "risk free." Kaplan assesses students during the first month of each program and determines whether they evidence the ability and rigor to succeed; if not, they are asked to withdraw, without any tuition owed or debt incurred. And any student who finds that the real experience during that period does not match his or her expectations for any reason can choose to withdraw, similarly without tuition obligation. A large percentage of those who drop out do so in the first term; the "Kaplan Commitment" leaves most of these students with no debt at all. Certainly one great way to ensure that students have real information—not just whatever they've heard from an admission advisor—is to let them experience the actual program and judge for themselves before they incur any financial obligation.

4. They Rip Off Taxpayers and Students.

Many of the criticisms I've addressed about private-sector colleges have been around for a long time. Lately, however, there's a new criticism of the industry: that its growth is coming at taxpayer expense, since the vast majority of its students rely on federal financial aid to fund their studies.

The argument that the taxpayer is being ripped off by private-sector education is the complete opposite of reality. From a taxpayer's perspective, private-sector education is easily the most efficient spending in higher education.

Critics of for-profits focus on the amount of federal financial aid (such as Pell Grants and student loans) that private-sector colleges receive, because private-sector schools receive a disproportionate share of these particular funds.[28] Typically, critics seek to characterize the entire value of student loans as "taxpayer expense," even though the vast majority of those loan dollars are paid back to the government. To be sure, if the government decided to forgive the entirety of America's $1 trillion in student loan debt, those loans would become taxpayer expense—but that's not going to happen. The reality is that because of interest payments, the government collects considerably more on student loans than it lends out, even after defaulted loans are considered. To state it even more clearly: the federal government makes money on student loans. Loan dollars are *not* the functional equivalent of the vast direct contributions the state and federal governments make to their public and nonprofit institutions; *those* dollars come right out of the taxpayers' pockets. Loan money is repaid to government coffers. Thus, the arguments that for-profits are spending vast sums of "taxpayer money" on things such as marketing, compensation, or shareholder dividends are simply inaccurate.

When you include the billions of dollars in support that public and private nonprofit institutions receive (federal, state, and local appropriations, per-student aid, grants, contracts, and other funding—sums that are *not* repaid to the taxpayer) with the student financial aid that traditional schools receive, and divide it by the number of students they enroll, it becomes clear that private-sector schools provide a bargain for taxpayers.

Robert J. Shapiro, a senior fellow at Georgetown University's School of Business and a former Clinton administration official, and his colleague Nam D. Pham have crunched these numbers. "Private for-profit institutions and their students receive less than 30 percent of the support per student from all levels of government provided to public institutions and their students," they write. And when it comes to direct support—government money contributed directly to institutions, as opposed to student financial aid that is based on where an individual student goes to school—the difference is even starker. "For every $1 in direct support for private for-profit institutions, per student, at federal, state and local levels, private not-for-profit institutions receive $8.69 per student and public institutions receive $19.38 per student."[29]

These data tend to get obscured by critics of for-profits, who prefer to focus on a single source of government aid: the student loans taken out by people who enroll in private-sector colleges. Private-sector college students borrow more money than students at other colleges for two reasons: they tend to come from lower socioeconomic groups and have less of their own resources on which to draw, and they receive less direct subsidy from the government than students at other colleges. As Shapiro and Pham write, "Students attending private for-profit institutions receive, on average, significantly smaller educational grants from government than recipients at public or private not-for-profit institutions. As a result, students at private for-profit institutions receive, on average, larger government-subsidized higher-education loans."[30]

Critics also focus on the fact that students at private-sector colleges, on average, default more frequently than other college students or graduates,[31] but there are good reasons for this. These students are more economically disadvantaged, and their overall financial situations are more fragile. This isn't true only at private-sector colleges, however: studies have shown that non-profit schools that also serve nontraditional student populations have nearly identical default rates, and that students' socioeconomic level is by far the dominant driver of defaults.[32] There is a very high (91 percent) correlation between institutional default rates and the percentage of low-income, Pell Grant students at an institution.[33]

Private-sector colleges are working to bring down default rates, but it's important to put this situation in perspective. First, *defaulted* debt is not the same as *unpaid* debt. According to the federal Office of Management and Budget, even when student loans go into default, on average, the government collects the full amount of those loans plus an interest component. According to the OMB, the government ultimately ends up collecting about 112 percent of the amount of *defaulted* loans, including the principal plus interest and fees paid.[34] This situation is not analogous to the housing crisis, in which homeowners defaulted and walked away from their homes. Those loans went bad; relatively few student loans do, even if some go into (temporary) default.

Second, if the goal is purely to reduce the announced default rate, it's possible to do so. If a hospital wants to decrease its mortality statistics, the fastest way to do it is to admit fewer people who are extremely sick and face a higher chance of dying. Likewise, if a college wants to minimize its default rate, the fastest way to do so is to enroll only affluent students—the Automatics whose parents will foot the bill, and maybe provide their children with a car and beer money along the way. But making college attainable only for the least risky, most affluent students is a surefire way to see America's rank in college attainment fall even lower than it is today. That's the direction in which some current proposals will lead—and those proposals will lead to outcomes that aren't good for anyone.

On the topic of whether for-profits are a drain on the taxpayer, however, the answer could hardly be clearer. After calculating the costs of student loan defaults, tax payments, and direct and indirect grants and subsidies by federal, state, and local governments combined (and excluding hospitals and related noneducation costs), Shapiro and Pham found that four-year public institutions receive $15,540 per enrolled student in governmental support, while private nonprofits receive $7,065.[35] Despite the fact that they have comparable or greater graduation rates and serve a higher-risk student population, for-profit institutions receive only $2,394 per student. Far from "ripping off" the taxpayer, private-sector higher education is the taxpayer's best friend.

5. The For-Profit Model Can Create Incentives for Bad Behavior.

No matter how much transparency regulators and institutions bring, there will always be some leaders who choose to manage for the short term rather than the long term—particularly when they hold the highly liquid equity stakes that the leadership of private-sector institutions sometimes receive as part of their compensation. This isn't a theoretical issue; it has happened.

Career Education Corporation, based near Chicago, operates a variety of for-profit institutions, including Le Cordon Bleu cooking schools and the Sanford-Brown Institutes, where Yasmine Issa trained to become a sonographer. By early 2011, Career Education Corporation had more than 116,000 students. During the first half of the 2000s, the company was growing extremely rapidly, and at one point its stock hit $70 a share.[36] But that growth, critics alleged, wasn't sustainable for one simple reason: its managers were overselling and misrepresenting aspects of its program to students. By 2005, disgruntled students and disgusted admissions reps were appearing on *60 Minutes* complaining that the school was hoodwinking applicants to get them to enroll. The U.S. Department of Justice spent several years investigating the company, which the *New York Times* referred to as "The School That Skipped Ethics Class."[37] The company ran into accreditation problems, and its stock price plummeted. For all the players in the industry, the case was a vivid reminder that schools that fail to deliver consistently on their promises to students aren't operating a good long-term business. Career Education brought in new management, which focused on a far more student- and quality-centered approach. It has made substantial progress, but has continued to have to deal with the damage its reputation received due to its previous problems.

Companies, like universities, are built to last forever. They don't end with the death of the founder, or if someone leaves; the structure is designed to enable continuity. If a company in the higher education market wants to build value over time, it has a powerful incentive to deliver results for its customers over time—just as any company does. Failure to do so will damage its brand, reduce its attractiveness, and ultimately diminish its profitability and value. Consistently meeting or exceeding student expectations will enhance the brand, make it more appealing, make it easier to attract more students, and thereby increase profitability. So the incentives for a company with long-term goals reside in delivering strong academic outcomes and improving student experiences.

The problem comes with those who enter the for-profit higher education sector with a short-term time horizon. While there are plenty of highly honorable players in the sector, there are a few who have little interest in the long-term outcomes of their students, in part because they don't intend to be in the business that long. Higher education, by its nature, is long term: the benefits a person gets from a college education are designed to last a lifetime. An investor who wants to make a quick hit can, at least theoretically, buy an institution, rev up the recruitment engine, reduce investment in educational outcomes, and deliver a strong short-term margin—and if he can then sell the institution at the height of its profitability and dump the problem on the next buyer, a dramatic return on investment is possible.

This is an area where regulation is appropriate, in order to reduce the upside for this kind of behavior. For example, if a buyer of an institution were on the hook for educational outcomes for at least seven years after acquisition—or, even better, for several years after it *sold* a school—there would be less incentive for that buyer to exploit the school and its students for short-term gain.

Likewise, schools risk encouraging overselling when they factor enrollment counts into the compensation structure for their admissions advisors. Even if those practices are isolated, they continue to provide fodder for negative news media articles and government investigators. Regulators have long limited such enrollment-dependent compensation, and new rules bar it altogether. For companies that take a long-term approach to delivering a quality education, this seems like an appropriate step.

WHEN I LOOK at the criticism that's routinely leveled at private-sector colleges, I'm struck by how Americans tend to greet many new things with suspicion and misunderstanding—and how quickly they condescend toward any institution that dares to serve non-Automatics.

Private-sector colleges aren't perfect. Like any industry, for-profit higher education contains good players and bad players, and even the good companies make missteps from time to time. But these acknowledged imperfections don't make it acceptable for critics, some of whom have a vested financial interest in doing so, to continue to criticize the work of the entire proprietary sector based on anecdotal bad data, faulty facts, and misinformation.

The real facts make it clear that private-sector colleges do a better job of educating students than many traditional institutions, particularly for the demographics they serve; that private-sector colleges make more efficient use of tax dollars than traditional colleges as a group; and that students choose private-sector colleges—sometimes at a much higher price than some alternatives—because the schools offer support, convenience, and outcomes that students value.

Over time, honest observers will begin to understand these facts. Some already do. "For profit colleges and universities are tax-paying, job-generating, investment-attracting businesses that serve to raise workforce educational levels—all attributes highly prized by most national, state and local governments," writes Guilbert Hentschke, a professor at the University of

Southern California. "At the same time, for profit colleges and universities can be viewed as recently-arrived, profit-seeking interlopers on the student markets of traditional colleges and universities whose relations with governmental bodies are of long standing."[38] Indeed, the fact that so much of this criticism is based on competitive fears will also become more widely understood as our industry matures.

It's important for policy makers to start looking at the real data, and to put them into perspective against the backdrop of a country that desperately needs to create more college graduates. If we really want to broaden the pool of students who can access higher education, we must be open to new approaches, even if some of those approaches challenge our assumptions about how higher education has "always been." That's particularly true since, as we have seen, what appears to have "always been" in American education is in many cases of relatively recent vintage, and was itself the product of debate and opposition. Private-sector colleges have room to improve, but they've become a vital player in America's higher education landscape. They are early in their development, and it would be a tragedy to hamstring them just as we're entering a hotly contested global education race. As I discuss in the next chapter, they may be the best hope we have of introducing the kind of educational innovation and efficiency that will enable the United States to lead the world in the twenty-first century as it did the twentieth.

The Learning Playbook

2036 and the Coming Twenty-Five Years of Change in Higher Education

In 2036, Harvard will celebrate its four hundredth anniversary. As ever, its commencement that spring will be a spectacle of pomp and circumstance, one based on centuries of tradition. As they did hundreds of years ago, the graduates will gather in Harvard Yard, forming columns through which the President's Parade will pass en route to the stage. Trumpets will announce a fanfare for Harvard's president, who, by tradition, is the only official whose entrance warrants that accolade, even if the president of the United States happens to be in attendance (and on this august occasion, she might well be). Upon the stage, the university president will sit in a Jacobean chair that's been used at every Harvard commencement since the mid-1700s. Two top students will give speeches, and the audience will mumble its way through the Harvard Hymn, its lyrics entirely in Latin. Degrees will be conferred, a benediction will be given, and family and friends will toast their graduates.[1] Commencement day, one Harvard alum wrote, is "a singular commingling of solemnity and festivity, tradition and modernity."[2] Chances are, one of the traditions that Harvard will celebrate on that day will be its four hundredth year as the nation's number one university—and, depending on who's assessing, a long run as number one in the world.

Harvard in 2036 will look and feel a lot like the Harvard of today. Students, many of them high school valedictorians or holders of perfect scores on their entrance exams, will still live in the brick residences that line Harvard Yard and the Charles River. They'll still crowd into Sanders Theatre for some of the large introductory lecture classes, such as Ec10, which might even be taught by some of the same faculty teaching at Harvard today. They will still read the *Harvard Crimson* (electronically, at least), and laugh at the antics of the *Harvard Lampoon*. They'll cross the river in late November to attend "The Game" against Yale. Their parents—many of whom are enjoying college today—will complain that their kids drink too much, sleep too little, and spend more time thinking about out-of-class passions like soccer or crew or theater than about their classes (until finals, at least). But these students will be having some of the best four years of their young lives, and moving on to becoming America's leaders in the latter half of the twenty-first century.

There will still be plenty of people who are eager to pay a premium for an education at Harvard and other elite institutions, just as today there are plenty of people who are willing to pay a premium for a Mercedes, even though they could get to work and the shopping mall in a Ford or a Kia much less expensively. People like what going to Harvard or owning a Mercedes says about them, and no one doubts the excellence that these brands represent.

But under the hood, during the intervening quarter century, much will have changed in American higher education.

THE EDUCATIONAL SYSTEM of twenty-five years from now will be unlike today's education in at least seven important ways:

1. It Will Be More Mobile.

One of the fundamental assumptions about traditional education is that it happens *somewhere*, and that somewhere is usually the campus. Of course, a lot of things used to happen somewhere but don't have to any longer: banking, buying music, finding someone to date. Over the last two decades, those activities have moved to a fixed screen, and today they're in the latter stages of moving to mobile devices. We are astounded at the quality of what we can get on our smartphones and tablet devices today, and there's no doubt that the ability to interact and communicate from mobile devices will improve dramatically in the decades ahead.

Millions of students already take courses online. A small percentage can now participate in their coursework entirely from a mobile device. Aside from the convenience, there are many elements of online education that are pedagogically superior to studying in the traditional face-to-face method. Among them: the data an instructor has about how a student is engaging with her course; the ability of an instructor to require responses from all students, not just one, to a question or dialogue; the ability of a student to raise sidebar questions with a teaching assistant during a class session, or to replay a complicated portion of a lecture; and the ability to supplement live classes with asynchronous message boards and projects.

It is not hard to imagine that as technology advances, mobile learning will become superior to face-to-face learning in most key educational respects. The perception of the quality of mobile learning will surely lag behind the reality, of course; observers will cling to the superiority of traditional methods long after those methods have been superseded purely in terms of learning outcomes. Even so, as they become aware of the strength of alternative means of learning, it will be harder for parents to justify the cost of shipping their sons or daughters off to a resort for four years with the ostensible purpose of getting an education they could get from home or the workplace. Students will have to confront directly how much of the cost of education is being spent on education; on brand and prestige; on building a network of future contacts; on socialization, friendships, and fun; and so on—and they will have the opportunity to pay for only those elements that make sense for them. The "bundled product" element of higher education—the fact that today, in order to get the education, you have to buy the football team, dining halls, and climbing walls—will start to break down as various players in the education marketplace start to sell elements separately. By 2036, it's a virtual certainty that many students—even eighteen- to twenty-four-year olds—will be purchasing education separately from the socialization experience of today's college.

2. It Will Be More Disaggregated.

Just as students will be able to acquire education without having to "buy" the campus experience, they will no longer be expected to acquire all of their education from the same provider. We don't usually think of today's university as an integrated product, but it is. The same entity provides the classrooms; hires, trains, and evaluates the instructors; offers, teaches, and provides grades for the courses; bundles the classes into degree programs; validates the completion of the educational experience; and offers a credential at the end of the process. At a residential college, that same entity houses, feeds, and entertains its student body. Today some students may start at one school and transfer to another, or take a summer course or even a semester abroad someplace other than their "home" college. But generally speaking, everyone must choose one integrated provider or move to another; they can't mix and match, buying part from one and another part from another.

All of this integration stems from convenience and tradition, but it will start to break down over the coming decades. If the University of Minnesota has a fantastic economics lecturer, why should he be limited to teaching Minnesota students? Couldn't he build his own following among all prospective students—become an economics celebprofessor? In fact, what's to keep him from building his own business surrounding his course, with his own teaching assistants, grading staff, proprietary textbook, and his own advertising to drive registrations? And what stops another institution, for-profit or nonprofit, from aggregating a group of celebprofessors into packages available to students? Or others from offering low-cost courses that could be aggregated into degrees? Or others from offering courseware that local instructors can use? Or still others from validating or certifying the learning experiences that students acquire elsewhere?

Even better, much of this may be offered for free. The Open-CourseWare movement is already putting entire courses online from instructors at top schools such as MIT, Johns Hopkins, the University of Michigan, and Tufts.[3] One can envision a world where future students will be able to acquire an entire college education at a fraction of the cost of getting a degree today—and get a validated credential at the end.

At present, the barriers to much of this are regulatory and accreditation rules that insist upon integration of teaching and validation. But over the next twenty-five years, as institutions find ways to demonstrate quality and reliability in a disaggregated environment, those barriers are likely to relax. And when that happens, students will have the option of experiencing higher education in ways that are out of the question now. They will be able to patch together low-cost courses to get an inexpensive, practical commodity degree. They will match star professors' courses from multiple sources into a high-powered education that is not tied to a single institution. Some, of course, will prefer an integrated experience that looks much like today's university; these are the students who will march in 2036 graduation ceremonies like the one that opens this chapter. Others will create a higher education that is tailored to their needs. What matters is that students will have far more choices, and much more ability to match an education with their needs, desires, and pocketbooks, than they do today.

3. It Will Be More Personalized.

Most of education today treats all students in a given class the same: they get the same assignments, the same lectures, and proceed at the same pace, regardless of their capabilities or background. Some students are bored because the course is moving too slowly; others are overwhelmed by what they feel is the blistering pace (or because they chose a course that was too challenging for them in the first place). From the institution's perspective, it's far less expensive to put a single professor in front of a room with a large number of students, but it's a remarkably inefficient process from a learning perspective. This common system exists because historically the only alternative would have been individual or small-group tutoring, which is too expensive to provide at scale.

To be sure, there are important parts of education that don't need to be highly personalized, because they involve the basic download of information. This recitation and imparting of information—how to calculate a differential, the structural difference between comedy and tragedy, what happened in the Battle of Stalingrad—is currently delivered thousands of ways by thousands of instructors in thousands of locations, at widely varying levels of specificity, engagement, and quality.

Particularly as students access more and more of their education through mobile devices and other technology, it will become much easier to standardize the basic download of information, using the most compelling instructors in highly produced segments with simulations, maps, illustrations, video, and avatars. At the same time, technology will allow educators to tailor educational experiences to the specific needs of each individual student. While completing standardized assignments, students will engage with dynamic, interactive coursework that zips through material they understand and targets their weaknesses. On these types of homework assignments, how a student answers question 17, for example, will determine which version of question 18 pops up next. Each interaction with a program will create and capture data that helps determine what the student should do next—and how that student handles each interaction will shape what the database recommends for future students.

Using these types of technologies, it will be possible to know how much time students spend studying, how they've answered every question asked in the review at the "back of the chapter" (a term that will go away), what issues they don't understand, how quickly they're progressing through a curriculum, and where they hit stumbling blocks. This information can be combined with an array of other information about a given student—academic background, financial information, career goals, performance on questions in previous courses, an employer's assessment of the skills the student needs to improve to win a promotion—to create models that will be custom-designed to suit students' academic strengths and weaknesses, learning styles, goals, time availability, life challenges, and more. These models will enable institutions to deliver the precise education each student needs, when she needs it, and in the format she is most able to understand. This technology will enable remediation of problems that today's professors wouldn't even know existed. It will let students progress quickly through subject areas they already know and pause and reflect on those they don't. Institutions will learn what works and what doesn't, and will create a virtuous cycle whereby each student helps inform what would be best for future students.

Faculty roles will evolve as these advanced forms of teaching take hold. Many faculty will move away from the large-class lecture and more toward coaching students on areas in which they need extra help, guiding students toward learning objectives, and building supportive, motivating relationships to help students advance toward their goals. In the future, "teaching" will consist of something that looks less like the "sage on a stage" that typifies instruction at many modern colleges, and more like something we'd now consider "tutoring." It's a change that will benefit students—and will make many faculty jobs more satisfying as well.

4. It Will Focus More on Learning Outcomes.

The students who throw their mortarboards in the air at the conclusion of Harvard's 2036 commencement will have earned their degree, just as the students who graduate this year will. But there will be a key difference. Today it's nearly impossible to answer two very simple questions about a college graduate: What did she learn, and how did she learn it?

We assume that if a student graduated from a good university, she must be reasonably smart and must have learned something. After all, she was smart enough to get in, she was exposed to impressive professors, and she managed to progress all the way to graduation. Doesn't that indicate that she must have learned something? Well, not necessarily. In fact, some economists argue that a key value of an elite college degree is the "signaling" value: that when Goldman Sachs decides to hire Cornell graduates, it's doing so not because the company is certain the applicant necessarily learned a specific body of knowledge at Cornell, but because competitive college admissions and the subsequent grading system effectively acts as a filter, so that hiring a Cornell grad provides reasonable certainty that an employer is getting the best and the brightest. Some wags go so far as to argue that a company that hired Ivy League grads and a company that simply hired students admitted to an Ivy League school (regardless of whether they actually enrolled) would probably wind up with an equally talented pool of employees.

The truth is, outside of those disciplines that have some common measurement at the end—nursing, medicine, law—it's hard to assemble data on what, if anything, anyone who has attended an American university has learned, or how they learned it. That's not to suggest that students don't learn (though I cited some studies in chapter 2 that do raise that question). It's only to say that what students learn is generally not measured by any common, comparable standard, and therefore it's hard to make comparisons as to where and how students are learning more. That makes it difficult to assess who is enabling better learning, and why. *Today's universities essentially do not compete with one another on what should be their core goal: enabling learning among their students.* The competition among universities tends to be on what are, at best, secondary or tertiary indicators of learning—metrics such as the caliber of the students they admit, the number of applicants to whom they deny admission, the pedigree of the faculty, the size of the library, or the quality of facilities.

Over the coming decades, measurement of student learning outcomes will become much more widespread and sophisticated. We will know not just precisely what a student has learned, but how he learned it—which is crucial for helping determine whether there could be a more efficient route for future students to achieve that learning outcome. The technology that personalizes education will be built around engines that enable and measure efficient and effective learning. Education will return to an idealized stage in which student learning is the key metric in evaluating education. Increasingly, institutions and courses will be evaluated not on reputation, tradition, or assumption, but on how effectively they help students achieve learning outcomes. Those that try to rely on the assumption that students are learning will steadily lose ground to those that can prove it; and those that can show they enable efficient, direct learning will have an advantage over those that can't.

One of the important outcomes of a focus on learning will be a return to a student-centric environment. Teaching faculty will be evaluated not on politics or reputation or even research, but on effectiveness in educating students. Universities will develop learning reputations, rather than riding on their history. Alumni will have a stake in the continued measuring of learning outcomes of their alma mater, as it will drive the reputation of their school. Legislators will want better learning outcomes for their own institutions compared with those of the next state, because an educated populace will drive the local economy. Learning organizations will at last compete on their effectiveness in enabling learning.

5. It Will Be More Accessible.

The trend in American higher education has been steadily and inexorably toward greater access. From the first northeastern colleges for students from elite families to the land-grant schools to the community colleges and the private-sector colleges, each new chapter has brought more prospective students into the mainstream—and each has led to a more educated populace and stronger economic growth. Many would argue that the rise in American higher education over the last century and a half has mostly been about improved access. There could be wonderful debates as to whether today's Harvard or Rutgers graduate is better educated than a graduate from fifty or a hundred or two hundred years ago, but it would likely lead to no decisive conclusion (as opposed to the clear answers to whether, say, today's automobiles or crop yields are better than they were a while back). What is certain is that the average farmer or office assistant has far more access to higher education than in generations past.

Even so, before we get too proud of ourselves on this point, we should keep in mind that of the more than 133 million people age 25 and over in the current civilian labor force, nearly 89 million do not have a bachelor's degree. About 50 million have never had any college.[4] In our increasingly high-tech and service-oriented economy, that's a lot of people who may not be prepared for the jobs the new economy is creating—and it suggests a continuing challenge for our country in the coming global marketplace. Other nations have surpassed the United States in educational attainment, and that gives them a big advantage in winning the twenty-first century. As President Obama said in his Austin speech in August of 2010, "Education is an economic issue when we know beyond a shadow of a doubt that countries that out-educate us today will out-compete us tomorrow."

The good news is that the changes in store over the next twenty-five years bode well for continued expansion of access. With the arrival of mobility and the forces enabling much less expensive delivery of quality education, such expanded access will be much easier to deliver. Prospective students will be able to obtain low-cost education tailored to their specific needs, and acquire exactly the education they need to compete in the workforce.

The potential bad news, at least for the primacy of the American economy, is that these same opportunities to expand access will exist globally, and those societies that take advantage of them will have an edge. The United States is no longer the leader in promoting access to education for its citizens. If the reflexive American predisposition to throw up barriers and heap condescension on new forms of education continues in the years ahead, we will find ourselves falling further behind the rest of the world in educational attainment.

6. It Will Be More Global.

With the rise of mobility, place will not matter nearly as much in the future. A student from Kuala Lumpur can take a mobile class as easily as a student from Kansas City, and at prices that will be affordable for many more students worldwide. The primary force that keeps international students out of American institutions, and vice versa—geography—will cease to be a barrier for students who seek a mobile education. This will lead to a more international flavor in those higher education institutions that embrace mobility. American universities, which have tended to be more insular than many around the world, will particularly benefit from this influx. Students will spend more time in their college years working with others from Hong Kong, Singapore, Adelaide, Abu Dhabi, Santiago, and Dublin than do American students of today. As a result, they will be more prepared for the global work environment they will face when they graduate.

Of course, just as American institutions will welcome more international students, foreign universities will be more attractive (virtual) destinations for American students. The already heavy competition among U.S. universities for American students will become even stiffer as top foreign institutions increasingly provide attractive value propositions. As universities increasingly compete on learning outcomes, those institutions that rank highly in a new world order will be more desirable to students worldwide.

American institutions start off with clear brand advantages in what will be an increasingly important competition for global higher education leadership. In a 2010 ranking of the top world universities, the United States had thirty-one colleges among the top one hundred,[5] and in a 2010 ranking by Shanghai Jiao Tong University, America claimed fifty-four of the top one hundred spots.[6] America also has global tech-industry leadership, a history of attracting international students, and the demonstrated successes of for-profit institutions in online education and other learning innovation. To the extent that policy makers further the goal of making America the home of large, global educational institutions—as opposed to putting up barriers— the United States can become the home base for worldwide higher education.

The race for education leadership matters. First, having students from around the world attending U.S. institutions will help acquaint and socialize those students to American systems and values, creating understanding and kinship that will be important in aiding U.S. diplomatic and policy initiatives for generations. Second, education is likely to become a major export product over the next twenty-five years. If students from around the world have access to a given class or program, the providers of that program will have access to a much larger market than the domestic market that is the primary domain of most universities today. The country that leads in attracting students has the potential to attract a massive inflow of tuition and other dollars from around the world, and put hundreds of thousands of people to work teaching those students. If other nations move more quickly to seize global education leadership, these benefits will flow elsewhere.

Just as the last twenty-five years have seen the world "flatten" for business, the next twenty-five years will almost certainly see it flatten for education. The outcome will be students who are more confident and comfortable dealing with people from different cultures—which will be a win for everyone.

7. It Will Be Cooler.

It's fun to imagine all the ways technology will make education more responsive, engaging, and interesting. Imagine simulations that enable students to experience how blood courses through the body, how a volcano erupts, or how a change in prices affects all competitors in a marketplace. Imagine robots and avatars that enable a student to travel to Germany in the age of Bismarck, to Craig Venter's lab as he worked to sequence the human genome, to Washington's headquarters on Christmas 1776, or to the Enron boardroom. Imagine project teams that bring together students from around the globe to solve a problem. Imagine virtual tutors that give lessons tailored to a student's specific shortcomings the day before the exam. Imagine neural imaging that helps instructors understand how learning is progressing, and diagnose and track learning deficits.

Still, the specific executions of these imaginings are less important than the more fundamental shift they will represent. The next twenty-five years offer an opportunity to transform the way students have learned for centuries. We will be able to deliver education to students where they are; based on their specific needs, desires, and backgrounds; focused on delivering outcomes that are matched to student and employer goals; to a much broader audience of students, and at lower cost, than ever before; and integrating a global population of potential students. It promises to be one of the most exciting eras in educational history, one likely to presage a new surge in global economic activity in the latter half of this century.

THE TRENDS I'VE described are, to one degree or another, inevitable. Over the last twenty-five years, we have evolved from a country that once lacked TiVo, disposable contact lenses, elliptical trainers, cell phones and laptops, prewashed salad in a bag, car navigation systems, and the Internet. Yet even as our day-to-day life has changed dramatically, the university experience is still pretty much the same. That's true for a reason: compared with other sectors of the economy, education is highly resistant to change. But it won't be able to resist that change over the next twenty-five years—at least not worldwide. Those societies that reward forward-thinking approaches to education will be the economic winners in the twenty-first century—and those that protect the status quo will see their economies suffer. The United States still has the best higher education system in the world, but for that to continue into the latter half of this century, policy makers will need to shift from being protective of tradition to rewarding specific types of behaviors.

In my view, higher education policy makers should seek to reward institutions that show measurable success in four areas:

- Learning outcomes
- Access
- Low costs
- Innovation

This is the tide that is coming in. Societies that promote these values will win; those that don't will fall behind. To avoid that fate, policy makers should cease rewarding attributes that are unrelated to these values—things like relative rankings, luxurious facilities, football teams, or the particular tax structure of an institution. The U.S. education system is already more bureaucratic and less nimble than that of many other countries. If we use regulation or accreditation to enshrine the status quo, we will seal our fate as a second-rate power. The nations that lead educationally will lead economically and, eventually, politically and militarily. It's that important to our future.

The question American observers should ask is: Who will have the courage to say that the system we have now will not lead the world in the future, and that innovation should be unleashed? Who will be willing to say that we are misallocating our investment in higher education, and that the focus should be on learning outcomes?

Let institutions fight it out on learning grounds: those that seek prestige should earn their acclaim through the demonstrated learning outcomes of their students. Let's be sure our crucial investments in expanding access to higher education are focused on delivering quality to the broader population that needs education, not just a seat in class. Let's embrace those who seek profits in delivering education, but only as long as they deliver measurable student results. Taxpayer subsidies should follow institutions that deliver demonstrable results on the four values. If an institution can deliver those results and still produce an exciting football team or climbing walls or corporate profits, bully for them, but these extras should exist as ancillaries to educational excellence, not as a primary focus of university leaders.

Our current higher education system funds institutions—and students—without regard to performance. Shouldn't we be using that funding mechanism to reward those who do better, and prod others to join that club? To support universities that drive down costs while improving outcomes? To encourage institutions that graduate their students at a higher demographically risk-adjusted rate? To promote the measurement and improvement of actual learning? To support the student who graduates quickly, rather than reserving more funding for those who linger? Our current simplistic, one-size-fits-all approach promotes spending in the wrong places and doesn't encourage the kind of innovation and excellence we need from our institutions of higher learning. We need much more nuanced, results-oriented federal and state funding systems that tilt dollars toward performance and away from mediocrity.

In the United States and other countries with developed higher education systems, we can expect opposition to rewarding institutions that increase learning outcomes, increase access, reduce costs, and boost innovations. Today, traditional universities hold enormous political power, and that gives them sizable influence over the regulatory environment that incentivizes—or, too often, disincentivizes—innovation. The question is how long the traditional players will hold on to this power, and how long they'll be able to hold back newer, more innovative approaches.

History tells us quite clearly that American higher education will not reform itself, and suggests that government will not reform its educational funding and oversight system without a major shove. It will have to be forced into change by crisis, and to my mind, such a crisis might come in one or more of three forms.

The first will be *budgetary*: in a time of shrinking budgets and decreased willingness to fund profligacy, state and federal legislators will be forced to make ever more difficult decisions regarding what gets funded and what doesn't. Eventually they'll stop funding ancillary activities and force colleges to focus their spending on learning.

The second will be *international competition*: the success of other nations in developing more effective higher education systems will create a Sputnik-like fear that the United States will lose the education race unless it refocuses its higher education system around student learning.

The third will be *domestic competition*: the rise of private-sector colleges and other new models will draw more students out of traditional institutions, forcing those institutions to change and adapt to a new competitive environment.

Regardless of whether a crisis forces major shifts, the U.S. education system is on a track to change. After a period of intense scrutiny, private-sector colleges will adapt to stricter regulatory oversight—a process that will ultimately be a good thing for students, the public, and the long-term success of these schools. But they will not merely be addressing today's issues, such as marketing or student loan defaults. Institutions like Kaplan are investing heavily over the long term, both to further and benefit from the coming advances in mobility, disaggregation, personalization, outcomes focus, accessibility, and globalization. Other types of institutions will also be working to win in the dramatically new environment the next twenty-five years will bring—and the competition among them will be healthy for students, our society, and the economy.

While the for-profits may face a pause in growth after new regulations are implemented, I'm confident they will then resume growing, continue to innovate, and, over time, will end up with educational results that put significant pressure on some traditional institutions. They're offering a disruptive product. Established players have moved too far upmarket and are overshooting too many potential consumers, and the private sector is simply following the rules of Econ 101 to provide supply to satisfy this unmet demand.

Ultimately, it all comes down to the playbooks.

Many years from now, Harvard will still be Harvard, because the Ivory Tower Playbook will continue to work for the nation's elite institutions. A lot will change over twenty-five years, but the human desire for prestige will not be one of them. The best high school students in the country will still scramble for admission to the most elite institutions, and those institutions will still attract the very best to teach them, build the finest facilities to house them, and cosset them with luxurious surroundings. Legislators will continue to fund these elite institutions because they do an effective job of educating and socializing the nation's future leaders.

Below that level, however, things are likely to change. If

tuition prices were to continue to rise at 5.94 percent—that's nearly twice the overall rate of inflation—as they did between 1989 and 2005, a bachelor's degree at a solid private college (think Rice University in Texas or Beloit College in Wisconsin, each of which cost about $33,000 in tuition per year today, not counting room and board) would cost around $645,000 in 2036.[7] There will be no one willing to pay for a Bubble Couch at that point: students will have lower-priced alternatives and won't pay up for an undifferentiated degree, while taxpayers will long since have run out of tolerance for such frippery. Outside of the elite, all institutions will have to compete in a world where quality education is accessible at reasonable cost. That will push not just traditional institutions, but community colleges and private-sector schools, too.

In many ways, private-sector colleges are most vulnerable to this change. They lack both the long-term brand recognition and the governmental subsidies of public institutions. In a competitive world in which learning is central, they will have to excel to survive. My guess is that many will not.

But other private-sector institutions have shown more nimbleness, more innovation, and more commitment to learning outcomes than just about any institutions on the American higher education scene. These institutions will have a distinct advantage in adapting to the new world. They will embrace mobility, personalization, and even disaggregation to provide services needed by the market. They will benefit from the slow-moving nature of the traditional system, and ultimately they will become successful case studies written by the generation of scholars who follow in the footsteps of Clayton Christensen.

It will come as no surprise that I believe private-sector institutions will join their land-grant and community college cousins as widely accepted and embraced parts of the American higher education landscape—even as all sectors are under attack from new models. Indeed, I am confident that the Private-Sector Playbook discussed in chapter 5 will lead some private-sector institutions to become among the nation's, and even the world's, most admired institutions over the next twenty-five years.

Competition will force all three playbooks to change in the next several decades. For all but the most elite schools, the Ivory Tower Playbook leads to unsustainable cost. As the track record of community colleges illustrates, the All-Access Playbook doesn't consistently deliver excellence in outcomes. The Private-Sector Playbook can be tightly aligned with learning, but it can also veer away from it. All institutions are going to need to bring forward something new: the Learning Playbook.

Most traditional universities started with a Learning Playbook; they generally were founded on the need to bring more educated students into the community. But with the expansion of access and money, they evolved into the prestige-driven approach that's been codified as the Ivory Tower Playbook. Learning and prestige were once very closely linked in the context of a university—in fact, the shift from one to the other was probably barely perceptible at first. But once the goal became focused on prestige rather than learning, the two diverged—because you can achieve prestige through better students, and you can attract better students through means other than enhancing learning. That's how we arrived at the *reductio ad absurdum* in which a university can build a twenty-five-person hot tub to enhance prestige.

The All-Access Playbook similarly started as a Learning Playbook, as community colleges opened and focused on practical skills that drove the economy. Over time, however, as community colleges instilled the novel belief that college should be available to all rather than just the chosen few, they became the college of last resort for those who couldn't go elsewhere. As legislatures tried to be more egalitarian, they pressed community colleges to expand, and the Learning Playbook morphed into an agenda that's all about access. Eventually, the attention on access squeezed the learning focus.

The Private-Sector Playbook started out with learning as a means to an end, a return on investment, but for the reasons I've set out, I think it's the incentive system that's most closely aligned with the Learning Playbook ideal. That is, in order to achieve a high return in the long run, private-sector colleges must focus on learning outcomes. The Private-Sector Playbook is the only one where stronger learning outcomes are a direct and necessary prerequisite to achieving the playbook's goals, at least over the long run.

Those who are charged with higher education policy should have their own Learning Playbook. They should explicitly reward and subsidize activities that further learning—not just deep learning for a select few, but quality learning for many. They should discourage and eliminate subsidies for activities that aren't linked with learning; and they might start with all those athletic complexes, luxury dorms, and over-the-top university centers.

WHILE I WAS finishing this book, I took a weekend off to spend with my wife in Maine. We flew into Boston en route to the scenic Camden region, about two hundred miles to the north. After renting a car, my wife and I got into the inevitable discussion: she wanted to take the scenic route and spend the day meandering among the cute villages, blueberry stands, antique shops, and country stores in out-of-the-way corners by traveling to our destination via the coastal roads of Maine. As the driver,

I wanted to take the highway, the most direct route, so we could get to our inn in Camden and I didn't spend the whole day driving. This choice represented a clear trade-off. We'd see more, have a more interesting time, meet more quirky characters, and have more stories to tell if we took the meandering route. On the other hand, we'd get to our destination more quickly by the highway—and once there, we could enjoy our day in Camden. We'd probably save gas, too.

Higher education has a similar debate. Private-sector schools and community colleges seek to take students by the direct route to their end goal: a degree and a set of skills they can apply in the job market. Traditional universities, as a general matter, want to lead students on a meandering course in which the journey is as important as the destination, where a stop along the way might truly take you on a whole different track.

During the preceding chapters, as we've toured traditional campuses, a few of my observations may have appeared overly critical of traditional education. But to be clear, my objection is to extravagance, not the meandering path itself. I believe that a broad liberal arts education is a wonderful way to expose students to new ideas they never would have seen "from the highway." The direct route in education, meanwhile, is sometimes viewed as "lesser," but it's responsive to the desires of students who want efficiency. Each route serves its purpose. You wouldn't want to have only one or the other as a possibility. Sometimes the same person wants one at one point (college), and the other at a different point (an online graduate program, for example). Indeed, in my Maine example, we ended up meandering up to Camden, since we had the whole weekend ahead of us, and taking the direct route back in order to make our plane—different solutions for different circumstances.

This is an important point. I love the traditional college experience, and I feel strongly about what it can do to expand the horizons of students who get the chance to experience it. It's the reason I love spending time on campuses and talking with students and professors in all types of institutions. I'm excited for my children to be able to go away to college, to learn from exciting professors, to meet new kinds of people and engage with new kinds of ideas, to participate in community service projects, to join clubs and play sports—in short, to grow as people and as members of society from the experience. But we need to make a distinction between those who are, in fact, getting a high-quality education that is expanding their minds, making them critical thinkers who (in the words most often used by proponents of liberal arts education) have "learned how to learn" and "know how much they don't know," and those who are buying a legitimized four-year resort experience, funded or subsidized by taxpayers, with some classes thrown in. I'm reminded of a quote attributed to the philosopher David Wood of Vanderbilt University: "College is the best time of your life. When else are your parents going to spend several thousand dollars a year just for you to go to a strange town and get drunk every night?" This quote might be funny if it were in fact only "several thousand" instead of "tens of thousands of dollars," and if it were only parents (and not taxpayers) who were footing the bill.

I've also tried to make clear that I admire those who have devoted their lives to the education of others, usually for all the right reasons. But I believe that the structure we've built rewards and encourages the wrong behavior. If you gave Nido Qubein of High Point University the task of building a learning-centered, mobile, personalized educational experience, I'd bet on him to do it. But even though that's where the world is going right now, it's not what the various constituencies at most colleges want, and it's not what educational funders require. So, instead, he's building gourmet steak houses and luxury cinemas, and handing out free ice cream. In his own way, he's doing exactly what the Ivory Tower Playbook incentivizes him to do, and in the eyes of his trustees, students, and alumni, he's succeeding beyond anyone's wildest dreams. He's no villain; to the contrary, in the context of the rules he's working under, he's a hero.

Those who work in higher education usually do so because they want to shape young minds and influence the future. They want education to be at the core of their institutions, and they often resent the way the system pushes them toward less important matters. Given the $430 billion our country spends on higher education, much of it coming from taxpayers, others should resent it, too. If we don't get ready for the education world of 2036, our nation risks being left behind in the decades to come.

But change is difficult. And the problem with changing the American higher education system, of course, is that it is not really a "system" at all. It's a set of loosely governed, autonomous institutions, most of which are insulated from normal competitive pressures by funding mechanisms. Each institution seeks to act in its own perceived self-interest, and any that try to buck the accepted playbook (e.g., refusing to build fancy dorms or competitive football teams) create problems for themselves.

Change will happen only if funders force it. We will have a Learning Playbook—a system that incentivizes learning outcomes, access, low cost, and innovation—if the government appropriators whose money fuels and shapes the market for higher education demand that it should be so. If higher graduation rates for a given student demographic mix leads to more funding, and lower rates to less funding, just watch how quickly universities prioritize graduation rates over climbing walls. If funding rewards measurement and improvement of learning outcomes, more students will end up learning more in college. Our education system in 2036 will be fashioned by those who are responsible for creating the incentives today. Accountability lies with the funders.

A key ally in the path to a new higher education playbook will be a well-regulated private sector that believes that strong learning outcomes attract students and capital and that has confidence in the power of disruptive innovation. Private-sector colleges may not have four hundred years of history behind them. They don't have billions of dollars in endowments, and they don't sing Latin hymns. When I presided over graduations at Kaplan University, I sat in a folding chair, not on a sixteenth-century Jacobean throne. But we have one major advantage: we're not afraid of change. And no matter what institutions lead the way over the next twenty-five years, there are a lot of changes coming.

Acknowledgements

've spent most of my life studying or working in the world of education—public, nonprofit, and private sector. This book emerges from the thousands of people I've met in the hundreds of educational institutions I've visited around the world. I've always been inspired by students who are trying to better themselves and their communities. If parts of this book are critical of our education system, it's because I so strongly believe these students deserve the best our society has to offer.

So many people have helped to make this book a reality, and while they are not responsible for the things that make you angry (that would be me you're mad at), they were often responsible for the things that make you think. I am particularly appreciative of the team at Kaplan Publishing, led by Maureen McMahon, Publisher, who urged me early on to write it. Jennifer Farthing, my editor, backed the project from the outset and cracked the whip when I fell behind my deadlines, but always did it with good cheer and backed it with insight and good ideas. Sheryl Stebbins served gracefully as editor of the final draft. Fred Urfer, my production editor, nicely got it into final form. And throughout the process, others associated with Kaplan Publishing played key roles, including: Tim Brazier, Jenna Dolan, Rebecca Geiger, Marcy Goot, Rod Hernandez, Annette LaRocco, Jacqueline Jones, Rena Kirsch, Piya Kishore, Michele Mazur, Siobhan McKiernan, Cassandra Pappas, Michele Pore, Babette Ross, Denise Roy, Brett Sandusky, John Scarnecchia, Carly Schnur, Ron Sharpe, and Michelle Sterk Barrett.

Matt Seelye is a great partner who led a group of remarkable professionals providing essential analytical support; much of the data (and plenty of ideas) cited in this book stems from their good work. Ivan Palacio, Zack Tillitski, and Jason Levin were key parts of this process.

Melissa Mack championed the book from very early on, and has long been an important source of support. So too were Mark Harrad, Johan de Muinck Keizer, and Vanessa Soman. I regularly got good ideas and thoughts from colleagues, including Janice Block, Becky Campoverde, Mark Coggins, Jeff Conlon, Edward Hanapole, Beth Hollenberg, John Lock, Greg Marino, John Polstein, Jim Rosenthal, Allison Rutledge-Parisi, Darrell Splithoff, and Jose Wehnes.

Don Graham, Peter Smith, Barry Currier, Wade Dyke, Geri Malandra, and Bror Saxberg read earlier versions of the manuscript, providing excellent feedback that helped make the book better. Each has been an important source of insights over the years, while Don in particular has been amazingly supportive and helpful in all kinds of ways.

Stephanie Kehrer keeps me on track, and tries to keep me on point, on a wide range of matters (including this book), while Marina Huettel keeps me on schedule. I appreciate them both very much.

I've been lucky to work with people who always inspire questioning, skepticism, and ambition. Jonathan Grayer heads this list, along with Robert Greenberg. I feel lucky to have been partners with them.

Daniel McGinn helped me shape my voice; his critical eye and journalistic instinct helped me immeasurably. I'm very grateful for his assistance and partnership.

I'm indebted to the many remarkable thinkers, innovators, and observers on the educational scene whose works and thoughts I've cited in the book. Many students and educators took time out of their day to be profiled for this book or to share their insights with me. I want to thank them for their participation in this project.

My wife Marcelle and our kids Danielle and Jake were unbelievably understanding as I wrote this book on weekends, holidays, late nights, and whenever I could find the time. Their love, support, and good humor means everything to me.

My mom and dad always taught my brothers and sisters and me to think for ourselves, and to value learning above everything else but family. My mom passed away while I was writing this book, and never got to read the manuscript. But her presence, and that of my dad, is on every page.

Notes

INTRODUCTION

1. Jeffrey M. Silber and Paul Condra, "Equity Research: Education and Training" (New York: BMO Capital Markets, September 2010), 111.

2. "History of UC Berkeley: 19th-Century Founding of UC's Flagship Campus," UC Berkeley, accessed November 22, 2010, www.berkeley.edu/about/hist/foundations.shtml.

3. Dave Weinstein, *It Came from Berkeley: How Berkeley Changed the World* (Salt Lake City, Utah: Gibbs Smith, 2008), 32–33.

4. "Facts at a Glance," UC Berkeley, accessed November 22, 2010, www.berkeley.edu/about/fact.shtml.

5. "DeCal," Democratic Education at Cal, accessed November 22, 2010, www.decal.org.

6. "Living at Cal: Clark Kerr Campus," UC Berkeley, accessed November 22, 2010, www.housing.berkeley.edu/livingatcal/clarkkerr.html; "Golden Bear Rec Center," UC Berkeley, accessed November 22, 2010, calbears.berkeley.edu/insidepage.aspx?uid=279f35b9-f898-40e6-bae1-831af606a609.

7. If you think that comparing the resort-like experience at Berkeley to a Napa Valley resort is hyperbole, try doing a side-by-side comparison of the amenities available at Berkeley and those at the Silverado Resort in Napa Valley. Silverado offers tennis courts, mountain biking trails, cardio classes, and yoga—and so does Berkeley. Silverado offers hiking trails nearby—but Berkeley offers an "Outdoor Experiential Education Program," with instructional sailing, windsurfing, and sea kayaking classes, along with backpacking

trips. The Berkeley Web site offers student testimonials of what it's like to live in the various residential areas on campus. "When I think of Clark Kerr, I think of condos with nice gardens," says Wendy, a freshman from Seattle. "The landscape is incredible." "Clark Kerr is sort of like a resort," says Stefano, a sophomore. "There are so many things you can do on the grounds." "Life at Clark Kerr: North/West," UC Berkeley Residential Living, accessed November 22, 2010, housing.berkeley.edu/resliving/life_ckc_nw.html; "Life at Clark Kerr: South/East," UC Berkeley Residential Living, accessed November 22, 2010, housing.berkeley.edu/resliving/life_ckc_se.html.

8. "Sports and Recreation," UC Berkeley, accessed November 22, 2010, www.berkeley.edu/life/sports.shtml.

9. "Massage," UC Berkeley Recreational Sports, accessed November 22, 2010, www.recsports.berkeley.edu/insidepage.aspx?uid=f66c87ca-1954-4991-89fa-6e2751031bcb; "Personal Training," UC Berkeley Recreational Sports, accessed November 22, 2010, www.recsports.berkeley.edu/inside page.aspx?uid=f31df0d1-da87-4474-87a8-51e57bc18438.

10. The Student-Athlete High Performance Center is part of a $500 million funding campaign for Berkeley athletics. In addition to the High Performance Center, the money will pay to renovate Memorial Stadium and for athletic scholarships. To help raise the money, Berkeley fund-raisers created various "giving opportunities"—a list of amenities and the price a donor would pay to have his or her name attached to a given amenity. For $2 million, your name could adorn the Piedmont Stair. For $1 million, you might get naming rights to the Football Equipment Room. For $750,000, you could claim to have funded the Offensive Coordinator's Office—or, if money is tighter these days, opt instead for the Tight End Coach's Office, for a mere $350,000. "Memorial Stadium Project," UC Berkeley News, accessed November 22, 2010, newscenter.berkeley.edu/features/stadium; "The Building," Cal Student-Athlete High Performance Center, accessed November 22, 2010, www.calhighperformance.com/content/index.asp?s=485&t=The-Building; "High Performance Center, Memorial Stadium Projects Taking Shape," California Golden Bears: Official Web site of Cal Athletics, last modified August 18, 2010, www.calbears.com/genrel/081810aab.html.

11. "Frequently Asked Questions on Plans for the California Memorial Stadium Project," UC Berkeley News, last updated June 17, 2008, www.berkeley.edu/news/media/releases/2008/06/17_stadium-faq.shtml.

12. UC Berkeley, "Facts at a Glance"; "Berkeley's Budget: Tradeoffs, Choices, and Challenges," UC Berkeley News, last modified March 1, 2010, berkeley.edu/news/media/releases/2010/03/01_gore.shtml; "Operational Excellence Homes in on Potential Savings," UC Berkeley News, last modified February 16, 2010, berkeley.edu/news/media/releases/2010/02/12_OE_interim.shtml; "Workforce Census, Spring 2010," UC Berkeley, last modified May 24, 2010, hrweb.berkeley.edu/files/WorkForceCensus_2010-04-30.pdf.

13. "Estimated Undergraduate Student Budgets," University of California Berkeley Financial Aid and Scholarships Office, accessed November 22, 2010, students.berkeley.edu/finaid/home/cost.htm.

14. "Campus Recreation," University of Illinois, accessed October 8, 2010, www.campusrec.illinois.edu; "Specs and Facts, ARC," University of Illinois, accessed October 8, 2010, www.campusrec.illinois.edu/facilities/arc/facts.html.

15. "Back to School," Roger Ebert, accessed November 22, 2010, rogerebert.suntimes.com/apps/pbcs.dll/article?aid=/19860613/reviews/606130301/1023.

16. Burt E. Powell, *The Movement for Industrial Education and the Establishment of the University, 1840–1870* (Urbana: University of Illinois, 1918), 105.

17. See, for example, my eulogy at Stanley H. Kaplan's August 2009 memorial service, at www.kaplan.com/shk/eulogy/Pages/default.aspx; see also Stanley Kaplan, *Test Pilot* (New York: Simon and Schuster, 2001).

18. Jonathan's accomplishments have been deservedly noted in the national media. "Behind the scenes and with little fanfare, Grayer has quietly transformed Kaplan from a stodgy test-preparation provider into one of the country's largest education companies, with one million students, 70 campuses, and an online law school," wrote Suzanne Kapner in a *Fortune* magazine story. "Sales in 2007 totaled $2 billion, compared with $80 million in 1994, the year Grayer was named CEO" ("Kaplan's Next Test," September 15, 2008). In the *Financial Times*, Francesco Guerrera wrote, "Under the Harvard-educated Mr. Grayer, a former marketing executive at *Newsweek*, Kaplan has replaced the august newspaper as the most important component of the Washington Post group" (July 11, 2008).

19. Donald E. Graham, remarks at UBS 37th Annual Global Media and Communications Conference, New York, December 7, 2009.

20. James Vaznis, "Asking More of Preschool," *The Boston Globe*, June 10, 2010, www.boston.com/news/education/k_12/articles/2010/06/10/asking_more_of_preschool; "Strategies for Improving the Early Education and Care Workforce in Massachusetts," Strategies for Children, April 2010, 4, www.strategiesforchildren.org/eea/1publications/SFC_WD_Report_Full_March_2010.pdf; Patricia Benner et al., "Book Highlights from *Educating Nurses: A Call for Radical Transformation*," The Carnegie Foundation for the Advancement of Teaching," accessed November 22, 2010, www.carnegiefoundation.org/elibrary/educating-nurses-highlights.

21. Steve Kolowich, "Online Cure for the Nursing Crisis," *Inside Higher Ed*, last revised February 2, 2010, www.insidehighered.com/news/2010/02/02/nursing.

22. Anthony P. Carnevale, Nicole Smith, and Jeff Strohl, "Help Wanted:

Projections of Jobs and Education Requirements Through 2018," executive summary, Georgetown Center on Education and the Workforce, Washington, D.C., June 2010, www9.georgetown.edu/grad/gppi/hpi/cew/pdfs/Executive Summary-web.pdf.

23. Ibid.

24. "The College Completion Agenda: 2010 Progress Report," College Board Advocacy and Policy Center, accessed November 22, 2010, 6, 9, 10, completionagenda.collegeboard.org/sites/default/files/reports_pdf/Progress_Report_2010.pdf; "Education at a Glance 2009 Summary of Key Findings," Organisation for Economic Co-operation and Development, accessed November 22, 2010, www.oecd.org/dataoecd/1/28/43654482.pdf; "Education at a Glance 2009 Key Results," Organisation for Economic Co-operation and Development, accessed November 22, 2010, www.slideshare.net/OECD/education-at-a-glance-2009-oecd-indicators.

25. "Remarks of President Barack Obama, Address to Joint Session of Congress," The White House, accessed November 22, 2010, www.whitehouse.gov/the_press_office/remarks-of-president-barack-obama-address-to-joint-session-of-congress.

1. HARVARD ENVY

1. Henry C. Shelley, *John Harvard and His Times* (Boston: Little, Brown, and Company, 1907), 126.

2. Samuel Eliot, Morison, *The Founding of Harvard College* (Cambridge, Mass: Harvard University Press, 1935), 106.

3. Shelley, *John Harvard and His Times*, 126, 128, 203.

4. Ibid., 232.

5. Morison, *Founding of Harvard College*, 219.

6. Ibid., 223.

7. "The Tale of John Harvard's Surviving Book." Harvard University Library Notes 1340, November 2007, hul.harvard.edu/publications/hul_notes_1340/john_harvard_book.html

8. John R. Thelin, *A History of American Higher Education* (Baltimore, Md.: Johns Hopkins University Press, 2004), 9.

9. Ibid., 1.

10. Ibid., 41.

11. Ibid., 20.

12. Ibid., 27–28.

13. Ibid., 31.

14. Ibid., 25.

15. Women who hoped to attend Harvard were instead enrolled in Radcliffe College, one of the Seven Sisters schools, chartered in 1894. It was not until 1963 that women were eligible to earn degrees from Harvard University, and in 1999 Radcliffe and Harvard formally merged. "Harvard University," Encyclopædia Britannica, November 17, 2010, www.britannica.com/EBchecked/topic/256300/Harvard-University.

16. Thelin, *American Higher Education*, 23.

17. Daniel McGinn, "The Master of Innovation," *Newsweek*, November 17, 2003, www.newsweek.com/2003/11/16/the-master-of-innovation.html.

18. Ibid.

19. Clayton M. Christensen, *The Innovator's Dilemma* (New York: HarperBusiness Essentials, 2003), xviii, xxix.

20. Ibid., xxix.

21. Coy F. Cross II, *Justin Smith Morrill: Father of the Land-Grant Colleges* (East Lansing: Michigan State University Press, 1999), 1–5.

22. Ibid., 12.

23. Ibid., ix, xiii.

24. Ibid., ix.

25. J. L. Van Zanden, "The First Green Revolution: The Growth of Production and Productivity in European Agriculture, 1870–1914," *Economic History Review, New Series* (May 1991): 215–39.

26. Cross, *Justin Smith Morrill*, 79.

27. Ray V. Herren and John Hillison, "Agricultural Education and the 1862 Land-Grant Institutions: The Rest of the Story," *Journal of Agricultural Education* 37, no. 3 (1996): 26–32, pubs.aged.tamu.edu/jae/pdf/vol37/37-03-26.pdf.

28. Cross, *Justin Smith Morrill*, 80–81.

29. Herren and Hillison, "Agricultural Education."

30. Cross, *Justin Smith Morrill*, 82.

31. Herren and Hillison, "Agricultural Education."

32. Cross, *Justin Smith Morrill*, 85.

33. Roger L. Williams, *The Origins of Federal Support for Higher Education* (University Park: Penn State University Press, 1991), 66.

34. Danforth Eddy, Jr., *Colleges for Our Land and Time: The Land-Grant Idea in American Education* (New York: Harper and Brothers, 1956).

35. "Fourth Annual Report of the President and of the Treasurer," The Carnegie Foundation for the Advancement of Teaching, New York, 1909, 103.

36. James K. Patterson, "A Retrospect," Proceedings of the 24th Annual Convention of the Association of American Agricultural Colleges and Experiment Stations (Montpelier, Vt.: Capital City Press, 1911), 34.

37. Isaac Phillips Roberts, *Autobiography of a Farm Boy* (Albany, N.Y.: JB Lyon, 1916), 219–20.

38. Eddy, *Colleges for Our Land*, 48.

39. Arthur J. Klein, "Survey of Land-Grant Colleges," *Journal of Higher Education* (April 1931): 169–76.

40. Eddy, *Colleges for Our Land*, 45.

41. James Bryant Conant, *The Citadel of Learning* (New Haven, Conn.: Yale University Press, 1956), 24.

42. Clark Kerr, "The New Race to Be Harvard or Stanford or Berkeley," *Change* (May/June 1991): 10.

43. Robert H. Frank and Philip J. Cook, *The Winner-Take-All Society* (New York: Penguin Books, 1996), 149.

44. Nina Munk, "Rich Harvard, Poor Harvard," *Vanity Fair* (August 2009), www.ninamunk.com/articleDetails.htm?doc=RichHarvardPoorHarvard.

45. "President Faust's Sept. 24 Address to the Community," Harvard University Office of the President, September 24, 2009, last modified, president.harvard.edu/speeches/faust/090924_openyear.php.

46. Information on the educational impact of Harvard's budget cuts can be found in the following three sources: Tracy Jan, "Harvard Labs, Classrooms Feel Pinch of Budget Cuts," *Boston Globe*, June 17, 2009, www.boston.com/news/education/higher/articles/2009/06/17/harvard_classrooms_labs_feel_pinch_of_budget_cuts; Julie M. Zauzer, "Slavic Language Classes Cut Due to Budget," *Harvard Crimson*, September 16, 2009, www.thecrimson.com/article/2009/9/16/slavic-language-classes-cut-due-to; Noah S. Rayman and Elyssa A. L. Spitzer, "Faculty Consider Pre-Registration," *Harvard Crimson*, April 7, 2010, www.thecrimson.com/article/2010/4/7/harris-korn-faculty-policy.

47. "Building Boom at Stanford," *San Jose Mercury News,* November 6, 2009; "Summary Minutes of the Forty-second Senate of the Academic Council," Stanford University Senate of the Academic Council, last modified November 5, 2009, facultysenate.stanford.edu/2009_2010/minutes/11_05_09_summary.pdf; John Wildermuth, "Stanford Construction Hums Along," *San Francisco Chronicle*, November 26, 2009, articles.sfgate.com/2009-11-26/news/17180511_1_new-buildings-new-science-center-engineering-quad.

48. Brian McNeill, "U. Va. Poised to Issue $300 Million in Bonds to Finance Campus Construction Projects," *Richmond Times-Dispatch,* April 4, 2009, www2.timesdispatch.com/news/2009/apr/04/uvaa04_20090403-

223316-ar-47315; Dan Huechert, "U.Va., Backed by Highest Possible Credit Rating, Sells $250 Million in Bonds," University of Virginia, last modified April 15, 2009, www.virginia.edu/uvatoday/newsRelease.php?id=8342.

49. Shannon Colavecchio-Van Sickler, "Medical Schools Get Okay, Not Cash," *St. Petersburg Times*, March 24, 2006, www.sptimes.com/2006/03/24/State/Medical_schools_get_o.shtml; "Resolution with Regard to the Future of Medical Education in Florida," Florida Department of Health, last modified March 23, 2006, www.floridashealth.org/Workforce/Workforce/Articles/BOG_Resolution_on_MedicalEducation_06.pdf; Shannon Co-lavecchio-Van Sickler, "Budgets Pinch Med Schools, *St. Petersburg Times*, February 11, 2008, www.sptimes.com/2008/02/11/State/Budgets_pinch_med_sch.shtml.

50. "Reject Medical Schools," *Palm Beach Post*, March 22, 2006.

51. Lisa Greene, "As Doctor Shortage Looms, Florida Schools Plan a Cure," *St. Petersburg Times*, November 12, 2005.

52. Charles Chieppo, "Law School a Bad Deal for Mass.," *Providence Journal*, December 9, 2009, www.projo.com/opinion/contributors/content/CT_lawschool9_12-09-09_S5GNE10_v8.3f889c3.html; "Highest Per Capita Lawyers," Avery Index, accessed November 17, 2010, www.averyindex.com/lawyers_per_capita.php; Paul Schwartzman, "From 2007 to 2009, D.C. Paid More Than $50 Million in Legal Settlements," *Washington Post*, October 11, 2010, www.washingtonpost.com/wp-dyn/content/article/2010/10/11/AR2010101100060.html.

53. From the *Boston Globe*, July 1, 2010: "Governor Deval Patrick signed a $27.6 billion spending plan yesterday for the budget year that begins today, slashing funding for services across state government, including public education, dental care for the poor, and developmental services for toddlers. 'The pain is widespread,' Patrick said as he signed the budget in his office, surrounded by stoic aides. 'Our budget reflects the difficult economic times.' Patrick blamed the tough economy, combined with a stalled round of federal stimulus money, for forcing cuts even on items he considered sacred a few months ago. The governor had submitted a budget in January that protected money for local governments and school districts. But the plan he signed yesterday cut local aid by 4 percent, or $160 million, affirming a reduction made by the House and Senate." Noah Bierman and Michael Levenson, "Patrick Signs a Painful Budget," *Boston Globe,* July 1, 2010, www.boston.com/news/local/massachusetts/articles/2010/07/01/patrick_signs_a_painful_budget.

54. "Trustees Approve Law School," University of Massachusetts, Dartmouth, last modified December 12, 2009, www1.umassd.edu/communications/articles/showarticles.cfm?a_key=2700.

55. David Yas, "Commentary: A Public Law School in Massachusetts? Maybe Now Is the Time After All," *Massachusetts Lawyers Weekly*, November 2, 2009.

56. Tracy Jan, "Strong Start for UMass Law," *Boston Globe*, July 6, 2010, www.boston.com/news/local/massachusetts/articles/2010/07/06/strong_start_for_umass_law; Martha Neil, "U Mass Welcomes 1st Law School Class," *ABA Journal*, August 19, 2009, www.abajournal.com/news/article/u_mass_welcomes_1st_law_school_class.

57. James B. Twitchell, *Branded Nation* (New York: Simon and Schuster, 2004), 124.

58. Mark Bauerlein, et al., "We Must Stop the Avalanche of Low Quality Research," *The Chronicle of Higher Education*, June 18, 2010.

59. Patrick Healy, "College Rivalry," *Boston Globe*, June 29, 2003.

60. Barb Berggoetz, "Indiana Universities Pay Top Dollar, Raid Other Schools to Get Star Professors," *Indianapolis Star*, November 23, 2004.

61. Healy, "College Rivalry."

62. Mark Levine, "Ivy Envy," *New York Times Magazine*, June 8, 2003.

63. www.law.stanford.edu/publications/projects/lrps/pdf/lomiowayne_rp4.pdf.

64. www.timeshighereducation.co.uk/hybrid.asp?typeCode=243; www.albany.edu/dept/eaps/prophe/data/International_Data/WorldUniversity-Ranking2004_ModifiedFromTHES.pdf.

65. www.nyu.edu/about/news-publications/news/2010/01/26/nyu_receives_record_number_of.html.

66. Berggoetz, "Indiana Universities."

67. Frank and Cook, "Winner-Take-All," 165.

68. Healy, "College Rivalry."

69. "President Faust's Sept. 24 Address."

70. Daniel L. Bennett, "Bureaucrat U," *Forbes*, July 13, 2009, www.forbes.com/forbes/2009/0713/opinions-college-tuition-teachers-on-my-mind.html.

71. John M. Guilfoil, "Harvard Accepts a Diverse Class of 2015," *Boston Globe*, March 30, 2011, www.boston.com/news/local/breaking_news/2011/03/harvard_accepts.htm.

72. Beckie Supiano and Andrea Fuller, "Elite Colleges Fail to Gain More Students on Pell Grants," *The Chronicle of Higher Education*, March 27, 2011, chronicle.com/article/Pell-Grant-Recipients-Are/126892/.

73. Jonathan R. Cole, *The Great American University* (New York: Public Affairs, 2009), 4.

74. Ibid., 6.

75. Ibid., 6–7.

76. Gap, notably, pursued both the high and low end of the market, purchasing Banana Republic as a premium offering and launching Old Navy as

its value brand. All three of those brands suffered ups and downs over the years, but as of mid-2011, Banana Republic and Old Navy were performing quite nicely, but the middle-market Gap brand was still struggling to find a way to woo customers into its stores. It has become a business school truism that being in the middle of a market—offering something undifferentiated, that's not quite premium and not quite value—is a dangerous place to be. Gap's experience provides evidence of this, and I'd maintain the same phenomenon works in higher education, too.

77. Peter Smith, *The Quiet Crisis* (Bolton, Mass.: Anker Publishing, 2004), 38.

2. CLUB COLLEGE

1. James O'Neill, "Colleges Use Resort Touches to Make a Play for Students," *The Dallas Morning News*, July 28, 2006.

2. "Time Use of Full-Time College Students Ages 18 to 24 Years, 2003–2006." Postsecondary Education Opportunity, last modified January 2008, www.postsecondary.org.

3. David Glenn, "New Book Lays Failure to Learn on Colleges' Doorsteps." *The Chronicle of Higher Education*, January 18, 2011, chronicle.com/article/New-Book-Lays-Failure-to-Learn/125983/.

4. "Trends in College Pricing 2010," The College Board, accessed November 22, 2010, trends.collegeboard.org/downloads/College_Pricing_2010.pdf.

5. Robert J. Shapiro and Nam D. Pham, "Taxpayers' Costs to Support Higher Education: A Comparison of Public, Private Not-for-Profit, and Private For-Profit Institutions" (Washington, D.C.: Sonecon, September 2010), 1, www.sonecon.com/docs/studies/Report_on_Taxpayer_Costs_for_Higher_Education-Shapiro-Pham_Sept_2010.pdf.

6. "Tax Brackets (Federal Income Tax Rates) 2000 through 2009 and 2010," Moneychimp, accessed November 22, 2010, www.moneychimp.com/features/tax_brackets.htm; "2010 Tax Bracket Rates," Bankrate, accessed November 22, 2010, www.bankrate.com/finance/taxes/2010-tax-bracket-rates.aspx. This calculation doesn't include foregone state income tax revenue, which would range from zero in the eight states that don't tax regular income to a high of 11 percent on top wage earners in Hawaii, which would create an additional subsidy of $110,000 for a million-dollar donor from the Aloha State.

7. Jennifer Cheeseman Day and Eric C. Newburger, "The Big Payoff: Educational Attainment and Synthetic Estimates of Work-Life Earnings," U.S. Census Bureau, Washington, D.C., July 2002, www.census.gov/prod/2002pubs/p23-210.pdf.

8. Melody Barnes and Randall Stephenson, "Education Is Key to Win-

ning the Future," *The Huffington Post,* March 21, 2011, www.huffingtonpost.com/melody-barnes/education-is-key-to-winni_1_b_837958.html. See also McKinsey & Company, "The Economic Impact of the Achievement Gap in America's Schools," April 2009, www.mckinsey.com/app_media/images/page_images/offices/socialsector/pdf/achievement_gap_report.pdf

9. Christine Lagorio, "Blackboard Cribs," *New York Times*, October 26, 2009; "Purdue University to Expand First Street Towers Complex," Purdue University News Service, May 14, 2010, www.purdue.edu/newsroom/general/2010/100514McMainsTowers.html.

10. Tracy Jan, "BU Dorm Offers a Study in Luxury," *Boston Globe*, September 2, 2009.

11. Anthony Bianco, "The Dangerous Wealth of the Ivy League," *BusinessWeek*, November 29, 2007, www.businessweek.com/magazine/content/07_50/b4062038784589.htm.

12. "July Existing-Home Sales Fall as Expected but Prices Rise," National Association of Realtors, last modified August 24, 2010, www.realtor.org/press_room/news_releases/2010/08/ehs_fall.

13. Jonathan Zimmerman, "First-Class Dorms," *Pittsburgh Post-Gazette*, October 28, 2007.

14. "Campus Food: Virginia Tech," Media Gallery in The Daily Beast, accessed November 22, 2010, www.thedailybeast.com/blogs-and-stories/2009-10-07/the-best-college-food/#gallery=804;page=2.

15. "Campus Food: Oregon State University," Media Gallery in The Daily Beast, accessed November 22, 2010, www.thedailybeast.com/blogs-and-stories/2009-10-07/the-best-college-food/#gallery=804;page=1.

16. "Campus Food: Wheaton College," Media Gallery in The Daily Beast, accessed November 22, 2010, www.thedailybeast.com/blogs-and-stories/2009-10-07/the-best-college-food/#gallery=804;page=12.

17. "Student Leisure Pool," Texas Tech University Rec Sports, accessed November 22, 2010, www.depts.ttu.edu/recsports/aquatics/leisure.php.

18. "History of High Point University," High Point University, accessed November 22, 2010, www.highpoint.edu/about/index.cfm?DeptCategory=6&PageID=1071.

19. "2004–06 NCAA Revenues and Expenses of Division I Intercollegiate Athletic Programs Report" (Indianapolis, Ind.: National Collegiate Athletic Association, 2008), www.ncaapublications.com/productdownloads/RE2008.pdf.

20. Joseph McCafferty, "The Money Bowl," *CFO*, August 1, 2006; "Boone Pickens Donates $165 Million to OSU Athletics," Oklahoma State University Stillwater, last modified January 10, 2006, osu.okstate.edu/news/osuhistoricgift_shutt.htm; Associated Press, "Pickens Donates Record $165

Million to Oklahoma State," ESPN, last modified January 10, 2006, sports.espn.go.com/espn/wire?section=ncf&id=2286807.

21. Curtis Eichelberger, "Fired NCAA Coaches Are Owed $79.5 Million as Costs Double over Three Years," Bloomberg, last modified April 6, 2010, www.bloomberg.com/news/2010-04-06/fired-ncaa-coaches-are-owed-79-5-million-as-costs-double-over-three-years.html.

22. Jodi Upton et al., "Big-Time College Athletics: Are They Worth the Big-Time Costs?" *USA Today*, January 15, 2010, www.usatoday.com/sports/college/2010-01-13-ncaa-athletics-subsidies_N.htm.

23. Dena Potter, "'Flutie Effect' Study Shows Success on Fields and Courts Really Does Mean More Applications," *Minnesota Daily*, March 23, 2008, www.mndaily.com/2008/03/24/flutie-effect-study-shows-success-fields-and-courts-does-mean-more-applications.

24. Joe Nocera, "Skybox U," *New York Times*, October 28, 2007.

25. Doug Lederman, "Bad Apples or More?" Inside Higher Ed, last modified February 7, 2011, www.insidehighered.com/news/2011/02/07/ncaa_punishes_almost_half_of_members_of_football_bowl_subdivision_for_major_rules_violations.

26. "Most University Presidents Agree Current Athletics Spending is Unsustainable," John S. and James L. Knight Foundation, last modified October 26, 2009, www.knightfoundation.org/news/press_room/knight_press_releases/detail.dot?id=353228; "Knight Commission on Intercollegiate Athletics" (Baltimore, Md.: Art and Science Group, October 2009), www.knightcommissionmedia.org/images/President_Survey_appendices.pdf; "First of Its Kind Survey Reveals Dilemma of Reform," Knight Commission on Intercollegiate Athletics, last modified October 26, 2009, www.knightcommission.org/index.php?option=com_content&view=article&id=418&Itemid=96.

27. "Regulate Spending of College Sports Like Charities," Knight Commission on Intercollegiate Athletics, accessed November 22, 2010, www.knightcommission.org/index.php?option=com_content&view=article&id=299.

28. Ken Belson, "Universities Cutting Teams as They Trim Their Budgets," *New York Times*, May 3, 2009.

29. Andrew Ryan, "Northeastern Calls an End to Football," *Boston Globe*, November 23, 2009, www.boston.com/sports/colleges/football/articles/2009/11/23/northeastern_calls_an_end_to_football.

30. Dave Marcus, "Hofstra Sets Game Plan, Off-field," *Newsday*, December 14, 2009; "Hofstra to End Intercollegiate Football Program to Invest in Academic Initiatives," Hofstra University, last modified December 3, 2009, www.gohofstra.com/ViewArticle.dbml?DB_OEM_ID=22200&ATCLID=204843540.

31. Libby Sander, "The Allure of the Gridiron," *The Chronicle of Higher Education*, last modified May 13, 2010, chronicle.com/blogPost/The-Allure-of-the-Gridiron/23947.

32. "Trends in Student Aid 2010" (New York: The College Board, 2010), 10, trends.collegeboard.org/downloads/Student_Aid_2010.pdf.

33. Ibid., data table for Figure 10b, trends.collegeboard.org/downloads/2010_Trends_College_Pricing_All_Figures_Tables.xls.

34. "Educational Endowments and the Financial Crisis: Social Costs and Systemic Risks in the Shadow Banking System" (Boston, Mass.: Center for Social Philanthropy at Tellus Institute, 2010), 6, www.tellus.org/publications/files/endowmentcrisis.pdf.

35. "Contributions to Colleges and Universities down 11.9 Percent to $27.85 Billion" (New York: Council for Aid to Education, 2010), 4, www.cae.org/content/pdf/VSE_2009_Press_Relsease.pdf.

36. Richard Vedder, *Going Broke by Degree* (Washington, D.C.: AEI Press, 2004), 40–41.

37. Mark Schneider, "Where Does All That Tuition Go?" American Enterprise Institute for Public Policy Research, accessed November 22, 2010, www.aei.org/outlook/100924.

38. Jane V. Wellman et al., "Trends in College Spending. Where Does the Money Come From? Where Does It Go?"(Washington, D.C.: Delta Project on Postsecondary Education Costs, Productivity and Accountability, 2009), 28–29, www.deltacostproject.org/resources/pdf/trends_in_spending-report.pdf.

39. See, for example, Glenn Reynolds, "Higher Education's Bubble Is About to Burst," *Washington Examiner*, June 6, 2010, www.washingtonexaminer.com/opinion/columns/Sunday_Reflections/Higher-education_s-bubble-is-about-to-burst-95639354.html; and Peter Wood, "The Bubble: Higher Education's Precarious Hold on Consumer Confidence," National Association of Scholars, last modified September 13, 2010, www.nas.org/polArticles.cfm?Doc_Id=1536.

40. Glenn Reynolds, "Further Thoughts on the Higher Education Bubble," *Washington Examiner*, August 8, 2010, www.washingtonexaminer.com/opinion/columns/Sunday_Reflections/Glenn-Harlan-Reynolds-Further-thoughts-on-the-college-tuition-bubble-100216064.html.

41. Wellman et al., "Trends," 17.

42. Vedder, *Going Broke*, xv.

43. Ibid., 64.

44. Sam Dillon, "Share of College Spending for Recreation Is Rising," *New York Times*, July 8, 2010.

45. Richard Vedder, "Learning from Socrates and Adam Smith on Financing Universities," *The Chronicle of Higher Education*, last modified July 20, 2010, chronicle.com/blogs/innovations/learning-from-socratesadam-smith-on-financing-universities/25555.

46. *Education at a Glance 2010: OECD Indicators* (Paris: Organisation for Economic Co-operation and Development, 2010), 220, www.oecd.org/dataoecd/45/39/45926093.pdf.

47. D. Bruce Johnstone and Pamela N. Marcucci, *Financing Higher Education Worldwide* (Baltimore, Md.: Johns Hopkins University Press, 2010), 108.

48. Ronald G. Ehrenberg, *Tuition Rising* (Cambridge, Mass.: Harvard University Press, 2000), 210.

49. Ibid., 252.

50. Ibid., 260.

51. Tamar Lewin, "Study: Foreign Students Added to Economy," *New York Times*, November 12, 2007, www.nytimes.com/2007/11/12/us/12international.html; "International Student Enrollment in US Rebounds," Institute of International Education, accessed November 22, 2010, www.iie.org/en/Who-We-Are/News-and-Events/Press-Center/Press-Releases/2007/2007-11-12-International-Student-Enrollment-in-US-Rebounds.

52. Richard Arum and Josipa Roksa, *Academically Adrift: Limited Learning on College Campuses* (Chicago: University of Chicago Press, 2011), 34.

53. Ibid.

3. THE (THEORETICALLY) PERFECT SOLUTION

1. "Remarks by the President on the American Graduation Initiative," The White House, last modified July 14, 2009, www.whitehouse.gov/the_press_office/Remarks-by-the-President-on-the-American-Graduation-Initiative-in-Warren-MI.

2. "Completion/Graduation Rates," Macomb Community College, accessed November 23, 2010, www.macomb.edu/About+Macomb/Completion+and+Graduation+Rates.htm.

3. Paul Osterman, "Community Colleges: Promise, Performance and Policy," paper presented at the American Enterprise Institute's Reinventing the American University Conference, Washington, D.C., June 2010, www.aei.org/docLib/Paul%20Osterman%20-%20Community%20Colleges%20Promise-%20Performance%20and%20Policy.pdf.

4. David Brooks, "No Size Fits All," *New York Times*, July 17, 2009.

5. "2010 Fact Sheet," American Association of Community Colleges,

accessed November 23, 2010, www.aacc.nche.edu/AboutCC/Documents/factsheet2010.pdf.

6. Zachary Karabell, *What's College For? The Struggle to Define American Higher Education* (New York: Basic Books, 1998), 5.

7. Anthony P. Carnevale, Jeff Strohl, and Nicole Smith, "Help Wanted: Postsecondary Education and Training Required," *New Directions for Community Colleges* (New York: Wiley, 2009) 21. For additional research on this topic see Anthony P. Carnevale, Jeff Strohl, and Nicole Smith, "Help Wanted: Projections of Jobs and Education Requirements Through 2018," executive summary, Georgetown Center on Education and the Workforce, Washington, D.C., June 2010, www9.georgetown.edu/grad/gppi/hpi/cew/pdfs/ExecutiveSummary-web.pdf.

8. Ibid., 24.

9. Gail O. Mellow and Cynthia Heelan, *Minding the Dream: The Process and Practice of the American Community College* (New York: Rowman and Littlefield, 2008), 19.

10. See, for example, Brook-Gunn et al. (2006), as referenced by James J. Heckman, University of Chicago, in "Reduce Deficits and Strengthen the Economy: Invest in Early Childhood Development" presented at the McCormick Forum, Chicago, December 16, 2010. www.heckmanequation.org/download.php?file=HeckmanLecture_notes.pdf

11. "Goal 2025," Lumina Foundation, accessed November 23, 2010, www.luminafoundation.org/goal_2025.

12. Martin S. Quigley and Thomas W. Bailey, *Community College Movement in Perspective* (Lanham, Md.: Scarecrow Press, 2003), 14 and xii; "History," Joliet Junior College, accessed November 23, 2010, www.jjc.edu/about/college-info/Pages/history.aspx; "IIT History – The Sermon and the Institute," Illinois Institute of Technology, accessed November 23, 2010, www.iit.edu/about/history.

13. George B. Vaughan, *The Community College Story* (Washington, D.C.: Community College Press, 2006), 40.

14. "Born of Controversy: The G.I. Bill of Rights," U.S. Department of Veterans Affairs, accessed November 23, 2010, www.gibill.va.gov/gi_bill_info/history.htm.

15. Ibid.

16. Diane Ravitch, *The Troubled Crusade: American Education, 1945–1980* (New York: Basic Books, 1985), 13–15.

17. Philo A. Hutcheson, "The Truman Commission's Vision of the Future," *Thought & Action* 107 (Fall 2007), www.nea.org/assets/img/PubThoughtAndAction/TAA_07_11.pdf.

18. Quigley and Bailey, *Community College Movement*, 3.

19. Ibid., 68.

20. Clyde Blocker, letter to the editor, *Austin American Statesman*, December 10, 1965.

21. Steven Brint and Jerome Karabel, *The Diverted Dream: Community Colleges and the Promise of Educational Opportunity in America, 1900–1985* (New York: Oxford University Press, 1989).

22. W. B. Devall, "Community Colleges: A Dissenting View," *Educational Record* 49, no. 2 (Spring 1968): 168–72.

23. "Notable Alumni," American Association of Community Colleges, accessed November 23, 2010, www.aacc.nche.edu/AboutCC/alumni/Pages/default.aspx.

24. "Occupational Employment Statistics" (May 2009 data), Bureau of Labor Statistics, accessed November 23, 2010, data.bls.gov:8080/oes/search.jsp?data_tool=OES.

25. "Ros-Lehtinen @Miami-Dade College to present to the Board of Trustees Congressional Resolution she authored celebrating college's 50th anniversary," Congresswoman Ileana Ros-Lehtinen, last modified October 21, 2010, ros-lehtinen.house.gov/PRArticle.aspx?NewsID=978; Michael Vasquez, "Broward College, Miami Dade College Celebrate 50th Anniversaries," *Miami Herald*, November 9, 2010, articles.sun-sentinel.com/2010-11-29/news/fl-colleges-turn-fifty-20101129_1_broward-college-miami-dade-college-50th-anniversaries; Joanne Bashford and Doug Slater, "Assessing and Improving Student Outcomes: What We Are Learning at Miami-Dade College," Community College Research Center, January 2008, www.achievingthedream.org/publications/research/Bashford_paper.pdf.

26. "Florida," Complete College America, accessed November 23, 2010, www.completecollege.org/docs/Florida.pdf.

27. "Graduation Rates of First-time Post-secondary Students Who Started as Full-Time Degree-Seeking Students, by Sex, Race/Ethnicity, Time Between Starting and Graduating, and Level and Control of Institution Where Student Started: Selected Cohort Entry Years, 1996 through 2004," National Center for Education Statistics, last modified June 2009, nces.ed.gov/programs/digest/d09/tables/dt09_331.asp.

28. Michael Vasquez, "Demand Soars at South Florida Community Colleges, but Not Enough Classes," *The Miami Herald*, July 3, 2009, *Miami Herald*, May 29, 2009.

29. "Public Community College Revenue by Source," American Association of Community Colleges, accessed November 23, 2010, www.aacc.nche.edu/AboutCC/Trends/Pages/publiccommunitycollegerevenuebysource.aspx.

30. Thomas Bailey and Jim Jacobs, "Inequality Goes to College: Can Community Colleges Rise to the Occasion?" *The American Prospect* 20, no. 9 (October 26, 2009), www.prospect.org/cs/articles?article=can_

community_colleges_rise_to_the_occasion; "K-20 Improvement Project," Michigan Department of Technology, Management and Budget, accessed November 23, 2010, www.nascio.org/awards/nominations/2010/2010MI2-Data%20info%20%20knowlede%20mgmt%20-%20k-20%20project%20final. pdf; "Welcome to the MCCA," Michigan Community College Association, accessed November 23, 2010, www.mcca.org; "Total Students," Michigan State University Office of the Registrar, accessed November 23, 2010, www. reg.msu.edu/reportserver?/ROReports/UE-TotalStudents&term_seq_ id=1104.

31. Kevin J. Dougherty, "Community Colleges and Baccalaureate Attainment," *The Journal of Higher Education* 63 no. 2 (1992): 189.

32. Bailey and Jacobs, "Inequality."

33. Dougherty, "Baccalaureate Attainment," 192–98; Kevin J. Dougherty, *The Contradictory College*, paperback ed. (Albany: State University of New York Press, 1994), 86, 93, 107.

34. Michael D. Summers, "ERIC Review: Attrition Research at Community Colleges," *Community College Review* 30 no. 4 (2003): 64–84, www. accessmylibrary.com/article-1G1-101612904/eric-review-attrition-research. html.

35. Thomas W. Bailey and Vanessa Smith Morest, *Defending the Community College Equity Agenda* (Baltimore, Md.: Johns Hopkins University Press, 2006).

36. Tamar Lewin, "Community Colleges Challenge Hierarchy With 4-Year Degrees," *New York Times*, May 2, 2009.; "Florida College Bachelor's Degree Programs," Florida Department of Education, accessed November 23, 2010, www.fldoe.org/cc/students/bach_degree.asp; David Moltz, "Not Just a Foot in the Door," last modified August 12, 2010, www. insidehighered.com/news/2010/08/12/baccalaureate; Michael Vasquez, "Colleges Push New Four-Year Programs," *Miami Herald*, July 5, 2010. www. miamiherald.com/2010/07/05/1716746/colleges-push-new-four-year-programs.html.

37. Lewin, "Hierarchy."

38. Mellow and Heelan, *Minding the Dream*, xvi.

39. Ibid., 69.

40. The seven factors are: GED instead of a high school diploma, delayed enrollment into postsecondary education, independent status, one or more children, single parent, part-time attendance, and working full time. For more information, see "Graduation Rates and Student Success: Squaring Means and Ends," Perspectives policy paper series, American Association of State Colleges and Universities, Washington, D.C., fall 2006, www.aascu. org/media/pdf/06b_perspectives.pdf.

41. See, for example, Hilary Pennington, "Funding Completion," *Inside Higher Ed*, February 22, 2011, www.insidehighered.com/views/2011/02/22/ hilary_pennington_on_why_completion_efforts_are_needed_even_in_ tight_economic_times.

42. "Achieving the Dream," Achieving the Dream Community Colleges Count, accessed November 23, 2010, www.achievingthedream.org.

43. "Turning the Tide: Five Years of Achieving the Dream in Community Colleges," MDRC, Community College Research Center, January 2011, www.mdrc.org/publications/578/full.pdf.

4. A CRUCIAL PART OF THE SOLUTION

1. "Postsecondary Institutions and Price of Attendance in the United States: Fall 2009, Degrees and Other Awards Conferred: 2008–09, and 12-Month Enrollment: 2008–09: First Look," National Center for Education Statistics, Washington, D.C., August 2010, 5, nces.ed.gov/pubs2010/2010161. pdf.

2. Jeffrey M. Silber and Paul Condra, "Equity Research: Education and Training" (New York: BMO Capital Markets, September 2010), 110, 134, 135.

3. Information on the size and scope of the University of Phoenix comes from the following sources: Robin Wilson, "For-Profit Colleges Change Higher Education's Landscape," *Chronicle of Higher Education* 56 no. 22 (February 12, 2010): A1–A19, chronicle.com/article/For-Profit-Colleges-Change/64012; Tiffany Stanley, "On For-Profit Colleges, Congress Gets Schooled—Again," *The New Republic*, last modified October 12, 2010, www.tnr.com/blog/jonathan-cohn/78333/profit-colleges-congress-gets-schooled—again; "How It Works: Learning Formats," University of Phoenix, accessed November 23, 2010, www.phoenix.edu/students/how-it-works/ how-learning-formats.html; Tamar Lewin, "Senator Calls for New Rules for For-Profit Colleges," *New York Times*, June 24, 2010, www.nytimes. com/2010/06/25/education/25education.html; "Speech: For-Profit Colleges and Federal Student Aid: Preventing Financial Abuses," United States Senator Dick Durbin, last modified June 30, 2010, durbin.senate.gov/show Release.cfm?releaseId=326085.

4. Wilson, "Higher Education's Landscape."

5. Richard Ruch, *Higher Ed, Inc.* (Baltimore, Md.: Johns Hopkins University Press, 2001), x.

6. James Coleman and Richard Vedder, "For-Profit Education in the United States: A Primer," policy paper, Center for College Affordability and Productivity, Washington, D.C., May 2008, 5, www.policyarchive.org/ handle/10207/bitstreams/20592.pdf.

7. Coleman and Vedder, "For-Profit Education," 5.

8. John Sperling, *Rebel with a Cause: The Entrepreneur Who Created the University of Phoenix and the For-Profit Revolution in Higher Education* (New York: John Wiley and Sons, 2000), 91–92.

9. James Traub, "Drive-Thru U," *The New Yorker,* October 20, 1997.

10. Ruch, *Higher Ed,* 1.

11. Ibid., 22.

12. Coleman and Vedder, "For-Profit Education," 11.

13. Gina Chon, "Dartmouth's Chief Tackles Endowment Hit with Tough Cuts," *Wall Street Journal,* March 25, 2010, online.wsj.com/article/SB10001424052748704211704575139721935298474.html; "Dartmouth Announces 4.6% Increase in Tuition, Room, Board and Fees for 2010–2011; Smallest Percentage Increase in Five Years," Dartmouth College Office of Public Affairs, last modified February 8, 2010, www.dartmouth.edu/~news/releases/2010/02/08a.html; "The Endowment (Fiscal Year 2010)," Dartmouth Strategic Budget Reduction and Investment, last modified February 17, 2009, budget.dartmouth.edu/faq/FY10/endowment.html; "A Message to Alumni from President Jim Yong Kim," Dartmouth Office of the President, last modified October 9, 2009, www.dartmouth.edu/~president/announcements/2009-1009-alumni.html.

14. Chon, "Dartmouth's Chief."

15. Terence Chea, "College Applications Rise, but Budget Cuts Cap Enrollment, *USA Today,* January 14, 2010, www.usatoday.com/news/education/2010-01-14-college-admissions_N.htm; Victoria Irwin, "Freshman Application Outcomes Announced," University of California, last modified April 14, 2010, www.universityofcalifornia.edu/news/article/23203; "2010–11 State Budget Increases Funding to CSU for the First Time Since 2007," California State University, last modified October 8, 2010, www.calstate.edu/pa/News/2010/release/Budget2010-11.shtml.

16. Ruch, *Higher Ed,* 77.

17. "Trends in College Pricing 2010" (New York: The College Board, 2010), 10, trends.collegeboard.org/downloads/College_Pricing_2010.pdf.

18. Robert J. Shapiro and Nam D. Pham, "Taxpayers' Costs to Support Higher Education: A Comparison of Public, Private Not-for-Profit, and Private For-Profit Institutions" (Washington, D.C.: Sonecon September 2010), www.sonecon.com/docs/studies/Report_on_Taxpayer_Costs_for_Higher_Education-Shapiro-Pham_Sept_2010.pdf.

19. See, for example, "The Degree Qualifications Profile (Indianapolis, Ind.: Lumina Foundation for Education, January 2011), www.luminafoundation.org/publications/The_Degree_Qualifications_Profile.pdf.

20. Barbara Means et al., "Evaluation of Evidence-Based Practices in Online Learning: A Meta-Analysis and Review of Online Learning Studies," U.S. Department of Education, Office of Planning, Evaluation, and Policy Development, Washington, D.C., September 2010, www2.ed.gov/rschstat/eval/tech/evidence-based-practices/finalreport.pdf. Emphasis added.

21. Guilbert Hentschke, "Innovations in Business Models and Organizational Cultures," paper presented at the American Enterprise Institute's Reinventing the American University Conference, Washington, D.C., June 2010, www.aei.org/docLib/Guilbert%20Hentschke%20-%20Innovations%20in%20Business%20Models%20and%20Organizational%20Cultures%20-%20The%20For-Profit%20Sector.pdf.

5. THE CASE AGAINST PRIVATE-SECTOR HIGHER EDUCATION

1. For details on the HELP hearing and copies of the statements of Senator Harkin and the various witnesses, see the HELP Committee website: Full Committee Hearing, "Emerging Risk? An Overview of the Federal Investment in For-Profit Education," U.S. Senate Committee on Health, Education, Labor, and Pensions, accessed November 23, 2010, help.senate.gov/hearings/hearing/?id=464686ba-5056-9502-5d95-e21a6409cc53.

2. "Remarks by the President on Higher Education and the Economy at the University of Texas at Austin," The White House, last modified August 9, 2010, www.whitehouse.gov/the-press-office/2010/08/09/remarks-president-higher-education-and-economy-university-texas-austin.

3. Robert Lytle, Roger Brinner, and Chris Ross, "Private Sector Post-Secondary Schools: Do They Deliver Value to Students and Society?" Parthenon Perspectives paper series, The Parthenon Group, Boston, March 2010, 6, 11.

4. See, for instance, Clayton M. Christensen, Scott D. Anthony, and Eric A. Roth, *Seeing What's Next* (Cambridge, Mass.: Harvard Business School Press, 2004), chap. 5.

5. Gregory W. Cappelli, Higher Education at a Crossroads (position paper, Apollo Group, Phoenix, August 2010) www.apollogrp.edu/Investor/Reports/Higher_Education_at_a_Crossroads_FINALv2[1].pdf.

6. Peter Goodman, "In Hard Times, Lured into Trade School and Debt," *New York Times,* March 13, 2010.

7. Daniel Golden, "Marine Can't Recall His Lessons at For-Profit College," Bloomberg, last modified December 15, 2009, www.bloomberg.com/apps/news?pid=newsarchive&sid=al8HttoCG.ps.

8. "Enrollment in Postsecondary Institutions, Fall 2008; Graduation Rates, 2002 and 2005 Cohorts; and Financial Statistics, Fiscal Year 2008: First Look," National Center for Education Statistics, Washington, D.C., April 2010, 14, nces.ed.gov/pubs2010/2010152rev.pdf.

9. Ibid.

10. Frederick M. Hess, et al., "Diplomas and Dropouts: Which Colleges Actually Graduate Their Students (And Which Don't)" American Enterprise Institute for Public Policy Research, Washington, D.C., June 2009, www.aei.org/docLib/Diplomas%20and%20Dropouts%20final.pdf.

11. U.S. Department of Education, National Center for Education Statistics, 2003–04 Beginning Postsecondary Students Longitudinal Study, First Follow-up (BPS: 04/06). For more information, see "Graduation Rates and Student Success: Squaring Means and Ends," Perspectives policy paper series, American Association of State Colleges and Universities, Washington, D.C., fall 2006, www.aascu.org/media/pdf/06b_perspectives.pdf.

12. U.S. Department of Education, National Center for Education Statistics, 2003–04 Beginning Postsecondary Students Longitudinal Study. Graduation rates include students pursuing associate's and bachelor's degrees.

13. Ibid.

14. Kaplan internal data for comparable student set (2003–04 cohort). Includes students with two or more risk factors (as defined by the U.S. Department of Education), pursuing associate's and bachelor's degrees.

15. Lytle, Brinner, and Ross, "Private Sector."

16. "Summary of Key Operating Statistics: Data Collected from the 2009 Annual Institutional Report," Accrediting Council for Independent Colleges and Schools, Washington, D.C., 2009, 12, www.eric.ed.gov/PDFS/ED509524.pdf.

17. Lytle, Brinner, and Ross, "Private Sector."

18. *Trends in College Pricing 2010* (New York: The College Board, 2010), 10, trends.collegeboard.org/downloads/College_Pricing_2010.pdf.

19. "Creating Opportunities," annual report, Apollo Group, Phoenix, Ariz., 2009, 2, www.apollogrp.edu/Annual-Reports/2009%20Apollo%20annual%20report.pdf.

20. Report by First Analysis Securities Corporation, Post-secondary Education Analyst Corey Greendale, June 24, 2010.

21. Ibid.

22. Ibid.

23. David L. Bennett and Zac Bissonnette,"The Red Herring Crusade Against For-Profit Colleges," Forbes.com, last modified August 11, 2010, www.forbes.com/2010/08/01/student-debt-profit-expense-opinions-best-colleges-10-bennett-bissonnette_2.html.

24. Daniel Hamburger, "The Vital Role of Private-Sector Higher Education," white paper, DeVry Inc., Downers Grove, Ill.,phx.corporate-ir.net/

External.File?item=UGFyZW50SUQ9Mzg4MTg3fENoaWxkSUQ9Mzkw
OTEwfFR5cGU9MQ==&t=1.

25. "For-Profit Colleges: Undercover Testing Finds Colleges Encouraged Fraud and Engaged in Deceptive and Questionable Marketing Practices," U.S. Government Accountability Office, Washington, D.C., August 4, 2010; revised and reissued on November 30, 2010. www.gao.gov/new.items/d10948t.pdf

26. Daniel De Vise, "Leading For-Profit College Responds to GAO Report," College Inc. blog, accessed March 20, 2011, www.washingtpost.com.

27. Subsequently, as of July 1, 2011, U.S. Department of Education regulations require such changes.

28. Some critics of private sector higher education have used a formulation asserting that proprietary colleges account for 10 percent of students in higher education, but receive 23 percent of federal grants, and account for 44 percent of defaults. (See, e.g., Statement by Senator Tom Harkin (D-IA), September 20, 2010). It's a strong sound bite, repeated frequently in the media, but not good data. The sound bite dramatically understates the percentage of for-profit students, and overstates the percentage of loan dollars defaulted by such students, falsely making it appear as though for-profit students are defaulting on disproportionately more dollars than other students.

Measured on a common basis, based on Department of Education data for 2008/09, for-profit higher education represents 20 percent of students receiving financial aid, 23 percent of student loan and grant dollars, and 24 percent of the defaulted dollars. For-profit students thus default slightly more dollars than their proportionate share, by a very small amount. (Source: U.S. Department of Education 2009 "GE-Date-Model" www2.ed.gov/policy/highered/reg/hearulemaking/2009/ge-data-model.xls)

The difference stems from the sound bite's contorting data to use number of students at a point in time (not borrowers going into repayment, a more appropriate measure) and then using percent of *students* defaulting rather than *dollars* defaulted. Since the average defaulted debt of a for-profit student is much lower than the national average, the sound bite significantly overstates the dollar amount of the defaulted debt.

29. Robert J. Shapiro and Nam D. Pham, "Taxpayers' Costs to Support Higher Education: A Comparison of Public, Private Not-for-Profit, and Private For-Profit Institutions," Washington, D.C., Sonecon, September 2010, www.sonecon.com/docs/studies/Report_on_Taxpayer_Costs_for_Higher_Education-Shapiro-Pham_Sept_2010.pdf.

30. Ibid.

31. For fiscal year 2008 (the most recent for which data are available), the rates are 6.0 percent for public, 4.0 percent for private, and 11.6 percent for for-profit. Source: Federal Student Aid, 2010, "Direct Loan and Federal

Family Education Loan Programs: Institutional Default Rate Comparison of FY 2006, 2007, and 2008 Cohort Default Rates," last modified September 19, www2.ed.gov/offices/OSFAP/defaultmanagement/instrates.html.

32. "Proprietary Schools: Stronger Department of Education Oversight Needed to Help Ensure Only Eligible Students Receive Federal Student Aid," U.S. Government Accountability Office, Washington, D.C., August 2009, www.gao.gov/new.items/d09600.pdf; Jacob P. K. Gross et al., "What Matters in Student Loan Default: A Review of the Research Literature," *Journal of Student Financial Aid* 39 (2009): 19–29.

33. U.S. Department of Education, www2.ed.gov/policy/highered/reg/hearulemaking/2009/ge-data-model.xls. Kaplan custom analysis of Cohort Default Rate by percentage of Pell recipients.

34. Office of Management and Budget, 2011, "Federal Credit Supplement: Budget of the U.S. Government, Fiscal Year 2011," Accessed April 22, www.gpoaccess.gov/usbudget/fy11/pdf/cr_supp.pdf. Table 4, p. 20.

35. Shapiro and Pham, "Taxpayers' Costs to Support Higher Education."

36. "Career Education Corporation, 2005 Annual Report," Career Education Corporation, Hoffman Estates, Ill., 2005.

37. Gretchen Morgenson, "The School That Skipped Ethics Class," *New York Times*, July 24, 2005, www.nytimes.com/2005/07/24/business/yourmoney/24gret.html; "Career Education Corporation Provides Update on Department of Justice Investigations," press release, Career Education Corporation, Hoffman Estates, Ill., April 30, 2007, www.allbusiness.com/services/business-services/4322274-1.html.

38. Guilbert C. Hentschke et al., *For Profit Colleges and Universities: Their Markets, Regulations, Performance, and Place in Higher Education* (Sterling, Va.: Stylus Publishing, 2010), 4–5.

6. THE LEARNING PLAYBOOK

1. Martin Hightower, "The Spirit and Spectacle of Harvard Commencement," Harvard University, accessed November 22, 2010, www.commencement.harvard.edu/background/spirit.html.

2. Ibid.

3. "OCW Consortium," OpenCourseWare Consortium, accessed November 22, 2010, www.ocwconsortium.org.

4. Gregory W. Cappelli, "Higher Education at a Crossroads," position paper, Apollo Group, Phoenix, Ariz., August 2010, www.apollogrp.edu/Investor/Reports/Higher_Education_at_a_Crossroads_FINALv2[1].pdf; "Employment Status of the Civilian Noninstitutional Population 25 Years and Over by Educational Attainment," U.S. Bureau of Labor Statistics, last modified August 9, 2010, www.bls.gov/web/empsit/cpseea5.pdf.

5. "QS World University Rankings 2010," Quacquarelli Symonds, accessed November 22, 2010, www.topuniversities.com/university-rankings/world-university-rankings/2010/results.

6. "Academic Ranking of World Universities–2010," Shanghai Ranking Consultancy, accessed November 23, 2010, www.arwu.org/ARWU2010.jsp.

7. The historic college inflation rate of 5.94 and the resulting calculation were done using the following Web sites: "Tuition Inflation," FinAid, accessed November 23, 2010, www.finaid.org/savings/tuition-inflation.phtml (for 1989–2005 information); "Historical Inflation," InflationData.com, accessed November 23, 2010, www.inflationdata.com/inflation/inflation_rate/historicalinflation.aspx.

Index

Berkeley College